Bright Levant

Bright Levant

Laurence Grafftey-Smith

STACEY INTERNATIONAL

Bright Levant

First published by John Murray

This edition published 2002 by
Stacey International
128 Kensington Church Street
London, W8 4BH
Tel: 020 7221 7166 Fax: 020 792 9288
E-mail: enquiries@stacey-international.co.uk

ISBN: 1 900988 429

A catalogue record for this publication is available from the British Library.

Printed and bound by IBT Global UK Ltd

For Jane

Contents

Illustrations

Author's Note

I have always thought it neither proper nor prudent to keep a day-to-day record of official involvements: in these pictures of other days around me, only memory sheds the light. But in my account of 'Egypt and the High Commissioners', memory has been valuably refreshed by such books as Lord Wavell's *Allenby*, Lord Lloyd's *Egypt Since Cromer* and Sir Ronald Wingate's biography of his father, *Wingate of the Sudan*. I gratefully acknowledge these illuminations of a familiar scene.

My transliteration of Arabic words—always a headache—will not be academically acceptable. I have not attempted the uniformity of *Husayn*, *'Abd Allah*, or *Sulayman*, preferring to write each name as it was spelt in each country at the time. French influence in Egypt imposed *Hussein*, with *Suleiman* or *Soliman*: in Iraq, such names were otherwise transliterated. But I have at least tried to use the same spelling for the same individual throughout.

For those illustrations which do not come from my own albums, I am much indebted to those—Lord Allenby, Lord Lloyd, Sir Ronald Wingate and the Hon. Mrs. Alexander Monro —who have rifled their family portraits for my use; to Mr. C. J. Edmonds for his photographs of Kurdistan; to Sir Reader and Lady Bullard for our derelict home in Jedda, and to Sir Hugh Stonehewer-Bird for his Jedda *Sûq*. The Middle East Archive of St. Antony's College, Oxford, yielded the two photographs of Cairo, and I have to thank the Research Department of the Arabian American Oil Company in Dhahran for their portrait of King Ibn Saud.

A special debt of acknowledgement is due to Mr. A. Rizkallah, for his study of an Egyptian *Felláh*, which appeared in the Cairo review *La Femme Nouvelle* of December 1950.

The T. E. Lawrence extracts are quoted by kind permission of the Executors of the T. E. Lawrence Estate, from *Seven Pillars of Wisdom*, pp. 65, 66, 72, 585 (Jonathan Cape, 1935).

Most of the typing of the book was done by Mrs. Joy Macrow, whose labours are most gratefully remembered.

When the late Sir Ronald Storrs produced his *Orientations*, I complained to him of his omission of the wealth of slightly malicious anecdote which had always spiced his small-talk. Many of my friends may be similarly surprised to find here a certain lack of pungency in comment. In these matters, the wisdom and experience of Mr. John Murray have been decisive: any fleeting regret for stories left untold has faded in appreciation of his unfailing patience and constant help, and in delight at my admission, as an unusually venerable runner, into his stable.

L. G.-S. 1970

Foreword
to this edition

The news that *Bright Levant* was to be reprinted filled me with gladness and gratitude.

I knew Sir Laurence for many years, but in an unusual way: he and I were friends who never met. The friendship began when he sent the typescript of *Bright Levant* (as the rules of the Diplomatic Service required) to the Foreign Office for vetting. The sections on the countries for which my Department was responsible were assigned to me to say whether anything in them might embarrass HMG or its friends. I quickly gave the all-clear and wrote to him, unintroduced, to say how much I had enjoyed the book. He sent me a kindly and gratified reply and from then until the end of his life we corresponded sporadically but warmly. I kept promising myself that I would go and see him; but though I knew that he was an old man, his letters were so spry and sparkling that I always felt there was plenty of time. Suddenly it was too late: so many squandered opportunities.

The first thing to say about the book is that he writes like an archangel. Not Lucifer of course (though there are some faint echoes of mischief) and not quite Gabriel; but what a blessed change from the gobbledegook that disfigures most English prose today. He is a phrase-maker, a wordsmith. Relish, for example, his description of Durrell's Alexandria as "a suburb of the European mind" and his own view that it was a town corrupted by "centuries of infiltration by seafaring sin". Bask in his list of Yezidi taboos: "lettuce, the colour blue, and buttons on shirt collars."

His book is full of wit and anecdote, yet at the same time he has much to say, profound and detailed, about the politics of the Middle East. Liberal by temperament, he is rightly critical of British imperial policies and social attitudes and deeply sympathetic to the Arabs (though frank enough about the warts).

My affection and admiration for this unseen friend are, I suppose, partly based on shared experience: both of us were trained Arabists, both were posted twice to Jeddah, both had at times the absorbing, now obsolete, job of Oriental Secretary in an embassy. He was luckier than I in seeing the Arab world before it was homogenised by the Macdonalds, the Hiltons and the package tours; unluckier because he spent most of his career, before the reforms of 1943, in the consular service, condescended to by the diplomats. I enjoyed better pay and more comfort but caught only a wistful glimpse of the old East before it faded into global uniformity.

His personality shines out of his writing: impish, quirky, courteous, generous, deeply decent. I salute his life and work with reverent applause and I promise new readers of this book that they are in for a treat.

Sir James Craig GCMG
May 2002

Chapter One

Introduction to the Levant

The perpetual kaleidoscope of Time, gently making nonsense of dynasties and institutions and established circumstance, confuses even the gazetteers. Where do the younger generation look to find Fashoda, Christiania or Mesopotamia, and who of my generation can recite the states and capitals of independent Africa? There was once a Near Eastern Question, but where today is the Near East? The Middle East, remote sixty years ago, now encroaches on the Mediterranean.

The 'levanter' wind still blows from the East; the Gulf of Genoa still flaunts its *Riviera di Levante*; the sun, indeed, still rises, but rosy-fingered Eos is now denied a local habitation. Kinglake went to the Greeks for the title of his *Eothen*, and he wandered in and painted the lands which for them cradled each day's dawn. There I, too, found a lifetime's enchantment.

A dictionary defines 'Levant' as . . . 'the Eastern part of the Mediterranean with its islands and neighbouring countries'. Whoever planned the responsibilities of the Levant Consular Service, before 1914 one of five watertight compartments of our Foreign Service, gave generous interpretation to the words 'neighbouring countries', for our parish ran from Morocco to Egypt; from the Yemen border to the Balkans; from western Turkey to eastern Persia. Three separate British consular services then covered all the world except those bits and pieces on which the sun never set; none of them offered me more delight than the service whose territory held the source of sunlight for the antique world.

Professionally speaking, the Levant was a rich mine of political experience, for something was always happening. Here, if not there, history was always being made. It was also an area of varied historical interest, where official postings and official journeys were to show me the sources of light of many civilisations. Memphis and Thebes became familiar haunts; Mecca and Byzantium and Babylon were all once part of my consular district. I was busy for most of my time in Bible lands, and this work brought unusual acquaintance with the misty survivals of ancient heresies : I had fanatically Nestorian houseboys; bought my groceries from worshippers of St. John the Baptist; picnicked by the shrine where Satan is Lord. Our parish was rich, too, in those marble palimpsests of religious record which always surprise.

In Damascus, where Saladin sleeps in a shade of myrtles, I was happy to visit the great Omayyad Mosque. It stands on the site of a Church of St. John the Baptist and is rumoured still to have his head. That church usurped the site of a great Temple of Jupiter, and this, in turn, replaced a temple to the god Hadad. And what before that? And after this, what? One glimpses long-dead faiths at Karnak and Pompeii and Stonehenge; but the portmanteau quality of the Omayyad Mosque, as of the Cathedral of Tarragona —where the High Altar stands on a Roman temple-pavement and a *mihráb* in the cloisters still marks the path of prayer to Mecca— seems to bear tangible witness to the smooth succession and supersession of divine dynasties, casting a shadow of the transitory across our mirror of the eternal.

To equip us for service in this widely interesting zone, we were given an intensive language-specialisation which, by opening windows on to many worlds, brought us a measure of self-confidence, if not self-esteem, rare on the lower rungs of the ladder. This is not a bad thing, if duly controlled. A further antidote to inferiority complexes was the rather murky tide of prestige which floated us in a régime of exterritorial jurisdiction. We had judicial functions unshared by our colleagues of the General Service and felt superior.

If I was happy in my service, I was perhaps particularly fortunate in the accident of time. Elizabeth Monroe, in her brilliant study of *Britain's Moment in the Middle East*—which I persist in thinking of as the Levant—fixes the limits of that moment as from 1914 to 1956. In 1914 I became a Levant student interpreter, and in 1956 I left Khartoum at the end of my last official assignment. In this context of reminiscence what matters is not the compulsions and evasions, the success or failure, of British policy during those forty-odd years; what matters is that I enjoyed every moment of them.

★   ★   ★

The year 1914 lay in a dim future when, in 1909, a family crisis tore me from the sixth form at Repton, shortly before my seventeenth birthday. My father in his Derbyshire vicarage hinted urgently at jobs in the Midland Bank or some insurance company, neither of which appealed to me. I preferred to sit for a newly-invented examination advertised for 'Junior Appointments in the Admiralty, etc.', success in which would put me somewhere between the Second Division of the Civil Service, which was by definition ancillary, and the plushier, University-bred First Division, for which I could not afford the academic formation. Strong hopes of early promotion to the First Division were dangled, and the path to a Permanent Under-Secretary's chair was shown on the map. Candidates were to be between 18 and 19½; this gave me time to attend a crammer's. The only one we could afford was unimpressive.

Unimpressive, too, were both teaching staff and students, who came from a broad spectrum of background. We played nap under the table during lectures. One young man from Charterhouse, Donald Gainer, was preparing for another examination, for something called the Levant Consular Service, and a series of exotic figures visited him daily to teach him languages. I found his curriculum irresistibly attractive.

Shortly after my eighteenth birthday in 1910 I sat with four hundred others in Burlington House to compete for six posts. All six were taken by established Second Division men, who were allowed to compete up to the age of 25. All six were in the Customs and Excise Department.

My father resumed his talk of the Midland Bank, but I beat down all suggestions and announced my ambition of joining the

Levant Consular Service. The examination required me to keep my Latin and Greek and English up to a high standard, to improve my French and to acquire Spanish, German and Italian. Arithmetic was also a subject. Leap-frogging the years, my mother and I wandered through the bazaars of Constantinople in a pipe-dream. My father asked how I would live while learning these various languages.

Fortunately, by arranging for my own exchange with a French and later a German girl; by tutoring the children of a Stralsund timber-merchant and a Spanish ambassador, and by sweating it out in the slave-labour of Berlitz schools in Paris, Madrid and Florence, I was able to arrange my further education without involving my father in more capital expenditure. Those were years of hard work, and of great fun.

Donald St. Clair Gainer, the 'onlie begetter' of my ambition, failed to pass his Levant Service examination but entered the General Consular Service after 1918. His most memorable service was as consul-general in Munich from 1932 to 1938, when Hitler declared him to be *persona non grata*. His Munich despatches provided the Foreign Office with priceless ammunition against the smooth assurances flowing from Nevile Henderson in his Berlin Embassy. My fellow-alumnus of Clark's Civil and Commercial College retired as Ambassador in Brazil, with the coveted 'G.B.E., K.C.M.G.' double.

By May 1914, I had spent rather less than four months in England out of rather more than three years and a half, and I had been speaking foreign languages, or teaching English to foreigners, all the time. The latter habit, though I did not realise it at the time, had given me a few alien mannerisms of speech. I rolled my 'R's' like a Scot; pronounced 'house' like *Haus*, and developed a feminized 'L' in words like 'silk' or 'milk', in the Italian manner.

When I was summoned from Florence to attend a selection board at the Foreign Office, these peculiarities of accent became an embarrassment. The Board did not distribute marks. Its object was to weed out sheep from goats and to admit to examination only those considered to be of the right representational timber. It would be impossible to revive it today. Its decisions were based

4

on impressions not ascertainable from any written paper. I assume that any serious physical deformity meant a black ball, and I suspect that there were other, less avowable, criteria.

Lord Dufferin, white haired and pinkly spruce, was chairman of inquisitors, and I was asked a number of questions which seemed only marginally relevant to consular labours. Did I hunt? What club, or clubs, did I belong to? (I was 22 at the time.) I waited to be asked how many duchesses I knew. Was I English on both sides, because I did not give that impression? Did I shoot? Was my mother, perhaps, of German stock? I understood, just in time, this interest in my bloodstream and explained the causes of my temporary accent. I was then given written authority to take the Levant Service examination in August.

Most conveniently, someone left me £100 in June, and I was able to afford a nine-week term at Scoone's, then the leading crammers for all Foreign Service examinations. The classics were dusted off and polished; arithmetical tricks were re-learnt; I was taught by the admirable André Turquet that grammatical correctness and perfect vocabulary are not enough to ensure that a phrase is French. The German tutor was better than any of us in finding the immediate English equivalent of any polysyllabic portmanteau-word. An aged cleric called Dawson-Clark, looking like Silenus, presided over our revels. I conscientiously wrote a weekly English essay, and read through the corrected versions the night before the examination. One of the subjects was set in our first paper; and this good luck followed me through that anxious week, and brought me to the top of the list.

The examination had one unusual discomfort. It was held at the beginning of August, 1914, when the lights were going out all over Europe. Concentration was more than difficult. Difficult, too, was our oral examination in German, when a figurative flag of truce flew between the examiner and his victim.

★ ★ ★

Cambridge, when I went up to Pembroke in October 1914, for a two-year course in Oriental languages at Government expense, was an empty shell. The mass of undergraduates had enlisted and were being pulped in the giant mixers of the Artists' Rifles, the Honourable Artillery Company and the Public Schools Brigade for early drainage into the mud of Flanders. Apart from the militarily unfit and the rare conscientious objector, the student population was limited to medicals, who were expected to qualify before joining up; undergraduates, mostly coloured, from overseas; and a few government-sponsored post-graduates like ourselves. Some Indian civil service cadets shared our Arabic lectures.

Non-academic activities had stopped. Organised games, except for an occasional scratch hockey-match, were dead. The Union was a shadow of itself. We were paid £200 a year, of which £30 a year went directly to the College for tutorial fees. This was not a generous wage, but the exceptional circumstances of the time saved us from much pleasurable expense on the various side-shows of University life. They also compelled us to work with unusual concentration. When all our friends were fighting, slackness would have been indecent.

My two colleagues, who had shared my good fortune in the examination, were Douglas Keane, a dark young man with a battleship chin, and Rex Gybbon-Monypenny, who was fair and musical and only nineteen. They both went to Caius. I preferred to join my elders of the 1913 batch, then beginning their second year, at the college where our Director of Studies held court.

This great man, Edward Granville Browne, Sir Thomas Adams's professor of Arabic, was also our constant friend. Physically considered, he epitomised the processes of evolution: he was short and broad in the shoulder, with a stoop, and grotesquely long arms dangled in his shambling walk. His finely chiselled face was a radiance of intellect and of love for his fellow man. I never met a kinder man. His benevolence was, indeed, all but universal: only one Russian Inspector of Customs, and Sir Edward Grey, the Foreign Secretary, were excluded from its blessing. He spoke Persian, Turkish and classical Arabic perfectly and at great speed, and his lectures were a continual excitement. Facts, theories, prejudices and esoteric pleasantries stormed the ear of his captive audience with the imparted urgency and the harmony in confusion of a pack of hounds' full cry. When this became too much for us, we would introduce a well-tried red herring into our question, and we could then relax, while he followed a familiar scent across Persia. His personal speciality was the Babi religion, which became the Baha'i religion after the founder's martyrdom. Gobineau's *Religions et Philosophies de l'Asie Mineure* is the *locus classicus* for these events. Browne preferred the cause of the saintly Subh-i-Ezel, whom Mohammed Ali el-Bab had nominated as his successor, to that of the more forceful half-brother who usurped his place. He gave me copies of all his books as a parting gift, and for many years we exchanged Persian greetings on the day of Nauruz.

The centenary of his birth in 1962 was officially celebrated in Persia, with ceremonies of pious commemoration, and at these a former Master of Pembroke represented the college which my old friend had made a Mecca for Oriental scholars of the world.

Our first morning of work was challenging, for we started Arabic, Persian, Turkish and Russian between breakfast and luncheon. Dropped into a conversation with the right intonation of casual throwaway, this detail has provoked admiration and some awe throughout my life; but it would be wrong to think of it as remarkable. Our programme looked glamorous and impressive; but we worked no harder than our friends who were studying Law or Medicine, and comparisons are odious.

We were instructed to study also the elements of Law, and to take a course in Ottoman History. This last subject was never attempted, for Ottoman History was already in the melting-pot.

Various *répétiteurs* worked with and on us. Arabic was taught by a graduate of Al-Azhar from Cairo; Turkish by a chubby Smyrniot who had to feel his way, experimentally, into the grammar and intricacies of his own tongue. Johnny Browne generally took us in Persian, though I remember a dim procession of unskilled assistants. Russian was in the hands of a sad, grey Scot called Goudy. He never struck a spark out of me, to my eternal regret. Huge chunks of ill-digested grammar were thrust morosely upon us, and I died somewhere near the aspects of the verb. After two terms, the Foreign Office decided that one of us

7

should abandon Arabic and Turkish and concentrate on Russian and Persian, with a view to specialised employment on both sides of the Imperial Russian frontiers with the Shah's dominions. I was offered this choice, but refused, preferring to keep alive my hopes of Constantinople. Keane was selected for the new job, and Mr. Goudy and his 'arse-pecked' verbs vanished below my horizon.

Of the 1913 batch of student interpreters, only Stonehewer-Bird, Bond and Jerram survived Cambridge. The first two shared my future stamping-ground, to our mutual pleasure; Jerram became a Russian expert and never came nearer to the Levant than Moscow.

Our passing-out examination, at the end of two years' sojourn at Cambridge, was to include French, and student interpreters had always been expected to spend at least six weeks in France, 'perfecting their knowledge of the language'. This pretext enabled the Foreign Office to send all three of us, during the Long Vacation of 1915, to consulates in France, to help out. I enjoyed my acting vice-consulship in Paris, struggling with invasions of four or five hundred people a day, all in need of British passports and visas, then a new phenomenon, and ostensibly preventing spies from reaching the British Isles. The experience was an expensive one, but no allowance for either travel or subsistence was made to us in respect of this period of initiation. When we returned to our studies, we all found ourselves impatient to get our second year over and to start real work abroad.

We were beginning to know something of the languages we studied, but Cambridge was, at best, a makeshift approach. We missed the 24-hour-a-day immersion in a foreign language which we had enjoyed in France and Spain, Germany and Italy; we missed the very special inspiration of leisure and casual conversation in a foreign air. Our contact with Oriental languages was limited to the lecture-room; outside the door, we were back in Cambridge. It had not always been so. In the years before 1904, Levant Service student interpreters had been whisked from the examination-room to a villa on the Bosphorus, where they spent two years working through the same curriculum as ourselves. They were enabled and encouraged to learn Turkish not from Hagopian's Grammar and an occasional tutorial only, but from life. In years past the French made similar arrangements for their cadets—*les jeunes du Roi*—destined for service in *les échelles du Levant*. Regrettably, an official visitor discovered our ultimate batch of these favoured few wearing pyjamas at noon and playing poker with a drunken Persian teacher. The stricter discipline of an English university was prescribed, and their successors were the losers.

We had no instruction in any branch of colloquial Arabic, and Arabic remained for us a dead language. I found that I was making less progress in Arabic than in Persian which lures the beginner with such promises as 'padar', 'madar' and 'biradar'—(for father, mother and brother)—or Turkish, which has the beauty of a Swiss chronometer. The future was to offer me opportunity to redress this balance.

In the event, we left Cambridge in the same order of seniority as we had come. Further examinations, at the end of our first and second years of foreign service, lay ahead of us, before this order of precedence crystallised into permanency.

*   *   *

Our highly specialised formation was designed to fit us for service in a geographical zone, the limitations of which combined with somewhat irrational conditions of work to produce a marked professional deformation. Most of my Levant colleagues would agree that all their colleagues, present company excepted, were slightly mad. We were a rather eccentric fraternity, united in our resentment of the snail-slow pace of promotion. In the General Consular Service, the *cadre* was a tunnel-shaped hierarchy, up which men moved easily from rank to rank. In our Service, the tunnel of opportunity became a funnel, and promotion involved long years of patience in vice-consular, and later in consular, posts, before one of the rare vacancies among consuls-general crowned all. I was not notably underprivileged, but I had to wait six years before becoming a vice-consul (£300 to £600) and eleven more before becoming a consul (£800 to £1,000).

The boundaries of our service were, very roughly, coterminous with those of a régime, that of the so-called Capitulations, which was for many years the bane of governments in Persia, Egypt, Morocco and the far-flung Ottoman Empire. The Capitulations were in no sense a capitulation: the word derives from 'capitula' (chapters), which were the articles by virtue of which the former caliphs of Islam and sultans of Turkey granted unilateral concessions of judicial or fiscal privilege to foreign governments. The practice goes back to Haroun al Rashid and his contemporary, Charlemagne, but the Capitulations interesting to us dated from 1536. Sultan Suleiman the Magnificent and François I of France shared a common dislike of the Emperor Charles V and his ambitions; and in that year the Sultan signed a treaty with France, approving the establishment of French subjects—hitherto practically outlaws, like all foreigners—in Turkey, and the appointment of French consuls, with exterritorial jurisdiction, to judge them according to French law.

Suleiman was not merely favouring an ally. Without such concessions, no foreign trader could settle in Turkey unless he accepted the rigours and mutilations of Shar'ia law. Now the lifeblood of trade and commerce could flow in.

Venice received similar concessions; and in 1583 England received her first Capitulations. As time passed, the main privileges granted included liberty of residence and of travel; freedom of religion and of commerce, and immunity from local jurisdiction. As a 'most favoured nation' clause figures in all the treaties, those privileges granted to any one power were applied to all the powers. As has been said, 'Every foreign colony in Turkey became an *imperium in imperio*. Among other traders, the English Levant Company became active up and down the eastern coasts of the Mediterranean. Shakespeare brings us news of one of the company's sea-captains, from a witch on a desert heath in Scotland: . . . 'Her husband's to Aleppo gone, master o' the "Tiger". . . .'

Like our colleagues in the Far East, where similar conditions existed, but unlike those in the General Consular Service, we of the Levant Service thus inherited from our merchant-venturing forebears a tradition of considerable prestige. Without our formal consent, no British subject could be touched by the local authorities. In our provincial (consular) courts our nationals received British justice, under British law. We were locally in the little tin-god-on-wheels class. Our course of Oriental languages had qualified us to serve in any part of the Capitulations area; the demand for strenuous earlier language-study was probably aimed at weeding out those with the necessary monkey-proficiency from the rest.

The few posts staffed in 1914 by our Service outside the area of exterritorial jurisdiction, such as those in Serbia and Bulgaria and Macedonia, were hangovers from earlier servitude to Ottoman domination. One is apt to forget how vast the Ottoman Empire once was. By the Treaty of Berlin, in 1878, Turkey was stripped of her nominal sovereignty over Serbia, Montenegro and Rumania; Bosnia and Herzegovina went to Austria; part of Bulgaria became an independent principality; Greece obtained parts of Thessaly and Epirus; and Russia obtained Kars, Ardahan and Batoum. The Levant Service had been instituted before then, in the middle seventies, and even after the loss of all these territories, it still served our consulates in a wide Turco-Arabian Ottoman Empire. My colleagues in Nish and Monastir, Galatz or Albanian Scutari, were inheritors of an historic Service connexion and tradition.

Long before the first World War, the Capitulations had become a scandal and a provocation of nationalist sentiment wherever they existed. The abuses of the system, which were built-in in Suleiman's first treaty, were glaring. On high government level, no fiscal measures were practicable which might affect nationals of the country concerned but not their alien next-door neighbours: hence, for example, no income-tax in Egypt. On the tabloid-newspaper level, no dopester or brothel-keeper of foreign nationality could be arrested unless a consular *cavass*, or orderly, in his uniform of scarlet gold-braided bolero and baggy trousers, complete with scimitar, accompanied the police to the scene. By the time he got there, the brothel had changed hands and a different foreigner owned it, or the wanted man had seen the red glow and decamped.

Foreign nationals were not all of honourable antecedents. It was British policy not to allow any British prostitute, for instance, to settle in Egypt; but this was only effective against the home-grown product. Malta and Cyprus contributed their quota of undesirables for our official protection. London, to be fair, always did its best to bend the Capitulations to the other country's interest: as each Egyptian law against drug-traffic appeared, H.M. Government issued an order in council applying its provisions to British subjects. Other countries were not so scrupulous. In one notorious case in Cairo, two Italians, a Greek and a young Egyptian Jew called Jacoel were involved in a pocket-knife murder, unexpected when they broke in to steal. The Egyptian was the only one to be hanged. The others, after condemnation in their consular courts, and release on appeal to Athens and Ancona, were back in Cairo in less than three months, buying haberdashery from the Jacoel family shop.

Constantinople being the capital of the sultans' empire, it was there that our Service was most importantly represented, by the First, Second and Third Dragomans on the staff of the British Embassy. They combined the expert knowledge and activities of Oriental secretaries with special responsibilities in the Ottoman law-courts. The rest of us, scattered over the most interesting and eventful countries of the Near (now Middle) East, performed a variety of consular duties in a variety of posts. The lonely vice-consul in Diarbekir or Van might hope in time to become consul-general in Smyrna or Alexandria, but not for a very long time.

After his various examinations the young consular assistant sloughed his Cambridge student interpreter's coat and was posted, after a brief run-in in Constantinople or Tehran, to Bitlis, Moham-merah, Van, or some other remote corner of the Persian or Ottoman Empires, where his only contacts were with local officials and the rare British banker or American missionary. Three years without leave, or two years and a half if the post were technically 'unhealthy', improved his colloquial Turkish but numbed his spirit. A few such tours, and he was no longer quite himself.

Alternatively, he might be posted to Port Said or Alexandria, where he did not even have to speak French if he did not want to, and where the bulk of his working day was spent in the company of merchant seamen. This waste of his training had its own frustrations. And at the back of his mind, wherever he was employed outside the embassies, was a possible nagging thought that consular work is basically all in the book, and that by opening 'Consular Instructions' the rawest vice-consul could do ninety-five per cent of the office work of the most experienced consul-general. I was 'Acting Consul-General' in Alexandria within a few weeks of joining up. In what legation or embassy would a third secretary of those days have been allowed to act as *chargé d'affaires*? By its nature, the work of a consulate is practical and ephemeral; more concerned with people than with policies. Very little carries over from one day to the next, and very little becomes a problem for month-long resolution. I always preferred embassy work, more closely involved with questions of principle and policy, and therefore, I thought, engaging more intimately than 'Consular Instructions' the effort of imagination and reasoned argument.

Many of my colleagues would not have been seen dead in an embassy, but there were some who suffered from an occupational disorder called 'consulitis', an inflammation of envy provoked by the status and privileges then assumed by some diplomatists vis-à-vis their consular subordinates. The word 'subordinates' reflects a state of affairs implicit in the fàct that all consulates in a country are under the authority of the Diplomatic Mission. Not only could too personal an assumption of authority by a young third secretary be galling to a veteran consul-general; some ambassadors were actively unfriendly. Sir Francis Bertie is said to have rebuked one of his staff, warning him that he might only continue to frequent the company of the consulate juniors at hazard to his own career.

Even within the Foreign Office walls, there was something of an atmosphere. The post of Head of the Consular Department seemed to be that least sought-after by the patricians. I can hardly believe that Lord Dufferin really rang for an office-keeper and demanded: 'A lot of blotting-paper, quick!' when one distraught and desperate consul blew his brains out during an interview. But any consul visiting one of his successors could be sure of seeing the Foreign Office List open at his name, to refresh a languid memory. There is now one combined Foreign Service, and no more nonsense.

★ ★ ★

The three successful candidates in the Levant Consular Service of 1914 were, though we ourselves did not know it at the time, the last of the student interpreters. No one who followed us was expected to pile language upon language.

The first intake after the 1914 war was drawn from service candidates whose military record was recommendation enough. Some of them had learned their Turkish the hard way, in the prison-camps of Anatolia. They were individually and collectively impressive.

A year or so later, the Foreign Office imposed an examination, searching but less specialist than ours, and sent those accepted to Middle East posts as probationers, to work in missions abroad while acquiring the local language. This was good, but rather invidious in effect, for the time spent in office work and the opportunities for useful study varied widely from post to post. Probationers in Cairo and Beirout, for instance, were able to follow special courses in Arabic in the local American universities, but those elsewhere had no such facilities.

The Levant branch of the consular service was then merged with the General Consular Service; but young men who were Levant vice-consuls in all but name still continued to staff exclusively Levant posts. They became known as the 'Minor Vices'.

One by-product of this movement away from intensive language specialisation was the staffing of Middle East posts with men of a broader academic formation, less exposed by their studies of history or philosophy or economics to the hazards of idiosyncrasy. Our own more distorted formation did, indeed, produce some strange behaviour: a full collection of Levant Service legends would make strange reading.

Mr. A. was reported, when his summoning bell remained unanswered, to have fired his revolver through the office ceiling to ensure his orderly's attention. Mr. B., by mastering the art of the farrier, was able to shoe his own and anyone else's horses and became popular throughout the Balkans for his skill. Mr. C., when in Mosul, shot and killed a Kurd, thus putting us one-up on any diplomatist in sight. Mr. D., posted to Sarajevo, failed to turn up there and was missing, until discovered, mother-naked, in a cave on a Greek island. The Foreign Office, always loath to deprive anyone of pension-rights which only became valid at the retiring age of sixty, was expansively indulgent to human weakness. Mr. D. was patched up and sent on to his consulate at Sarajevo as if nothing had happened.

Mr. E., a keen student of things Romany, became blood-brother to every gipsy brigand in Bulgaria and offered them lavish consular sanctuary to the constant annoyance of the Varna police. Gipsies played a part in the life of Mr. F., also, for when his Italian colleague in Durazzo called on him by appointment, this officer was discovered in a bath with a gipsy girl. Mr. G. was a poet and wrote 'Hassan' before dying in a Swiss sanatorium. Mr. H. left his post, and the Service, forcibly enclosed in a Foreign Office bag. Mr. I. also left the Service and became a wagons-lits porter at Toulon, where he touted for my attention and left me with a tricky tipping problem. He later became an earl.

I would not have it thought that this catalogue is comprehensive. There are plenty more letters in the Levant alphabet.

Still less would I wish it to be thought that eccentricity was the dominant of behaviour in a great Service. We produced giants. Men like G. H. Fitzmaurice and Sir Harold Satow, Sir Reader Bullard, Sir Andrew Ryan and Sir Walter Smart would have been outstanding in any walk of life; in a Foreign Office context, they were all of the finest ambassadorial timber. A recent obituary notice in *The Times* referred to the Service as a 'corps d'élite'. If an emphasis of the anecdotal in any way disparages these and many other great men, may I never be forgiven.

Various amalgamations of what had been watertight compartments of activity finally culminated in one sprawling Foreign Service, and I began to fear that the last flicker of 'zoning' and specialised language-training must disappear. Wisely, the Foreign Office set up a 'Middle East Centre of Arabic Studies', first in Jordan and later in the Lebanon. It has done excellent work, and Whitehall shares its benefits with the larger oil companies and business firms. Its students are well-grounded not only in the language but also in the history, politics and economics of the Arab world, and they have the advantage and pleasure of trying out their Arabic on ploughmen in the fields or bank clerks in the restaurant. They are part of the local scene.

Arabic is only one Oriental language, and Shemlan (1970) is not Stamboul (1904). But the wheel seems to be edging to full circle, and we are not so far from those early Levant student interpreters, living in their villa on the Bosphorus.

I have always envied those men, because the languages they were studying were alive around them. Their instructors were peasants and pashas. They rode the countryside from Therapia to the Black Sea. They swam in Leander's wake. By a freemasonry of speech, more seductive than any clash of creeds, they were enabled to share the daily life of an Oriental people; sharing the exploration of the pungent, twilit bazaars; the amber-mouthed water-pipes and rattling backgammon boards of the coffee-house. All of us, when the years brought dust and disenchantment, might find a welcome to the meadows of sleep from Scheherazade and Aziyadé and Hajji Baba of Ispahan. But how can I not envy those men, talking and learning in that place of cypress-trees and minarets and bright water; able to live the sweet language they were learning there, where Europe meets Asia under that pearly Ottoman sky?

Chapter Two

Egypt and the High Commissioners

1

October relieves the oppression of Cairo's summer heat and brings cool sparkle to a clearer air. On a bright autumn morning of 1916 it was pleasant to me and to my friend Bond, to walk to work from our all but unfurnished flat in the rue de l'Ancienne Bourse. This exercise is now a procession of memories, for most of the scenery of our walk is today unidentifiable.

Leaving the building where Mr. Killingbeck on the ground floor displayed his treasures of baths and bidets, we turned into the rue Kasr-el-Nil, near the point where Cairo's one and only first-war bomb later killed pretty Madame Merzbach and her little pug-dog. The Turkish pilot had taken risks, flying his packing-crate from distant Gaza and landing behind the Pyramids before attempting the return journey. We skirted the Savoy Hotel, still General Headquarters, British Expeditionary Force, and the unlikely home of a large number of general officers directing remote operations beyond the Canal. Thus we came to the Maidan Soliman Pasha.

The Pasha, marmorean in the swaddlings and fez and baggy trousers of his day, stared stonily at a city where his name had been a legend, waiting for Groppi's second tea-shop to open at his feet. He had trained tens of thousands of Sudanese soldiers and had led them to rout the Turks in Syria and to threaten Constantinople itself. But before entering the service and accepting the faith of Mohammed Ali Pasha, for whom these wars were fought, he had another name, his own; and Colonel de Sève's French cavalry sabre and other relics of the Napoleonic wars were shown to me by his descendant, Abdurrahim Sabry Pasha, whose daughter was to marry King Fuad. Queen Nazli

passed on to her son this trace of French blood, and Farouq's
wife, Queen Farida (née Zulfiqar), may well have added another
European strain to her daughters' heritage. Many of the best
Zulfiqars in Egypt descend from a Greek sailor, captured during
the sea-fight at Navarino, who became a Moslem, and prospered.

There were very few shops in the rue Soliman Pasha when we
walked past the Mohammed Ali Club to a raucous cornering of
tramcars in the Maidan Ismailiya and turned towards the bronze
lions guarding the Kasr-el-Nil bridge. On our right lay the
Khedivial princess's palace that had become Kasr-el-Nil barracks,
where British troops paraded and kicked footballs about to the
admiration of urchins. Refusing the lions, we walked down the
rue Eyyoub, all of one side of which was a walled garden. This
led us into the aristocratic quarter of Kasr-el-Doubara, with
its new Semiramis Hotel, open only for six winter weeks each
year, and on the left the stately pleasure-domes of Casdaglis,
Rolos and Hararis. Beyond the hotel, along the Nile, lay the
great garden and palace of the Khediveh-Mother, and our street
was named after her. Her nearest neighbour was the British
High Commissioner, Sir Henry McMahon, the first of Britain's
representatives in Egypt to bear that title. The Residency, where
he lived and we worked, marked the end of our walk.

The Nile road ran on in a ribbon of palaces and villas behind
which there was nothing at all. An immense *terrain vague* stretched
dustily to Prince Mohammed Ali's cactuses and saracenic walls.
The tortuous maze of Garden City did not exist, even on paper.
By the same token, there was then no block of flats on Gezira,
where pashas and senior British officials had their elegant villas
and the Royal Flying Corps their headquarters in the Gezira
Palace hotel. That palace had been built by Khedive Ismail for the
brief sojourn of the Empress Eugénie, and its gardens, spreading
from the rue Boulaq along the Nile to the main Gezira road,
later became a suburb of expensive flats; but in 1916 the Elephant
and Castle and all the other good addresses were a banana-
grove. In another direction, Maadi was still an oasis of gardens,
where Mesdames Devonshire, Nimr and de Kramer rivalled in
roses.

Lord Cromer had lived for long in the rambling house in the rue Maghrabi that became the Turf Club; but when the Khedive offered attractive terms to all willing to settle in the then undeveloped Kasr-el-Doubara quarter, the British government built their Residency there. It was never a comfortable house, for it lacks the main north exposure which Cairo imposes, and suffers from an afternoon glare of sun. It is long and low and rather small. An unimpressive garden then stretched down to the Nile where strange flotsam washed against its wall. This, until 1914, was not only the home and residence of Cromer, Gorst and Kitchener; it also provided office accommodation for all their personal, diplomatic and service staff. The British Agent and Consul-General ruled Egypt and, in effect, the Sudan, with the assistance of one senior Foreign Office Counsellor, one Foreign Office Secretary, an Oriental Secretary, a Military Secretary and an Archivist. Our embassy staff later approached three figures.

In Lord Kitchener's day, a ballroom had been added, between the north wing of the house and the road, and into that room, chicken-cooped with partitions, the wartime Chancery had overflowed. It accommodated the Head of Chancery, Mervyn Herbert; two Second Secretaries, John Cecil and Hugh Lloyd-Thomas; an Honorary Attaché, Jack Gordon, and two Levant Consular Assistants, Bond, whose flat I shared, and myself. The Counsellor, Sir Milne Cheetham; the Military Secretary, Jimmy Watson; Ronald Storrs, the Oriental Secretary, and the High Commissioner worked in the house. There was no clerical staff at all.

Because the Foreign Office considered it neither proper nor prudent to unveil before the eyes of hirelings the mysteries of even the humblest Chancery chores, the young scions of Carnarvon and Exeter and their companions, after two years of war, were doing, not only most of the drafting, but all the typing, cyphering, accounts and archiving of an office which later filled a five-floor block. Only the Oriental Secretary and the Head of Chancery were exempt from these duties. This was wasteful. Craig, the Archivist, had Second Division origins. He was on leave: I was there to help Bond, who normally assisted him, to fill the gap. All of us, during my stay, might plausibly have concentrated on less ancillary duties; Bond and I, who had had hundreds of pounds of Government money spent on our Cambridge course of Oriental languages, might usefully have devilled for Storrs. Bond was Acting Archivist and I was Acting Archivist's mate; few tasks in Chancery are less distinguished, but such were the hazards of Foreign Service at that time. One of us wrote up correspondence-registers and card indexes; the other clipped and unclipped thousands of papers from the files, eight hours a day, seven days a week. I never sat down.

Four *cavasses* (orderlies) in scarlet and gold bashi-bazouk finery, and six *murasalas* (messengers) in sober blue, completed the human element of the room's population. A whiff of Whip-snade—and rather more than a whiff when a hot sirocco wind blew for fifty days—came from the ballroom floor, where a Saluqi bitch, an Irish wolf-hound and a Sealyham had their established places.

Valuable assistance was given by Lady Cheetham, both in typing and archiving; but her habit of indexing most things under 'T' (for 'The') was embarrassing. She was the step-daughter of Mouravieff, Imperial Russia's last ambassador to Italy, and she gave me my first peep at *l'âme slave*. One aspect of this was revealed when she found two small frogs between her ball and the hole on a Gezira green. She raised her putter and slew first one and then the other, before holing her putt. She also won the game, for her opponent was too shaken to offer further resistance.

The High Commissioner, to take first things last, was Lieut.-Colonel Sir Henry MacMahon, who had served in the Indian Political Service, ending up in Delhi as Foreign Secretary to Government. His distinguished career in India, where he demarcated the still controversial line of the frontier with Tibet and China, had left him with no knowledge of Arabic, or indeed French; and he never concealed a basic ignorance of things Egyptian and a real lack of interest in them. He rarely visited the sultan or met the cabinet, preferring to leave everything to the various British advisers, whose voluminous reports on this or that aspect of affairs we editorially topped and tailed and sent to London as being Sir Henry's own considered views. His only

Professor E. G. Browne with Staff and the last Levant Student Interpreters, Cambridge, 1915

Demonstrations, 1919

Ballroom-Chancery, Cairo, 1920

visible enthusiasm was locusts. He had had some success with locust control in India, and would discuss his methods with all and sundry. Hence a nickname, 'Loki', which also became the combination of the Chancery safe.

His main handicap was an assumption, then general in Egypt and probably in London also, that he was only in Cairo to keep the chair warm for Lord Kitchener, who had moved from Egypt to the War Office. McMahon was slight, sunbaked and spectacled; always courteous, but, in that job and at that moment of time, rather lightweight. This was most obvious in relation to the Arab revolt, for which he had political responsibility.

He had signed (I use the word advisedly) the famous letter* to the Sherif Hussein in Mecca which was to be the basis of Arab opposition to the Balfour Declaration. Officers of the Arab Bureau, the agency of this British involvement in Hejaz operations, passed often through our ballroom. We learned to recognise Hogarth and Cornwallis, who were Cairo-based, and their men from the field, Davenport and 'Skinface' Newcombe, Garland and Lawrence. Unfortunately, between Sir Henry McMahon and the G.O.C., Sir Archibald Murray, and between Cairo and Sir Reginald Wingate in Khartoum, disputes were frequent and bitter. Neither the Lieutenant-General at G.H.Q. nor the full General in the Sudan, appreciated the military appreciations of a Lieut.-Colonel in the Residency. Some Arab Bureau demands set an upper and a nether millstone turning.

*   *   *

Our work did not allow us much free time, but we had more leisure than our 56-hours-a-week schedule might suggest. We were in the office every day from 8.30 till 1.30 and from 5 p.m. till 8, unless there was something requiring overtime. The afternoon gap gave time for cables to come in for evening deciphering and it enabled us to spend the hottest time of the day at the Gezira Sporting Club, or shopping. I joined the club, and was still a member when Nasser requisitioned most of it.

* This letter is more comprehensively considered in a later chapter, see p. 153.

Another first step into a world that was to become familiar was an invitation to dine *en famille* in an Egyptian house. My host was a young expert on co-operative societies whom I had met on the ship coming out, and his large and pleasant wife was a niece of the redoubtable Madame Zaghlul Pasha. Turkish and Egyptian ladies being still strictly *harim* the experience of receiving a male and alien guest was not without its terrors for my hostess. The evening was spent more or less on tiptoe, and the occasion was never referred to in conversation with third parties.

In November we were asked to procure and to send to Buckingham Palace sets of the new Hejaz stamps, inspired by T. E. Lawrence, which were intended to boost the morale of Sherif Hussein in Mecca. On instructions we obtained blocks of sixteen stamps each of each type of stamp at each stage of printing, and these were enveloped for despatch by our next diplomatic bag. Then the whisper of a case of smallpox in the Survey Office, where the stamps had been printed, cast a diplomatic secretary for the role of an unwilling regicide. He assumed, hardly plausibly, that the royal tongue would moisten the mucilage of some 400 stamps, for attachment to the royal album. He boiled the whole batch in a saucepan to sterilise it, thereby removing the last trace of gum, and we had to start all over again.

When Lady McMahon was already at sea on her way to join him, Sir Henry read in a Reuter's telegram the news that he had been replaced by Sir Reginald Wingate, the Governor-General of the Sudan. Five of the six High Commissioners under whom I served in the Cairo Residency left Egypt before they expected to, at Whitehall's instigation; McMahon's dismissal was only the most cruel of this series. But it was a reflection of the hard fact that the British Agent and Consul-General whom he had replaced would not return to Cairo, and that McMahon's chair-warming tenancy must cease.

That great soldier, Field Marshal the first Earl Kitchener of Khartoum (there were nineteen distinguished letters after his name), was on his way to Russia to persuade the Tsar how best to keep his country in the war, when a German submarine sank HMS *Hampshire* with all on board, off the Orkneys, on June

5, 1916. He had been famous for many years, and had raised over five million men for the armed forces of Britain. He was mourned like a monarch, even by some of his enemies, who were many. His former Military Secretary, then still employed in the Residency, was distraught.

In such an atmosphere of respectful distress it was startling to find one small group who found some comfort in his passing. The local Syrian and Jewish collectors of porcelain and *objets d'art* told me that the very forceful endeavours of Kitchener's self-appointed agent, Ronald Storrs, to persuade them that their prize pieces would add welcomely to Lord K.'s own collection, had always been embarrassing, and sometimes impoverishing.

McMahon was appointed, after the war, when General Smuts' suggestion of mandates was under discussion, to act with Hogarth as a British delegate on a fact-finding mission ordained by President Wilson. The object was to ascertain the feelings of the people of Syria and the Lebanon, then a cockpit of conflicting Arab and French claims; but French opposition to this initiative availed to stultify it. Only the American delegates performed their task, and their report, firmly gallophobe, placed them on a Damascus blacklist and was soon, by French manœuvres, made obsolete.

Sir Henry lived to a great age, as Chairman of the Y.M.C.A. and of the National Bank of Persia. I doubt if he ever revisited Egypt, where his passage had hardly raised a ripple. But twenty years after he left us, Mohammed Mahmoud Pasha, one of Egypt's more distinguished politicians, told me that our best man had, of course, been McMahon. I asked him why he made this judgment. 'Because', I was told, 'we never knew what he was thinking.' This accepted excuse for a parrot's taciturnity made a strange eulogy of my first High Commissioner.

*   *   *

The first Lord Lloyd of Dolobran, the most old-fashioned thinker among Egypt's six High Commissioners, is at pains in his massive apologia to disclaim any intention of reviving 'Cromerism'. Indeed, he affects to ignore what the word can mean. But his

book more than once defines nostalgically what most people
would recognise as a rather flattering version of our proclaimed
line of policy in Egypt before the 1914 war: to safeguard certain
imperial interests vital to us; to fulfil certain responsibilities to
third parties; to secure the humane and stable administration of
the affairs of the Egyptian masses; and, in a remote future, to
hand over to some efficient and potentially stable Egyptian
Government. Already by 1910, this intention of terminating the
occupation had, according to Wilfred Blunt, been expressed in
twenty-four official declarations and pledges; when Turkey
entered the war in November 1914, the Occupation was a
museum-piece of *l'éternel provisoire*.

On November 6, 1914, Sir John Maxwell, Commanding British
Troops in Egypt, had proclaimed that Britain took upon herself
the sole burden of the war, without calling on the Egyptian
people for aid therein. Twelve days later, His Majesty's Government announced that '. . . Egypt is placed under the protection of
His Majesty and will henceforth constitute a British Protectorate . . . the suzerainty of Turkey over Egypt is thus terminated.'
Next day they announced that they had deposed Abbas Hilmy
Pasha, the Khedive of Egypt, and that Hussein Kamel Pasha,
eldest living prince of the family of Mohammed Ali, had accepted
the title of Sultan of Egypt. Abbas Hilmy had been *Son Altesse*;
the new dignity carried the ugly handle of *Sa Hautesse*. Large
marquee-type curtain hangings bearing the Arabic inscription of
Dar-el-Himaya, or 'The House of the Protectorate', soon orna-
mented the verandah and balcony of the Residency; they remained
there, an insult to all Egyptian guests, long after the British
protectorate had disappeared.

Prince Hussein Kamel was unique in Egypt in being without
an enemy, and he was beloved by the fellahin. His friendship with
Wingate was of long standing, close and constructive. He travelled
to Aswan to meet Wingate on his way up from the Sudan in
order to tell him personally how strained were relations between
the Palace and the Residency, and how deeply resented were the
attitudes of arrogance and independence which he observed in the
British advisers to his cabinet. Wingate was able, by tact and

firmness, to restore some confidence and goodwill to official relations, and thereby to secure more willing co-operation from the Egyptian government in matters concerning the conduct of the War. The Sultan's death in October 1917 was, indeed, a tragedy.

The successor to the Khedives was surrounded by a large family of the dynastic stock. There was the elegant and epileptic Prince Mohammed Ali, brother of the ex-Khedive, who was lavish in his advice to the Residency. There was the Sultan's own son, Prince Kemaleddin, who lived in sullen seclusion in a palace near the Kasr-el-Nil bridge which later became the Ministry of Foreign Affairs. There was Prince Youssef Kemal, who was always away shooting big game somewhere, with some handsome young man in attendance. There was Prince Haidar Fazil, who wrote French verses; and Prince Omar Toussoun, whose dislike of all things British combined with a strict austerity of morals to make him the favourite of all respectable Egyptians. Many of the others were later demoted by Fuad and became *Nablis*, in a new order of precedence which reflected Fuad as Sun. These included Amr Ibrahim, who built the charming Moorish villa opposite the Sporting Club entrance; Abbas Halim, the first leader of the Egyptian Labour party, who was, in 1916, flying with Mackensen in Rumania; Ismail Daud, in whose house in the Delta exclusive male entertainments were performed by an esoterically trained domestic staff; and a host more. The royal family frayed out further down into the eccentric, the raffish and the criminal. One princeling was coming out of Cartier's in Paris as my friend Robert Rolo went in, and he mentioned this casual meeting to M. Cartier. He was assured that the prince was a client, but that it was not the prince who had just left the shop. Mr. Rolo had played too much baccarat with the young man to be mistaken, and said so. 'I am sorry to hear it,' remarked Mr. Cartier. 'He told me that he was the prince's secretary, and I gave him a handsome commission on the deal.'

★   ★   ★

The population of Egypt (five million in 1863) was, in 1916, slightly over fourteen million—less than one-half of today's figure. This included about one million Copts, the native Egyptian Christians descended from first century converts. The consonants in CoPT and eGyPT vouch for their ancient origins.

The mass of the population, professing Islam, contained a few elements of pure Arab and Turkish stock, and some rare traces of mixed heredity. Statistically considered, it remained over-whelmingly and impressively Egyptian, sharing a language and a religion with the Arabs. Give or take an occasional history of immigrant blood, the Egyptian fellah, for all his Moslem faith and name, remains a blood-brother of the Copt whom he is tempted to despise. It is instructive, and indeed essential, in estimating Egyptian reactions to stress or challenge, to be guided by ex-perience of specifically Coptic behaviour, for there are archetypal national characteristics which no change of religion can basically affect. Similarly, I found it prudent, when involved in Dacca or Chittagong problems, to consider what the citizens of Hindu Calcutta, rather than those of Moslem Lahore or Peshawar, would do. The Bengalis of East Pakistan are devout Moslems, but their racial origins often dictate their attitude.

When Amr ibn 'Aas and his proselytising Arabs invaded Egypt (A.D. 639–641), most of the (largely pagan) native popula-tion, and some of the (Jacobite Monophysite) native Christians, accepted Islam. Many Christians fled south, to Upper Egypt, and even to Ethiopia whose Church they founded, and they survived to hold the faith preached by St. Mark, whom they claim as their first Patriarch. They suffered great humiliation through the centuries in Egypt, as serfs. Only in the mid-nineteenth century, when public education offered hope of better things, did they, like the Hindus in early British India, grasp eagerly an opportunity to equip themselves for the government posts of clerk or account-ant which Egyptian Moslems were still too proud, or too Koranic-ally prejudiced, to accept. During Cromer's time, the influence of the Copts in certain branches of the Administration, notably as *Bashkátibs* (Head Clerks) in the administration, and as technicians in the state railways, was preponderant. Their Christian profession

26

led some of them then to claim, without success, a position of favour and privilege in official British calculations. Very properly, the Coptic community was always represented by one member of whatever cabinet was in office.

One prosperous survivor from the earlier dispensation, Gallini Fahmy Pasha, who in his old age married the reigning Miss Europe, assured me that, as the child of serfs, he had been sold for two *keilas* of maize, at the age of three.

★ ★ ★

Between the descendants of Mohammed Ali the Great and the indigenous inhabitants of Egypt was a class whose disappearance was to be virtually complete in my own lifetime: the Turco-Egyptians, mostly of pure Turkish stock: the heirs of the men who had governed Egypt for a hundred years. They provided the social *élite* of the country; the ministers of the cabinets which came and went; the Mudirs or Governors of the provinces or the four towns. They studied law at French universities and soldiering at Sandhurst and St. Cyr. Even the laziest and most decadent of them possessed a natural authority then lacking in the pure local product. At their best they were very good indeed. But, as the Aràbi rising had shown, and as Zaghlul Pasha's hold on the country was to confirm, these pleasant people were as remote from Egyptian hearts as they were alien in origin and blood. You need Nile blood in the veins to be a successful demagogue in Egypt, and if there is a whisper of the darker Sudanese strain, as in Neguib Pasha, no Turk or foreigner stands a chance.

In 1916, the cabinet, by this historical monopoly, was of exclusively Turkish stock, except for the necessary Copt. Hussein Rushdy Pasha, the diminutive Prime Minister, had a Sorbonne-trained legal mind, which made him a good one. He had bristling white hair and moustachios, and wore pince-nez, thus creating an overall effect of Monsieur Delcassé in a fez.

Adly Yeghen Pasha, whose blood was as good as any Khedive's, seconded him, as Minister of the Interior. Had extremism and irresponsibility not been allowed to bedevil Egyptian politics,

Adly might well have given his country service matching his own very impressive presence. He was tall and square-shouldered, of handsome charm, and he had a dignity and courtesy rare outside the circles of archdukes and highland lairds. He had complete integrity—a precious attribute in Egypt—great wealth and much wisdom. But a fatal strain of laziness, or lack of ambition, or perhaps an aristocratic distaste for the dustier corners of the arena, frustrated all hopes placed upon him, and condemned the Moderates, whose leader he became, to perpetual insuccess. He was a little too good for the rough and tumble of politics.

Ismail Sirry, the white-bearded Minister of Public Works, was a graduate of Cooper's Hill. He had been recommended to a British Prime Minister by Egypt's nationalist firebrand, Mustafa Kamel, in 1905, as being ministerial timber. So had Yehya Ibrahim Pasha, who was in 1916 a rather dim figure; his chance came later, when Fuad needed a subservient tool. Two other Turco-Egyptians in the cabinet, Ibrahim Fathy Pasha and Ali Hilmi Pasha, had no moral right to be there at all. A well-liked Egyptian Christian, Yusuf Wahba Pasha, represented the interests of the Coptic community.

The most astute operator of them all, Ismail Sidqi Pasha, who had been in this cabinet, was dropped from office in 1915, after a scandal—by no means his last—involving Yehya Ibrahim's daughter and a *dahabiyya* on the Nile. His extreme intelligence and ruthless skill were to give him not one but several comebacks, and even a severe stroke failed to cramp him for long. He was *capable de tout*, which in Egypt means a lot, and he was never visibly put off balance, being 'unflappable'. Something about the cut of his moustache made the creamy smile with which he greeted bad news or good a little feline. He was one of the rare Egyptian politicians whose conversation was an intellectual excitement.

Three of Rushdy's ministers, and the son of a fourth, followed him as Prime Ministers of Egypt. Twilight in that Circassian world did not fall until Gamal Abdel Nasser, son of a village postman in Upper Egypt, seized the reins of power and surprisingly persuaded his fellow descendants of the Pyramid-builders that they were Arabs.

I remember Rushdy Pasha, returning from Europe by sea,

being enchanted at the sight of a pretty young thing whose skirts were whipped vertical by the sea breeze. He was then an old man and all but *gaga*, but he had not abdicated a proper interest in such delights. He rose from his deckchair and tore the rosette of the *Légion d'Honneur* from his button-hole, throwing it over the ship's railings and crying: *Oh Vent! Je te décore!*'

Another wind has blown away all that *panache*; all the Toussouns and Shirins; the Izzets, Monasterlis and Sherifs; the Elwis, Daramallis and Yeghens: all that gay Circassian world. Egypt has no use for them.

Absent from the cabinet was the only indigenous Egyptian Moslem ever to have been a minister, Saad Zaghlul Pasha. Cromer had made him Minister of Education and had paid tribute to him in his farewell speech, and his name now rings through the history books; but in 1916 the Residency had forgotten it.

Each Egyptian minister, except the Minister for Waqfs (Religious Foundations), had a British adviser at his elbow, whose advice he was expected to take, or else. The aim of these advisers was, presumably, good administration and a gradual training for autonomy, and they were a distinguished and talented body of men. Lord Edward Cecil, who was Financial Adviser, has written of his experiences as an Egyptian official from the angle of humour; but he was a heavyweight, and that noble head, looking like its own marble sculpture, always impressed. Sir George Grahame, a professional diplomatist, was at the Interior; but he was soon sent to the Embassy in Rome. Most forceful of them all, Sir William Brunyate, ruled as Judicial Adviser, before succeeding Cecil at the Finance. Here was a man born to provoke Egyptian hatred to an extraordinary degree, with a reputation for harsh speaking and churlish intolerance unbecoming to his role. Hardly less unpopular was the portly, bearded Dr. Dunlop, whom Cromer had beckoned from relatively lowly circumstances to organise Egypt's education service. These men and others of the advisers— Sir William Hayter was a shining exception—seemed to have allowed the excitements of legislation by martial law to go to their heads.

29

British officials in the Administration tended to become the handmaidens of General Headquarters. If Sir John Maxwell had never excluded Egypt from the war-effort; if Egypt had been a British Colony, this tendency to consider her no longer as a country to be instructed and trained for autonomy, but as one whose interests must be subordinated to the British cause of serving G.H.Q., might have been patriotically acceptable.

There were, in any case, rather too many British officials; Cromer's firm criterion of quality had been quantitively diluted. We had not only the Inspectorates of Finance and Interior, Public Works and Irrigation, Agriculture and Education; we had hundreds of schoolmasters and schoolmistresses; engine-drivers; station-masters; lighthouse-keepers; traffic police; shorthand typists, and a host more; all paid by the Egyptian Government and established for Egyptian pensions. They wore the official *tarboush*, or fez, which gave distinction to the homeliest English face, and they were very thick on the ground. This may have served some short-term convenience, but it was obviously bad policy after nearly forty years of British occupation. Where example is everything, swollen numbers increase the risk of indifferent performance, quickly observed by the populace. A point is reached, somewhere down the scale, where indigenous graduates and craftsmen feel that they could do the job as well or better: and more cheaply.

As so often, it was a question of *la manière*. A calculated disregard of official courtesies, with a humiliating assumption of the right to rule, caused resentment and ill-feeling, which soon became an inflamed and angry sense of injustice. What, if anything, did Sir John Maxwell's Proclamation mean?

This was the world to which Sir Reginald Wingate came from the Sudan in December 1916. It was a world he knew better than most men.

During the Boer War, schoolboys advertised their patriotism by displaying in the button-hole of their Norfolk jackets a selection of buttons carrying 'Portraits of British Generals'. In my prep-school, this tenuous association with Kitchener and 'Lord Bobs' was the prerogative of the older boys; lesser dogsbodies made do with Redvers Buller, Baden-Powell and the others. I used to carry on my chest a small picture of a portly person in a tall fez, with a regimental bandmaster's white waxed moustache which survived the years. This was 'General Wingate, Sirdar of the Egyptian Army'. I have no reason to believe that he ever went near South Africa, but I liked the look of the fez.

Wingate was a political and military heavyweight, with a close and informed experience of Egyptian affairs and personalities covering over thirty years. It was he who had planned with skill and patience the intelligence side of the reconquest of the Sudan, from 1896 to 1898; and he had been for seventeen years Governor-General of the Sudan (an Anglo-Egyptian condominium), and Sirdar, or Commander in Chief, of the Egyptian Army. He was respected and admired throughout the African Moslem world and wherever Arabic echoes sounded. He was also popular as few overseas administrators can be with the great British public, for he was part of the myth of Gordon, of Kitchener of Khartoum and of the River War; and his translations of the books of men who escaped from the Khalifa's captivity were best-sellers. In 1884, as a young A.D.C., he saw General Gordon off from Cairo on his last journey to Khartoum. Sixty-nine years later, in 1953, an Anglo-Egyptian Agreement permitted the present independence of the Sudan, and in that year Wingate died.

He was preceded to Cairo by some who were to become well known there; a (to me repulsive) creature, Lady Wingate's whale-headed stork, *balaeniceps rex*, a rarity from the Bahr-el-Ghazal; and a black personage in blue and silver uniform, soon known as the 'Popinjay', who was our new master's personal *cavass* and golf-caddy.

Before Wingate himself arrived, our archivist had returned from his home leave, and this released me for service at the British Consulate-General in Alexandria.

I left Bond in sole occupation of the little flat. One-and-a-half wars and thirty years later, he collected from me the consular fee charged for Performance of a Marriage. Kind things were said to me on my departure by all in the Residency, but I noticed a recurrent note of pity in these farewells. I might have been going to some minor martyrdom. This was, in fact, the thought in everyone's mind, for my consul-general in Alexandria had a reputation for aberrantly eccentric behaviour and innate arrogance, exceptional even in the higher ranks of the Levant consular service.

2

Thanks to the art and industry of Lawrence Durrell, the city of Alexandria is now a suburb of the European mind. Its streets and palaces, its harbour and slums, lie shimmeringly reflected in the memory of a poet who was four years old when I first lived there. His is the Alexandria of the second World War, but it is closer to the image of the city I knew in 1916, despite the social and architectural scene-shifting of twenty-five years, than to the gaunt and echoing Alexandria of today. Penury and despair have reduced the proud hierarchies of Levantine dominion. The elegance, corruption and aristocracy of wealth has vanished in an emigrant stampede. There is a new and different vulgarity of behaviour. Where was a Greek colony is now the shadow of an Omdurman market, for Africa has engulfed the last bastion of the Mediterranean.

For the governor, the municipality, the public health authorities and the police, Alexandria, then as now and always, was a large sprawling Egyptian town, whose labyrinth of tangled streets swarmed with hundreds of thousands of half-submerged Egyptians, living in poverty and dirt and ribald gaiety; like most Egyptians, fanatical rather than religious, and more vicious than most from centuries of infiltration by sea-faring sin. The bright sheen of corruption which gave its patina to the so-called native quarter was a sediment of the scum of the maritime Levant.

Within this territory, the White Highlands of society and commerce were occupied by the heirs of Athens and Rome and Phoenicia, and the commanding heights by the Greeks. The Greeks were, in fact, at home. Greek palaces and graves lay beneath the waves that lapped the lighthouse of Ras-el-Tin; their lovely Tanagra figurines graced the local museum shelves; the city's very name gave them right of domicile, and Alexander—

if legend was true—was buried where the Nabi Daniel mosque then stood. They dominated the town's economy at every level. Their leaders, the Sinadinos, Benachis, Choremis, Sinanos, Vlastos and Zervudachis, shared their consul's registers with little men who made their main meal off a tomato and two slices of beetroot in the rue Adib, before starting off again on their life's work as middlemen in the toilet-paper or boot-lace business.

The Italians, too, were ubiquitous. The British and French, much respected and very successful businessmen, were in, but hardly of, this community. The British retained too dogged an insularity, and the French too patriotic a nostalgia, to make total surrender to an alien ambience. The Belgians, outside the *Parquet* offices, were apparently only interested in tramways. The thousands of Christian Syrians and Lebanese, Jews and Armenians, who supplied the mass of the population of this little world, gave it its specific Levantine quality. Many of these, eagerly shaking off their local citizenship, had acquired, by hook or crook, some foreign nationality: Jacques Suarès was a Portuguese, and represented Portugal in the consular corps; others of his family were French or Italian or had remained 'local subjects'. The de Menasce family had been given Austrian passports, and so found themselves to be enemy aliens in wartime. There was continuous pressure to move under the spacious canopy of the Capitulations, which gave to foreign nationals its protection and shelter.

The detachment of this, the dominant element in the city's life, from the rest of Egypt, was remarkable. The Alexandria we knew was as Mediterranean a town as Genoa. It stretched, residentially, from Mohammed Ali Square up the rue Cherif Pacha and along the rue Rosette, into the fastness of the *Quartier Grec* and on, out of the town, where its villas mapped the whole suburb of Ramleh. In all this area, there was an occasional Egyptian laundry but hardly one Egyptian shop. At the corner of the rue Cherif Pacha and Mohammed Ali Square stood the temple of Levantine Alexandria, the Bourse. Beyond that, another world began. In the Mohammed Ali Square, in 1921, an Italian sailor was dowsed in petrol and burned alive by a cheering mob, merely because he was a European.

I confess to finding the people who inhabit Durrell's Alexandria less easy to recognise than his city. Never did I meet those Levantine socialites, graduates of some advanced Pelman Course, who cap six-page quotations from an old book with seven-page quotations from a forgotten bread-and-butter letter, and pass on to recall, in word-perfect and patient antiphony, a forty-minute conversation of years past between third parties in the children's brothel of the rue des Soeurs. Nor do I easily accept a Copt called Narouz, or the hypothesis of Coptic complicity in Zionist terrorism.

In the bulldog-kennels of the Union Club, the word 'Levantine' had a pejorative connotation. It implied the elevation to a principle of mere financial success; a blurring of essential standards; a certain moral suppleness, and probably the wrong attitude during shipwreck. Smyrna was always regarded and quoted as the example to avoid. Constantinople—'he's a Constantinople Scot!' —and Gibraltar were hardly less condemnable; and even our leading businessmen, if such birthplaces were, however distantly, discernible in the branches of their family-tree, were suspect. The cardinal rule was that boys should always be sent home when quite young to be educated in England, before joining the family firm.

The British colony, indeed, had its own strict conventions of behaviour. They were helped in their struggle to abstain from the pollution of idols by the circumstances of Egyptian history. Their fellow-crusaders in Turkey, the Whittalls and Lafontaines and other descendants of the Levant Company's staff, did not enjoy, in their battle for spiritual survival, the immense support of a Cromer, determined to inspire in every British subject in Egypt a sense of individual representational responsibility and prestige. As a result, my distinguished compatriots in Alexandria, the Peels and Aldersons, Carvers and Barkers, displayed the more rugged British virtues in almost uncomfortable manifestation.

Nothing could have been kinder than my reception, as a young consular dogsbody, into this strange new world. Once there, having a natural appetite for the exotic, I at once gravitated towards the *Quartier Grec*. I was, fortunately, never expected to return one-twentieth of the massive hospitality offered me: an unattached young man seemed to be always welcome. The monotony of my consular days was changed, after dark, for a glittering round of dinner-parties and dances, presided over by heavily jewelled dowagers and populated by a flower-garden of lovely girls, bringing to my eager experience the heady intoxication of Oriental beauty in its adolescent perfection. Prince Ahmed Fuad was often among those present, spilling his coffee on the carpet with the best of them—('*Ça porte bonheur, Monseigneur!*')—until destiny whistled him to a throne.

Subconsciously, I suppose, my pleasure in those days was increased by the novelty of intimacy with a very wealthy society. I was twenty-four years old, and I had never before been part of a world where drawing-rooms were museums of Meissen and Sèvres, Persian carpets and French paintings; where French chefs, in private houses, controlled a kitchen staff of fifteen; where girls paid £40—(multiply by 4 or 5 today)—for a Cherhuit frock, which they threw away after wearing it three times; where Lebanese matrons used diamond and emerald bracelets as Admirals might use gold braid on the sleeve, to impress and overawe. All this, sometimes ostentatious, affluence gave to the invitation-cards of Donna Vittoria Sursock, or Madame Sinadino, or the two little Countesses de Zogheb, a gilt-edged quality of attraction.

Dinner-parties and dancing and bathing-picnics were not all that Alexandria had to offer. The 'Lena Ashwell Concert Party', marooned in Egypt by a wartime ban on travel in the Mediterranean, brought us the nightingale voice of Marjorie Ffrangçon-Davies. Georges de Menasche played the piano, and there was good talk to be had outside the circle of established residents. The nuisance of the Capitulations had produced in Egypt a special judiciary, to hear 'mixed' civil, but not criminal, cases between foreigners and Egyptians; and the many foreign judges on the bench of these 'mixed courts', whose court of appeal was in Alexandria, helped, as did the consular corps and local British officialdom, to leaven the Levantine lump.

My own favourites in these mixed court circles were Judge and

Mrs. Pinkney Tuck, who brought to a Ramleh suburb the graces of Virginia. Their son Kippy was then a stripling, learning to mix mint-juleps. Their daughter, after much thought, had refused to marry an English officer. The young man sailed next day from Egypt and was torpedoed within sight of the Tuck's house. He swam most of the way ashore, put his question again and was accepted. Kippy, later a successful American ambassador to Egypt, told me that they lived happily ever after.

Every community has its licensed buffoon. We had Johnny Sinadino, a small, middle-aged man with a long prehensile nose, who cast himself always for the predestined victim of circumstance. He was a shrewd businessman, but after dark he liked to make people laugh. His own laugh was unique, a high repetitive brain-fever-bird note, which was immediately contagious. As soon as this treble cackle was heard in a theatre, the show was made; nobody could resist it. But when Johnny decided to raise a gale of laughter by going to a very English party with a mahogany girdle round his waist and a miniature gilt cistern over his head, pulling his little gilt plug-chain to spray his hostess with French perfume, no one was amused.

There was then no Corniche Road to limit bathing opportunities to a few concrete-cabined beaches, and one could find, along the stretch between Stanley Bay and Glymenopoulo, delightful coves, or odd corners where one could bathe off the rocks. Transport was by the Ramleh tram-line, which ran for miles, forking at Mustafa Pasha to San Stefano in one direction and to Victoria in the other. Most of the stations along this light railway took their names from members of the original board of directors, whose villas had imposed these halts; and this business association of Mr. Bulkeley, Mr. Glymenopoulo, Mr. Zizinia and Saba Pasha survived their deaths in tram-ticket memorial.

Beyond San Stefano, civilisation ended in desert and peasant cultivation. There was no road across the sands; no Sidi Bishr beaches; only the far palace of Montaza. But one could follow the road on to Aboukir, and there survey the scene of Nelson's victory, and the mosque which old Sir George Alderson had built, to counter-balance the little church he had built near Stanley

Bab-el-Zuweileh, Cairo

Egyptian Felláh

Cairo mosques

Bay. He had an old hulk moored in the middle of the bay, the remains of a Crimean War hospital ship, and from its creaking deck, where Florence Nightingale may have inspected homing casualties, one could plunge and plunge again. In late summer, the Nile flood comes roaring down from Abyssinia to pour thousands of tons of precious silt into the Mediterranean at Damietta, and the sea becomes richly phosphorescent for miles along the coast. A moonlight picnic on Sir George's 'Noah's Ark' was then an unusual entertainment. The oars of the boat taking us out across Aboukir Bay churned liquid light, and every swimmer cut himself a golden silhouette of glow-worm spray as he moved against the darkness. To dive deep down, eyes wide open, was to swim into the sun.

3

Mr. Donald Andreas Cameron, C.M.G., His Majesty's Consul-General, Alexandria, found much to dislike in life, but nothing more intensely than his own middle name. I never heard it explained, but its suggestion of alien blood was a cross to be borne. Once, when Madame Melas, the wife of a Greek court chamberlain, came into the office, Cameron greeted her with the declension of her name: *Melas ... Melaina ... Melan.* She properly thought this rather discourteous, but smiled charmingly and said: 'I see you have not forgotten your Greek, Mr. Cameron!' 'Madame!' he replied, 'Don't be impertinent!' He probably thought that she said: 'You're'.

He exemplified all too well some of the Levant service distortions. He was a man of fine intellect, who knew, among other things, just what Napoleon was doing at every moment of his life. He had served for some years as a Judge in the Native Courts in Cairo, where all proceedings are in Arabic, and he had written a valuable dictionary of Arabic judicial terminology. He had also written a good little history of *Egypt in the Nineteenth Century.* He would today have made a powerful Ambassador. The best he could hope for then was his £1,500 a year, the top of the service's salary scales, yielding a £750 annual pension. And to ensure this, he had to spend his days doing work that offered singularly little scope for his talents.

He enjoyed, and exploited, a reputation for extreme eccentricity. He shocked the last departing guest at one of his garden-parties by saying: 'My wife died last night. Goodbye!' At another party, he had welcomed effusively an uninvited gate-crasher and escorted him amicably, arm on shoulder, around the flower-beds. When they reached the garden door, Cameron flung it open and waved the man through to the street, saying: 'Have a look at this! The view from the outside is much admired!'

He was a distinguished old gentleman, then aged sixty-three, tall and portly; with glazed and chilling eyes and a large expanse of dewlapped cheek. Being rather bald, he wore a little black *calotte* in the house, which lent to his promenading of the office-corridors a heavily ecclesiastic air. In the morning, he was always on the prowl; and, if he paused on his way to inspect the shipping office, he would ask the general public in the central waiting-room some surprising questions.

'Good morning, Madam! How many children have you? What? Unmarried? Then why did you try to deceive me?'

I watched him once deal with a little bald Maltese who sat there quietly, with his hat on his knees.

'Put on your hat, Sir, you'll catch cold! I wear a skull-cap my-self.'

After protestations, the man put on his straw hat and remained uncomfortably different from all around him. Cameron, returning from the shipping office, was shocked to see evidence of such patent disrespect. He stared at the man and tapped his own head, as a hint. The man smirked and tapped his hat, to show that all was still well. This went on for three exchanges of tapping, which on Cameron's side became more and more violent. Finally, he exploded:

'And who the devil are you, Sir, to wear your hat in His Britannic Majesty's Consulate-General? *Awad!*'

The cavass appeared.

'Throw this person out!' Out he went.

After luncheon this activity ceased. He rarely came down to the office in the afternoon. Once, after tennis, I ran upstairs to his flat to ask for instructions in an emergency. They were never given. I was told, rather stumblingly, never, never to come upstairs in tennis shoes.

He wrote innumerable short notes, which he left silently on my desk. I wisely never replied in writing. He had kept every reply received from the vice-consul whom I was replacing, and these, grateful or angry in tone, he would display to me as evidence of the young man's unstable and inconstant character.

Until near the end, he was kind to me. He taught me the basic consular routines; pruned away the extravagances of my drafting; told me of the strange life of Suakin during the Mahdist troubles. Our Maltese pro-consul, Paul Cassar, completed my education.

Most of my work was concerned with the registration f British subjects; the administration of the Merchant Shipping Acts, and the affairs of the provincial court.

We signed seamen on or off; took charge of them when they were submarined or left ashore, sick; found passages for them as Distressed British Subjects; toothcombed their personal effects after death, before forwarding them home, to remove dirty postcards or any feminine photograph which might not be that of the wife. As there was a war on, every morning brought fifteen or twenty bleary-eyed men off ships in harbour, arrested for being drunk and disorderly somewhere in the Gueneina Quarter. This was Cameron's job.

'Name? Baines? Ten shillings fine, Baines!'

'Name? McNeill? Ten shillings fine, McNeill!'

'Name? Cameron! One pound fine, Cameron, for disgracing my name!'

He affected the greatest contempt for drunkards, and when he heard that the Commandant of Police, Hopkinson Pasha, had given his name to a long drink at the Union Club, he nearly burst with emotion. I had already noticed the sweet stench of the cachous he had begun to suck.

I rarely sat alone in court, but I enjoyed the experience when it came. I was happy enough to handle straightforward simple cases, but was always uneasy when some Cairo lawyer was involved, fearing that I might do something stupid with the laws of evidence. Cameron was impressive on the bench, where, for some reason, he always doffed his skull-cap.

In one case, involving broached cargo, the master and mate of the vessel had given lengthy and circumstantial evidence, but Cameron was bored by their zeal. He turned to the accused, a young Norwegian, and said: 'What is your name, my boy?'

'Pederson, Sir.'

'What is your nationality?'

'Norwegian, Sir.'

'Then listen, Pederson. Do you know just what the penalty is in a British Consular Court for Norwegian boys who broach cargo in British ships, in an Egyptian harbour, in time of Martial Law?'

The boy trembled. 'No, Sir,' he stammered.

'Neither do I!' said Cameron. 'Go away, all of you.'

He adjourned the court on another occasion, when old Tadros, the marshal, whispered that the next witness to be summoned was momentarily off the map. 'Oh!' said Cameron, thinking of the outside lavatory, 'he's out in the yard, is he?' It was revealed that Mr. Farrugia was, in fact, in the Holy of Holies reserved for Cameron and myself. The court was adjourned and the *calotte* resumed. He strode across the passage and thundered on the door behind which Mr. Farrugia cowered. 'What are you doing in my W.C., Mr. Farrugia?' he bellowed. Mr. Farrugia had not the courage to give him two guesses. As blows rained on the door, he climbed trouserless through the window and ran for home. We had to get a locksmith to open the door, and Mr. Farrugia's evidence was never taken.

My least favourite chore was the viewing of bodies before an inquest. Cameron passed this to me, after having had to examine a personal friend who fell from the third storey of his house. Bloated bodies from the sea, and slashed throats, gave me some grisly official moments.

Perhaps the least popular formality imposed on travellers arriving in Egypt was the enforced promenade past a cubby-hole from which an Egyptian clerk called out your name from the ship's passenger-list, held out his hand for fifteen piastres and ticked your name off, all without once looking up at you. You had then successfully passed the International Quarantine Board's medical examination. As United Kingdom delegate on this Board, which had its seat in Alexandria, I was on the receiving end of this racket and was rewarded with an extra allowance of fifty pounds a year.

We met ostensibly to prevent plague and cholera from entering the Hejaz during the annual pilgrimage, but little was done to protect the Hejaz from Egypt itself, where plague was endemic. We published a report, *Marche de la Peste*, every week. The Board's main interest lay in its other duty, to prevent plague or cholera from spreading to other countries after the Haj. One precious souvenir of pilgrimage was water from Zem-Zem—traditionally the source of succour of Ishmael, founder of the Arab race (Gen. xxi. 19). Suspect because of the risk of pollution upstream— and Egypt's last cholera epidemic had been traced to a tin of it— this water was anathema to the board. Tins and bottles were relentlessly seized, and returning pilgrims firmly herded into quarantine stations, whose revenue paid my perquisite.

Our chairman was a grossly obese charmer called Granville Pasha, who had a mind like a needle and ran the Alexandria municipality in his spare time. If he would have made a good Sancho Panza, his Secretary-General, Zananari Pasha, looked like a miniature Don Quixote. He was a very lean man with a Cyrano-esque nose; a native of the Ionian Islands and so, by historical accident, holder of a British passport. As he was assumed to sway the Board's decisions, he had received from all the maritime Powers except Britain an impressive collection of decorations. These he flaunted on ceremonial occasions, together with the medals of all five degrees of the Ottoman Orders of both the Mejidieh and the Osmanieh. He made his entry at official parties shimmering like a Christmas tree.

There was an obtrusive medical angle to our decisions about a 'clean' or 'unclean' Pilgrimage, and about a wide range of epi-zootic diseases, and I was supported technically by our local Scottish doctor. I threw a fly over my colleague, who was also our consulate doctor, and I was told, rather improperly, that my personal explanation of my consul-general's habits was all too well grounded: 'Liver like a bit of old rope!', I was informed. Apart from Mr. Cameron's Adenese servant, the doctor and I remained the only people to hold this key to his eccentricities. I was not happy about the situation, for any adverse report from my chief might blast me out of the service by return of post.

Our consular building, resting like so many in Alexandria on buried ruins, was gradually settling. Every evening, I pasted sticking-paper over cracks in the wall, and found it ruptured next morning. Now it seemed that the head of the house was also sinking slowly into collapse.

In late 1917, my colleague and predecessor as vice-consul, with whom Mr. Cameron was at feud, arrived in Alexandria on leave from his Intelligence duties with our forces in Mesopotamia. After a good luncheon at the Union Club, he visited the consulate at 2 p.m. and found the iron gates shut. Cameron called from the balcony of his flat to tell him to come back at 3 o'clock, when the office would reopen. The temporary captain thereupon climbed over the high gates and forced his way into the office. On a table, he found a batch of the forms we used to issue to persons author-ised to enter the Canal Zone. He had completed one: '*Name:* Donald Andreas Cameron. *Nationality:* Alleged British, but probably Greek', when Cameron came down to ask what was going on. The confrontation was stormy.

Cameron complained to the military authorities that the captain had done this and that 'while bestially drunk'. There was a judicial enquiry, and the Judge Advocate found that the word 'bestially' was not proved. A writ was then issued in the Cairo consular court, and this was sent to my consul-general to serve on himself. It all took a lot of sorting out, before the Residency managed to stop the nonsense.

The first Sunday in 1918 was ordained by the Archbishop of Canterbury to be a Day of Repentance and Prayer, at home and overseas. Cameron and I, in top hats and frock coats, attended a special service at St. Mark's. But the Maltese community, as always aggressively loyal, insisted that they also should repent and pray, if that was likely to bring the end of the war any nearer. They hired the cathedral of St. Catherine's and the Roman Catholic archbishop as well; and we were invited to be guests of honour at this pious act of religious solidarity. Cameron's afternoon was mis-spent, and by the evening, he was swaying.

We drove to the Cathedral, black in our frock-coats and top hats, and were given a front pew to ourselves. The great church was packed. Behind us were four pews full of R.C. army chaplains; there were large naval contingents, and all the Maltese in the world. When the archbishop began the service, Cameron began also, and he and I were in conversation for the next three-quarters of an hour. My contributions were whispered; his were loud and clear. I have never been so painfully embarrassed in my life.

'What's he doing now, Mr. Grafftey? What? Changing his clothes again? Good Gracious!'—turning to the chaplains behind us—'Can any of you gentlemen tell me why he should have to keep changing his clothes? . . . Are you kneeling, Mr. Grafftey?'

'Yes, Sir.'

'I'm delighted to hear it. I thought you had your bottom on the chair!'

When the service ended, he rose and put on his top hat.

'Just going up to shake the Archbishop's hand,' he announced.

I persuaded him at last to take his hat off; and he did, in fact, go up to the altar and shake hands.

On the way down the aisle, where the whole congregation was waiting for us to leave, he asked me merrily what I was doing later that night: 'Have a bottle of champagne on me,' he urged. It may be amusing now, but it was terrifying then.

I had not much longer to stay with Mr. Cameron.

The Alexandria winter can be cold and raw, with a bitter rain from the sea. I used to make sure of dry feet in the office by wearing spats on my walk from the boarding house, half a mile away. Cameron noticed them one day and was heavily humorous. That night, at eleven o'clock, a Consular orderly brought round to me an all but indecipherable note from him, saying that he would not allow me to appear again in his office wearing spats, '. . . the

Anathema Maranatha . . . the *ne plus ultra* of contempt'! If I were to appear in them again, it would be his sorrowful duty to instruct the cavasses to tear them off me.

I heard next day that he had read this ultimatum to the orderly, before giving it to him for delivery. I was very angry. I wrote him a note, my first, saying that it was difficult enough to keep discipline in the office during his absences upstairs, and that this would be impossible if he chose to discuss my clothes and habits with the native staff. He sent this note off to the Residency in Cairo and asked to be relieved of my presence without delay. I had a most friendly letter from Sir Milne Cheetham, sympathising with what he guessed might be my emotions and saying that he would be happy to have me back in the Chancery. A vice-consul from the Cairo consulate was sent to replace me. With delight, I took the train back to Cairo.

Mr. Cameron survived for some months as consul-general, but his attitudes during a luncheon-party given for the Duke of Connaught attracted the critical notice of our Military Secretary, who reported them. I was summoned by Sir Milne Cheetham and ordered to tell all I knew. Cameron was recalled to London, but apparently no one in the Foreign Office felt able to tell him why. He lived in rooms in Swiss Cottage, and, having sent each of his daughters a postcard saying that her allowance would stop that day, he married his landlady. This did not last long, and he moved on to the Italian Riviera. When Mussolini began his revolution, my old chief, the Donald and the Cameron dominant, launched a one-man campaign against Fascism, and had some success in the local estaminets and bars trolling his version of the Fascist *Giovanezza*, which went: '*Violenza! Violenza! Viva la Schiavitù!*' He managed to make his escape from the back door of his hotel as the castor-oil boys came in at the front, and he slipped over the frontier to Menton. There, after a year or two, a losing battle was lost.

'Dear Mr. Grafftey, Read the bee-yoo-tiful Poem in today's "Egyptian Gazette", signed LORENZO, WHO can the POET be?'

'Dear Mr. Grafftey, Very nice, BUT NEVER "Jeudi, le 5 mars", ALWAYS "le jeudi 5 mars". PLEASE.'

'Dear Mr. Grafftey, What a bee-yoo-tiful despatch! I shall have the draft framed in GOLD, with glass on BOTH SIDES!'

There were many small, and a few considerable kindnesses. Nowadays nobody consults the Arabic Dictionary, and *Egypt in the Nineteenth Century* has long been out of print. The historian of Napoleon, the Judge of the Native Courts, His Majesty's Consul-General, the unhappy, domineering old man, has gone. Fifty years later, I still find it painful to think of him, foundering, like some great ship, in a sea of loneliness, frustration and despair.

4

Much had happened in Egypt during my term of service in Alexandria; not least, the death of Sultan Hussein Kamel in October, 1917, and his succession by his younger brother, Prince Ahmed Fuad. Hussein Kamel's son, Prince Kemaleddin, refused the throne, ostensibly for reasons of temperament but really because his wife, Princess Nimetallah, was a sister of the deposed ex-Khedive. The selection of Fuad seemed to be dictated by considerations, held as cogent in London, which experience has more than once shown to be misguided. Wingate himself would have preferred more pressure on Kemaleddin.

It is natural, but unwise, where the elevation of Oriental princelings is in question, to expect some return of gratitude for favour shown to a relatively impoverished candidate. In the Arab world with which Egypt shares some of her conventional thinking, it may be hazardous to have known a rich man when he was poor. Generally speaking, anyone claiming past acquaintance in a period of which the prince, or merchant-prince, does not wish to be reminded, is no friend. One notable exception to this rule was King Abdul Aziz Ibn Saud, himself a most exceptional man.

A strong argument against promotion from penury is the habit of extortion and face-grinding all too easily acquired by jumped-up potentates determined never to be poor again. An associated parsimony usually deepens the public animosity provoked by this behaviour, and the new ruler's unpopularity soon rubs off on to his foreign sponsors. Finally, he tends ever more ruthlessly to frustrate and thwart any liberal measures favoured in London, if these appear to diminish his own potential of total authority and self-enrichment.

Prince Ahmed Fuad had spent his childhood and youth sharing the Italian exile of his father, the Khedive Ismail Pasia, deposed in 1870. He had very little money of his own, and in 1917 he owed large sums all over Egypt. It was in his preference for policies, and in his selection of human instruments, promising advantage to his material interest, that the new Sultan, and later King, of Egypt most notably failed to play ball. When he died in 1936, he left over seven million pounds as his personal estate.

He was a man of ambition and strong character, and he had a shrewd judgment of other people's weaknesses. He used to greet and welcome a succession of British High Commissioners with the words: *'Enfin Londres m'envoie un gentleman!'*, which always gave pleasure. He never lacked for lackeys, on every level, and he used patronage and the fount of honour with most damaging effect. Through his Nubian valet, Idris Bey, who controlled a network which included everybody's doorkeeper, house-boys and cook, he was remarkably well informed. After one farewell party involving most of the Residency staff, he asked Lord Lloyd if he knew just where his two aides-de-camp had been at 4 a.m. that morning.

His Italian upbringing had denied him the opportunity of learning Arabic—he spoke Italian, French and Turkish—and he had a taste for cosmopolitan company, with a pro-Italian bias in matters of opera, investment and mistresses. No one has, however, explained how King Fuad's gallant appeal to one lady: *'Pourquoi tous les autres et pas moi? . . .'* could possibly have become known.

His father's tastes, also, had been expansively cosmopolitan, and various stories of Ismail Pasha's alcove-life were told me by Felix de Menasche, who had them from his father. Ismail Pasha's lively interest in the introduction and expansion of the Egyptian railway system seems to have strangely influenced his amours. He had an arrangement with King Umberto of Italy whereby they exchanged mistresses, and the Khedive was embarrassed when one of these arrived, inopportunely, from Rome. But wounded feminine pride was assuaged by his command: *'Donnez-lui quarante locomotives!'* This sounds like a weighty *pourboire*; the lady was happy to be commissioned to supply forty railway-engines to the Railway administration.

Later, when visiting Vichy, Ismail instructed his chamberlain to 'send for Schneider'. An important railway-contract was under competition at the time between British and French interests, and the chamberlain, a partisan of the French cause, happily contacted M. Schneider, of the Creusot Iron Works, who travelled hot-foot across France. The announcement: *'Altesse! Schneider est là!'* prompted Ismail to reply: *'Faites-lui prendre un bain!'*; and a gaunt, middle-aged industrial magnate duly conformed to this instruction. There was mutual astonishment when the Khedive opened the bathroom-door, expecting to find Hortense Schneider, the reigning queen of the demi-monde. That contract went to Britain.

One factor encouraging Ronald Storrs, as Oriental Secretary, to press the choice of Fuad for the Sultanate was Fuad's own manifest desire to play some part on the world-stage. He had lent his name to a university-extension project in Cairo, and had been a candidate for the throne of Albania. If one must admit that he was by no means the worst possible sultan, there need be no suggestion that he was anywhere near the best.

Egyptian postage-stamps made the sweeping curve of his moustache familiar to the world. A no less individual characteristic was a high spasmodic bark which frequently interrupted his speech, discomforting to any uninitiated listener. I once saw a curtseying lady bowled over by it. It was caused by a bullet lodged in his throat some years before the War by his brother-in-law, Prince Ahmed Seifeddin, whose sister, Princess Shevekiar, Fuad had divorced.

As I heard it, Seifeddin tracked his cousin to the Silence Room of the old Khedivial Club—now a block of flats—and in that inappropriate setting opened fire, driving two obese pashas who were reading their newspapers to burrow vainly under their armchairs.

A sergeant from the British main guard next door to the club broke up these proceedings. He was adjured, before giving his evidence, to bear in mind that both accused and victim were princes of the reigning dynasty; but truth must out. His evidence allegedly opened with the words: 'Hearing sounds of gunfire from the club, I turned out a file of the guard and proceeded to investigate. I saw the nigger standing at the top of the marble steps. I closed with him, and overpowered him.'

Seifeddin toiled in a convict-gang in the Toura quarries; but his presence there was deemed unseemly, and a medical certificate of mental disequilibrium was produced. He spent the next thirty years in a one-man asylum, near Ticehurst. His escape, between the wars, caused intense despondency in Abdin Palace. His estates were of the richest: over 40,000 acres of the best land in Egypt (one multiplied by ten for the income in £s), and as their revenues were collected by King Fuad himself, much was at stake. After an alert involving every British and European port, Seifeddin and the two male nurses who had accompanied him on his escape turned up in Constantinople, to rejoin his sister, then living there with her fifth husband. The party had left the Ticehurst grounds; taken a bus to Folkestone and a day-excursion to Boulogne, where no passports were required. It was as simple as that.

Sultan Fuad's first request to Wingate had been a sensible one. He asked for the dismissal of two cabinet ministers, Ibrahim Fathy Pasha and Ali Hilmi Pasha, who were either grossly immoral or grossly incompetent, and their replacement by two respectable Egyptians of nationalist sympathies: Saad Zaghlul Pasha and Abdel Aziz Fahmi Bey. His prerogative gave the Sultan the right to appoint his ministers, but His Majesty's Government claimed the right to be consulted. Wingate urged London to agree to the proposed changes. London, having no crystal ball to tell them what Zaghlul would mean to them in years to come, refused to allow any change at all. The first offer of the Sibylline books had been made, and rejected.

*   *   *

In Cairo, everything looked much the same, except the Savoy Hotel, whose top brass now adorned the business side of the Canal; and the Was'a—the notorious red-light quarter of the Fishmarket, where Sheikh Ibrahim ruled supreme. This little friend of all the world was an Upper Egyptian, grossly fat, who lived softly in woman's clothes and had his bejewelled thumb in every kidnapping or abduction pie likely to yield girls and boys for his shop-windows. Between his pimps, his cutpurses and that legendary but ever-elusive donkey on the one side, and the Australian troops on the other, hostilities had flowered into a night of violence. Pianos had sailed through upper windows; imitation French sofas had gone up in smoke. But Australia had not been allowed to finish the job; and the feud went on. An assistant provost-marshal told me how he had found, in the 'black' Was'a, a lonely Australian, obviously dead-drunk, propping up a brothel wall, and had told him to get along out of it, quick. The man gave him a wink that would take the paint off a barge and said: 'Get along out of it, quick, yourself!'—or words to that effect; 'I'm a bleeding decoy!' Sure enough, four more husky Australians with entrenching tool handles, were just round the corner, waiting for some Egyptian fish to nibble at the bait.

Before leaving the red-light quarter, a tear may properly be shed for the waste and disease caused by the functioning of the biological urge in those Egyptian conditions. In the macabre 'boy-meets-girl' scenes one witnessed every day, the quality of the Anzac troops on leave from Palestine made the poor pox-stricken sepulchres on their arms unusually offensive. As an alternative, Hitler would have shipped out a few cargoes of German spinsters for the warriors' rest. The Nazi prescription for superfluous women was: '*Die Mutterschaft wird ihnen amtswegen zugefuehrt!*'

French soldiery abroad were officially provided for. When General Sarraut, in Salonika, offered General Mahon a share in these facilities, on Tuesdays, and was coldly asked never to mention the matter again, he admitted defeat and offered Fridays as well as Tuesdays. When I was worried, in Baghdad, by rumours of thefts of nurses' stockings in the R.A.F. station at Habbaniya, and asked the A.O.C. if some official safety-valve would not be the lesser evil, I was reminded that all British soldiers and airmen would probably fall in love with whatever was offered, and want to marry it. Perhaps this is all, now, a little old-fashioned?

*   *   *

In Chancery, there had been some changes and even some additions while I was away.

Ronald Storrs, the Oriental Secretary, had left Cairo, in the uniform of a Brigadier-General, to become the second Governor of liberated Jerusalem. The first, Borton Pasha, ex-Postmaster General of Egypt, had collapsed after some forty eight hours of very hard work. Storrs, a controversial personality, had been succeeded by Keown-Boyd, Wingate's Private Secretary in Khartoum, who accompanied him to Egypt. He was a first-class Oriental Secretary, but he became more important later, on appointment as Director of the European Department of Public Security—an awkward title for a most awkward job.

'K.B.' had acquired in the esoteric mysteries of the Sudan Civil Service the exact skill and experience, and the perfect temperament, required for a post which imposed not only the diplomatic and advisory functions of an old-style Adviser to the Ministry of Interior—such duties were never mentioned—but also direct administrative responsibility for all developments affecting the welfare and lives of British and other foreign residents in Egypt. The period of his activity was one of peculiarly stormy political weather; but he lived at the heart of the cylcone, indefatigable, imperturbable, affable and commonsensical, winning the respect of all Egyptians and the affection of most. Those who only knew him after the Anglo-Egyptian Treaty of 1936 had liquidated his office, when he himself turned to new interests as a business tycoon, lack the perspective in which to judge what was a remarkable personal achievement.

The additions to our staff were most welcome. A senior Inspector of Finance, A. T. Loyd, had been seconded to direct our new War Trade Department, made necessary by growing problems of certificates of origin, war contraband, black-lists and the rest. Wingate was authorised to borrow from the army the services of any officers who could declare a firm intention to apply for Foreign Office service after the war, a characteristic limitation. Most valuably, we now had a qualified and comely clerical assistant, also lent by the Finance. She was scrupulously conscientious and gave the Residency her instant loyalty.

These additions were welcome in 1917; but the real breakthrough came shortly after the war, when we were told that six ex-officers might be engaged at a salary of £300 each, and as much clerical assistance as £2,000 a year would buy. After that, Parkinson's Law took over, and staff proliferated.

My pleasure at being posted back to the Residency was more than mere relief at escape from the strain of service under an unpredictable chief. I was always happier in a chancery than in a consulate. The work itself was a major attraction. After the routine duties of a busy shipping consulate, it was stimulating to return nearer to the official heart of things, where major policy was debated; to handle 'Most Secret' papers, and to read Lawrence's despatches from Arabia in the edition of the *Arab Bulletin* not circulated to our allies. Our working hours were approximately double those of a consulate, and we never had a Saturday afternoon or a Sunday off. The interest was unfailing and exciting.

With all this, employment on the High Commissioner's staff carried some local prestige: an aura of authority surrounded even the humblest third secretary. Our master still carried Cromerian weight in Egypt, and when we accompanied him outside Cairo, it was always by special train. We left the splendours of diplomatic uniform to others; when attending the High Commissioner's audience with the Sultan, we wore morning dress and top hats. The Sultan himself called once a year on the High Commissioner. When His Highness went to Alexandria in June for the summer, and the cabinet followed him, the Residency followed them, thus allowing us for three and a half months to enjoy the cool breezes and beaches of Ramleh. This was financially disastrous, for the cost of summer lodging was high and there was no allowance to cover it. But it was worth the expense.

When I was first in Alexandria, the little house which was the summer residence of the High Commissioner or his deputy stood solitary in sand at the top of Mustapha Pasha hill; premises in Glymenopoulo were rented for the office work. But later, with the hospitable connivance of the Alexandria munipality, all that sand was transformed into a desirable site of lawns and flower-beds. Chancery offices were built next door to the summer resid-ence, and a few select villas shared with us an aristocratic eminence. For some years we were accompanied on our annual excursion to and fro by a massive iron safe, and this became the pride and challenge of one muscular Girgawi porter, who crawled beneath it from train to lorry and from lorry to office, like a herculean ant. But one day something snapped, and like an ant he was crushed to death.

Minor perquisites included first-class passes over the Egyptian state railway network; valueless to us, because our pressure of work prevented their use. Also a racket permitting us to charge to the British Treasury our (horse) cab-fares to and from the Resi-dency. This blew up in our faces when John Cecil developed a Saturday afternoon habit of charging the equivalent of three pounds for the hire of a car from the Heliopolis racecourse to the office. There were no taxis or motor-buses in Egypt until well after the end of the war.

I lived for a time in a pension called Rossmore House, run by two Scottish ladies who charged only £14 monthly for good board and lodging. To save money a colleague, Marmaduke Kelham, and I shared a large room. He was a most elegant young man, a postscript to the Yellow Book, always impeccably dressed. Only when a shoe-lace once gave trouble did I observe that the Savile Row façade concealed, on the lower floor, a criss-cross of darns and patches. Later, on his first day of consular work, when con-fronted with four impatient British subjects all demanding advice on different matters, he smiled disarmingly and explained: 'I'm sorry, I'm a stranger here myself!'

He drifted into rather undesirably raffish Levantine company and returned once, in the early hours, very much the worse for wear after some experiment with dope. He could not breathe properly and made distressing moaning noises when he tried to get air. I had nothing specific to offer, but I was able to lend him a bottle of hair-tonic from which, with noises like a haunted house, he proceeded to inhale some remotely alcoholic essence until relief came. Later I moved to a flat in the rue Abbas Daramalli Pasha, behind Sultan Fuad's private palace, and shared it with two British schoolmasters.

That Turf Club joke about the man who concealed his employment in the Egyptian Ministry of Public Instruction because he preferred his mother to continue thinking that he played the piano in a brothel (which, with other venerable classics, Major Jarvis revived in *The Back Garden of Allah*) would have been valid after Egyptian Independence, when the English teachers were, by nationalist policy, humiliated and treated as the merest ushers. Earlier, the standards were very high, and many schoolmasters moved from the 'P.I.' to the gilded hierarchies of Interior and Finance. All were good university graduates, and they interested themselves in the welfare of their students, out of school as well as in their classrooms. After Independence, no contacts except in class were permitted; and because a degree was still required, the meagre salary offered limited recruitment to the lower levels of Redbrick output.

My personal preoccupation during late 1918 was the last of the five examinations which determined the seniority *inter se* of our 1914 service entrants. I offered the 'Advanced' Arabic examination of the Egyptian civil service, only irksome because it involved a switch from the Latin presentation of Arabic grammar to that preferred by the Arabs themselves. This enabled discussion of a grammatical point in Arabic with one's teacher, but it meant learning a vast number of new grammatical rules, because, for an Arab, the language of the Holy Koran admits of no exceptions, only rules. My Scottish examiner, who used to wither the Egyptian students of English in his care by asking them: 'What like is a camel's fuit?', was merciful, and I passed.

Colloquial Egyptian Arabic contains, like Maltese, Phoenician remains, and it feminises all vowel-sounds. A Moroccan needs an interpreter in Cairo; but each region of the Arabic-speaking world thinks its own dialect the language of Paradise. Some British officials in Egypt were brilliant linguists. Those working close to the fellahin were better than most; and the police, who had to interrogate scallywags from every corner of the land, day and night, were remarkable.

Our diplomatic service secretaries had their own, very different, Arabic examination, generally conducted by the Sudan Agent in Cairo. He told me of one Head of Chancery whom he asked for the phrase: 'Come here!', and received the correct answer: *'Ta'ala hina'* (which in its Syrian version of *'Ta'ala hón'* is probably the origin of our 'Tally-Ho!', brought back by the crusaders). He then asked his victim how he would say: 'Go there!' 'Well, old boy', was the reply, after thought, 'I should go there myself and shout: *'Ta'ala hina!'* Success, as in this case, brought the diplomatist an allowance of £100 a year.

*　　*　　*

When I chose the Consulate-General in Alexandria rather than the Tehran Legation for my first foreign posting, I hoped that my presence in Egypt might find me poised for post-war transfer to Constantinople, for long the plum of Levant service appointments. But the issue of the war frustrated this ambition. By March 1918, the Ottoman Empire was in ruins. Enver Pasha, Talaat Pasha and their Young Turks had followed the Padishahs with their standards of gold crescent and horsetails, their Grand Vizirs and Chief Eunuchs, their Janissaries and Mutes of the Bowstring, into the dustbin of history. By that time I was well content to have chosen Egypt.

Sir Edmund Allenby, known as 'The Bull', had succeeded Sir Archibald Murray and had made a triumphant entry into Jerusalem. This event was reported in the *Journal du Caire*, a newspaper edited by the venomous Monsieur Vayssié, in a two-page story which contained no mention at all of Allenby or of British troops, suggesting that the whole Palestinian campaign had been waged and won by the handful of French staff-officers who followed Allenby through the Jerusalem Gate. This was a museum-piece of French pre-Entente thinking. Now Jerusalem was the headquarters of at least four Occupied Enemy Territory Administrations, and a heavyweight Zionist commission probed relentlessly for the future. None of this seemed to interest the Egyptian man in the street, but the educated classes began to take new hope from the thought of new liberties won in the Arab world.

The Russian Revolution had, as yet, no echo in Egypt. It relieved us, however, of a tiresome chore. Because Baltic communications were cut by the Germans, Foreign Office cables of a certain secrecy-grading for St. Petersburg came to Cairo for re-ciphering in a different code and onward despatch via the Far East. The new cipher was an unwieldy book, with no alphabetical pagination to facilitate handling. Exhausted by this supplementary labour, John Cecil sent to our Embassy in St. Petersburg a personal message in this highly secret code: 'Must-we go-on us-ing this take-third- interpretation bloody cipher?' The reply was immediate and crisp. 'Yes, you lazy here-insert-word-already-spelt-beginning-with bug!' The British taxpayer never knows what he pays for.

5

One file in our archives, a large one, contained matter sent to us by the adviser to the Ministry of the Interior under the routine heading, which no one in his office found strange, *'Compulsory volunteering'*. These reports concerned the recruitment of Egyptians for the Egyptian labour corps, which was employed by the military authorities not only in Egypt but in Palestine, Syria and Mesopotamia. The pay of the labour corps was considered good; there was no question of *corvée* or slave-gangs. The scandal, for there is no other word, lay in the method of recruitment adopted. As with the requisitioning of fodder and animals and cereals for the British army's incessant needs, recruitment was in the hands of young officers, and they, being ignorant of Arabic, not unnaturally relied on the co-operation of the village headmen, the Omdas, who form the lowest cog in the Egyptian administrative machine. These men are but human. Far too many of them, when asked to supply a contingent of volunteers for the labour corps, produced for possible death and mutilation, certainly for exile from family life, their own personal enemies, or their relations, or anyone unable to buy exemption; and they collected twice as many thousand *keilas* of grain or fodder as were asked for, hiding the balance in their own barns. All this they explained to their people as hardships imposed by the tyrannical *askaria*, the British soldiery; and the fair prices paid for the stuff requisitioned rarely reached the fellahin themselves.

Too many British inspectors had been allowed to join the Forces; otherwise they might have spotted and nipped in the bud these evils of the Omdas' rake-off in the requisitioning of food-stuffs and their discriminating methods of recruiting. As it was, while we were winning the war, we were losing the fellahin.

'Compulsory volunteering' had already, by mid-1917, produced nearly 90,000 men for the labour corps. Under pressure from London, this total was stepped up to 125,000 men. The War Office even called for general conscription, which Wingate was only able with great difficulty to prevent. That would, indeed, have been a flagrant breach of the assurances given in 1914, that Egypt would not be called upon for aid in the war. Meanwhile, in rural Egypt, a major revolution in thinking was kindling and spreading. As thousands of breadwinners disappeared, leaving their families un-protected; as man after man returned from Palestine or Iraq maimed, or not at all; the British military authorities became an object of cursing in every village. The same peasantry who owed most to Lord Cromer and to the impartial justice of his Civil Service found themselves suffering at his compatriots' hands, or so the headmen explained things to them. I cannot believe that the post-war appeals to nationalist, anti-British sentiment would, without this, have found an echo among the fellahin who were to be its indispensable instrument of violence.

Egyptians have a unique reputation for inactivity in mere misery. They must wax fat before they kick. Cotton, the country's staple crop, had doubled in price by 1918, and the Egyptian Treasury had a kitty of £E100 million at the war's end. This prosperity provided an essential element for active revolt. Incidentally, another grievance was born when General Headquarters dictated a cut of thirty per cent in the area of cotton cultivation of Egypt, in order the better to secure army needs of foodstuffs and fodder.

The Residency itself made one major blunder, when Lady Wingate was imprudently allowed to sponsor an appeal for the British Red Cross. The result was foreseeably unfortunate. In order to gain credit with a Residency still known as Cromer's House, Omdas squeezed their villagers till the pips squeaked, and a further excuse for resentment was provided. I remember one Omda swaggering into Chancery to claim a favour of some kind. His argument was that he had raised a total of over £7,000 from his village for Lady Wingate '. . . *wa kull millieme bi-zor!*', meaning that every penny had been forced out of its donor. He was ejected from the building, but the harm was done. Later, the Red Cross returned to us some thousands of pounds of this 'dirty money', and the Oriental Secretariat used it, anonymously, for charitable purposes.

During the second World War, when I was again in Cairo, I did what I could on my own level to ensure that such mistakes were not repeated. They were, in fact, made unlikely by the shift in military needs. But the many new mistakes then made proved that an abyss separates the political from the military mind.

Justice demands, as a footnote to any suggestion of the fellahin's indebtedness to Lord Cromer, that I should record a conversation between two peasants which I overheard on the platform of Damanhour station in the spring of 1918. One had asked the other which were the better, the English or the Germans. The question was interesting to an English listener later to be involved in 'psychological warfare'; the answer was: '*El-itnain awlad kelb!*'— They are both sons of dogs. Egyptians say of their country: '*Ma yathmarsh el-khair*', admitting that in Egypt 'an act of kindness bears no fruit.'

The revolution in rural feeling, later so tragically manifest in the bloody revolt of March 1919, was apparently unobserved by the Administration, and therefore unrealised by the Residency.

The paramountcy given to the recruitment of labour alarmed the High Commissioner more because of its clash with assurances given at the beginning of the war, and its unfavourable effect upon local political thinking, than because of its effect upon the fellahin themselves. I recall no anxiety about requisitioning processes.

Wingate was above all concerned to extract from His Majesty's Government some indication of their post-war intentions regarding Egypt. He was not given an answer about this, and had had no glimpse of future British policy when the war drew to its close.

*   *   *

Suddenly, the name of President Wilson, and the blessed word 'self-determination', echoed through the streets of Cairo. A joint Anglo-French declaration promised this self-determination to the Beduin of the desert and to all the other peoples liberated from the Turkish yoke. Hopes in Egypt ran high. On November 8 Zaghlul Pasha, who had been vice-president of the suspended legislative assembly, asked Wingate to allow that body to sit again. He had been seeing much of the sultan and the cabinet since London decided to reject him as a Cabinet Minister in 1917, and it is certain that they were anxious to keep in with the more overtly nationalist group associated with him. Armistice Day came and went. The ceremonial parade of the morning was followed by a *Walpurgisnacht* of riotous military celebration from which the military police were conspicuously absent. Besotted troops roamed the streets, wielding entrenching-tool handles, while their officers, among other feats of strength, rolled up the great hall-carpet of Shepheards Hotel, with the German-Swiss manager inside it.

Two days later, on November 13, Saad Zaghlul, Abdel Aziz Fahmy and Mohammed Shaarawi called on the High Commissioner and presented Egypt's case for complete autonomy. They undertook to make an alliance of perpetual peace and friendship with Great Britain, whom they regarded as Egypt's best friend and ally. They accepted the principle of some continued British financial supervision. But they asked for independence, which they held was as much due to Egypt, particularly in the light of her considerable contribution to our war effort, as to any Hejazis or Syrians. The interview was friendly and frank. Wingate told them that he could not, of course, answer for his government, and he advised them to go gently.

He suspected at the time that this *démarche* was made with the knowledge and approval of the sultan and the cabinet, and this was immediately confirmed to him by Rushdy Pasha, the Prime Minister, who hastened to propose that he and Adly Pasha should go to London to present Egypt's case to H.M.G., and that Zaghlul and some of his friends should accompany them. Neither Rushdy nor anyone else could have contemplated a visit to London in the circumstances, unless public opinion in Egypt were satisfied that Zaghlul and other 'nationalists' were associated with the mission.

We were at the point of balance.

Wingate at once urged acceptance of the proposal on London, in a letter to Lord Hardinge, then Permanent Under-Secretary at the Foreign Office, and a cable to the Secretary of State, Balfour. The Egyptian temperature rose, and he approached London again, with forceful arguments for his case. It was November 27 before a reply was received. His Majesty's Government ruled that no 'nationalists' should be permitted to leave Egypt. They said that they might find time to receive Rushdy and Adly, but not for some months yet.

In these exchanges, Zaghlul, who had been moderate, open and above-board, was labelled by Whitehall as 'extremist' and 'anti-British'; and Wingate was informed that his own reception of the 'extremist' leaders on November 13 had been unfortunate. He offered his resignation, which was refused.

His Majesty's Government said they were surprised and embarrassed by the Egyptian demand for independence, but their embarrassment is more easily explicable than their surprise. They had been warned. They had, alas, too much on their plate already. Peace treaties had to be considered and concluded with both Germany and Turkey, and the priority of an Egyptian grievance in this welter of preoccupations seemed invisibly low.

In Wingate's *Life* by his son, the suggestion is made that he was handicapped also by the relative inexperience of the Lloyd George Government in Egyptian affairs. For nine years, Asquith and Grey had been in day-to-day touch with reports from Egypt. Their successors of 1916 lacked such perspective. Unfortunately in early December 1918, both Balfour and Lord Hardinge moved from the Foreign Office to Paris, where Lloyd George followed them. From then until the signature of the Treaty of Versailles, the British delegation to the Peace Conference was effectively responsible for British relations with the thirty-seven states represented in Paris. Lord Curzon was left in Downing Street to handle relations with such countries as Egypt, not represented at the Peace Conference. His competence was duly limited, and the essential co-ordination with Paris was not always assured. Curzon had had no official employment from the date of his retirement as Viceroy of India in 1905 until his appointment to Lloyd George's cabinet in 1916. He was, from his Indian experience, inclined to equate nationalism with Revolution. Egyptians, like Indians, must be either loyal or disloyal. He was the last person to sympathise with 'anti-British' views on the future of Egypt.

On hearing London's dusty answer, Rushdy and Adly at once resigned. They and the Sultan insisted that Egypt's case must be heard before a peace treaty with Turkey created a new *fait accompli*, and that nationalist opinion must be represented. Wingate began to despair.

I blush to recall that his Chancery refused to be downhearted during these historic exchanges. Late on the evening of December 31, 1918, it was noticed that we had sent 1,998 telegrams to the Foreign Office during the year then ending. This figure (now peanuts) was then so monstrous a record for the mission that we decided it deserved to be rounded up. But no one could think up any excuse for further cabling. Eventually, I drafted two cables. The first said: 'Following for Perkins begins I agree ends' and the second said: 'My immediately preceding telegram Please cancel.' We then separated, to dance the New Year in.

★   ★   ★

The breakdown of government in Egypt seemed certain, so long as the sultan supported the resignation of his ministers and London refused any concession to their demands. Martial law in Egypt could only work up to a point. The advisers, for all their great authority, were impotent; they could only operate through the Egyptian ministers whom they were paid to persuade. It was with relief that Wingate received a belated but promising compromise-suggestion from the Foreign Office on January 1, 1919. This proposed that he should come at once to London, and should be followed within a week by Rushdy and Adly Pashas. It was still considered unlikely that the two ministers would be given a hearing before March; but it was hoped that their presence in London might have a calming effect on Egyptian public opinion, where nationalist propaganda was being stepped up.

Wingate had a fortnight of argument with the sultan and his ministers before he obtained their interest in this proposal. Rushdy and Adly still insisted that Zaghlul and his friends should accompany them, even if these men could not be officially received by His Majesty's Goverment; and this request Wingate pressed London to accept. There is a school of thought which holds that the two ministers were being Machiavellian in their insistence on Zaghlul's presence in London during their own mission there, hoping to secure for themselves from His Majesty's Government some positive accretion of Egyptian authority, and to present Zaghlul to his country as a person of no influence, returning empty-handed to Cairo. This theory is attractive, but unrealistic. Both ministers knew the strength of the nationalist appeal, and they did not even wish to take a line in opposition to it. They certainly hoped to influence Zaghlul's views in the direction of moderation, to secure their acceptance; but they would never be able to do so unless they were seen by the country to be in friendly touch with the nationalist leaders.

Having said his say, Wingate left for London. Lord Curzon kept him waiting a fortnight for an audience. Wingate then took to the interview a draft telegram for despatch to Cairo, embodying the recommendations he had made; and he warned Curzon that their refusal would inevitably mean an aggravation of nationalist agitation and probably some intimidation of the sultan. Curzon obdurately refused to have any truck with Zaghlul and his associates: he dismissed them as of doubtful standing and antecedents, disloyal, and not entitled to any measure of countenance and recognition. Explaining this in a telegram sent to Cairo, he added that Rushdy and Adly might still come to London, though he disliked their habit of seeking to impose their own conditions. It was a truly Curzonian cable.

The Egyptian cabinet resigned again. The Sultan's first gesture towards their replacement provoked, as Wingate had warned, immediate measures of nationalist intimidation. In alarm, Fuad appealed to the Residency for protection.

On March 7, Sir Milne Cheetham, now once more acting as High Commissioner, gave me an envelope to take by hand to General Headquarters. I might have done better to throw it into the Nile, for it contained a request for the immediate arrest and deportation to Malta of Zaghlul Pasha and three of his friends: Mohammed Mahmoud Pasha, Ismail Sidqi Pasha and Hamed el Bassel Pasha. Next morning, on March 8, the Egyptian Revolution began.

Early that morning, we heard that the students of the Law School were inciting the students of other faculties to join with them in strikes and demonstrations, and reports of rioting and affrays with Harvey Pasha's police kept coming in. The distant din of shouting seemed to come nearer, and I went out with John Cecil to stand at our railings and look down the Sharia Lazoghli, which ran off opposite us at right angles to the Sharia el-Walida. Suddenly we saw two little figures running across the far end of Lazoghli, and both threw up their hands and fell sprawling while still in sight. Police and British troops had been ordered to fire; these were the first two men killed.

The older students began it; the schoolboys followed, and the mob flocked in with them. In the girls' schools, whole classes of adolescents chanted in blind hysteria from one lesson's end to another. Long-hoarded photographs of the poor Denshawai dead, swinging by the neck in 1906, were brought out of hiding, reproduced by the thousand, and circulated as being yesterday's news. Coptic priests preached in Mosques; Moslem *Ulamá* preached in churches; William Makram Obeid, private secretary to Zaghlul, lent his new Oxford eloquence to this rare solidarity. Violence erupted all over the country.

Immense offence was given by a remark said to be made by Sir William Brunyate, the arrogant financial adviser, that 'any Egyptian revolution can be drowned in a gob of spittle'. Even if apocryphal, the attribution of this phrase suggests some defect in personal relations.

Cairo was isolated. Alexandria and the Delta had their tragedies; but even Tantah, the most fanatical town in Egypt, did not rival the brutalities of Upper Egypt, where liberty's new servants wore their most savage face. The Sa'idi, or Upper Egyptian, is notoriously hot-blooded, and life is cheaper there than north of the Barrage. Feuds between powerful landowners there are bloody; bandits hide in the sugar-cane, and men are men in the least civilised sense.

Dick Graves, an ex-Levant consul, then an Inspector in the Egyptian Ministry of Interior, was travelling by railway, sharing a carriage with an American woman-tourist for whom he had already developed a strong antipathy, when the train stopped at Beni Suef station and was attacked by a raging mob. Graves and the lady climbed out on to the track, and were hustled by a heroic little ticket-collector into a stores-shed and there locked in. Mr. Smith, of the Railways, was pulled out of his carriage at the rear of the train and butchered; his wife managed to escape by lying hidden in the river mud. The ticket-collector swore the oath of divorce that the shed was empty and the key long lost; but the mob thrust their blades through the woodwork, just on chance, and those inside had some bad moments.

A group of British officers returning from a holiday in Luxor— on which they had neglected to take their revolvers—might have got through if their train had not been stopped at Deirut for the ritual handing over and exchange of batons. Soda-water bottles were poor weapons against a mob of murderers, and by the time the train pulled out, almost all were dead. Down the line at Mellawi, where another crowd, led by a recently returned student

of the Agricultural College at Wye, waited for them, a scene of
Punjab-like horror was enacted. Only the action of the town-
harlot brought the mob to some sense of shame. She protected
what was left to protect, and later received a British pension for
life. When retribution came, and the ringleaders were about to
be hanged, one of them received by his last morning's post the
prize awarded him by the College at Wye as the most promising
student of his year.

We had been issued with revolvers and told to carry them
everywhere, but this I refused to do, knowing that it would
make me more of a danger to myself and my friends than to any
enemy. I confess that the sight of one colleague prodding a poor
gharry-driver in the bottom with his revolver, made me aware of
what some Egyptians found distasteful in the British character.

But I was always careful to keep out of the path of demonstrations.

The *muzdhara*, or demonstration, now a common European
phenomenon, has always been a favourite Egyptian formula:
it may grow round a coffin or a banner or just grow and flow
through the streets. The only safe rule in Egypt is never to allow
one, because an innocent procession easily turns into an angry
mob, if provoked; and there are always elements in it eager to
pay off old scores against Greek grocers or Armenian cobblers
or Coptic and Jewish drapers. Such processions used to file every
morning and every afternoon past the Residency, many thousands
strong, solemnly spitting in our direction and shouting '*Al-
Istiqlal el-tam*'—Complete Independence—and for Zaghlul Pasha.
In so large a demonstration, one cheer-leader can only look after a
few hundred marchers, and others followed at a strategic distance,
calling out slogans for the mob to echo. Opposite the Chancery,
at the corner of the Sharia Lazoghli, stood the house of the United
States representative, Mr. Hampson Gary, and some demonstrations tried to combine adulation for President Wilson, who then
held the future of the world in his praying hands, with condemnation of King George V. In the intervals of expectoration in
our direction the cry was raised: '*Fa'l yahya al-ra'is Wilson*'—
'Long live President Wilson'—and clamorously echoed. One

choirmaster, anxious to include Mr. Hampson Gary personally in these prayers, waved towards the American Building and began: '*Fa'l yahya*', but he couldn't remember the name. He turned to a friend and asked what it was. The crowd, happily, thus picked up a name which they thought conveniently pronounceable, and shouted: '*Fa'l yahya Ismu ay! Fa'l yahya Ismu ay!*'—Long live What's-his-name!

The revolt of March 8, 1919, was not merely an explosion of anger at national humilitation in the persons of four strangely representative men. A twist of peculiarly Egyptian thinking was in the fuse. Egyptians have a great talent for believing the paradoxical or improbable rather than the straightforward explanation of events.

Mohammed Mahmoud Pasha himself told me why, before March 8, the masses withheld their support of nationalist appeals, clamant since November: it was because they saw through the trick. Zaghlul and his friends were obviously British stooges, put up to distract attention and sympathy from the real nationalists, the pre-war Watanists. What right had men who had not fought before 1914 with Mustafa Kamel Pasha, Mohammed Farid Bey and Shaikh Abdel Aziz Shawish to claim to speak for Egypt? But the discomforts of arrest and deportation in March guaranteed their sincerity; and the mob reached for a *fass* (the heavy Egyptian hoe) or a cudgel. Independence ceased to be a newspaper headline, or a debating-society argument, and became a country-wide explosion of emotion.

After a fortnight, General Bulfin had restored order almost everywhere and he was rumoured to be considering the confiscation of certain bank-balances.

It was then, as old Dr. Fares Nimr of *Al Moqattam* was to tell me later, that the Wafdist leaders in Egypt, many of whom were very rich men, yielded to their fears. They sent Yusuf Suleiman Pasha to see Dr. Nimr to request him to arrange a meeting with General Bulfin. They were ripe for capitulation. They had no understanding of Russian developments, but they knew all about *la jacquerie*, and doubted whether a peasant revolt was really in the best interests of Egypt or themselves. They did not enjoy the pressure from behind them, and had, indeed, long expected, and hoped, to be summoned by the British and given some excuse to call a retreat. They did not even know what the First Eleven men in Malta would want them to do. And now, this talk of confiscated bank-balances!

An interview was arranged, but all General Bulfin could tell them when they met was that General Allenby's appointment as Special High Commissioner had that morning been announced and that he could not anticipate the General's line of policy. The Wafdists waited in anguish for a week. They need not have worried.

Lloyd George and his Government were seriously disturbed by the explosion of Egyptian revolt. Bloodshed and violence had done what poor Wingate's arguments failed to do. Allenby had his instructions, and he therefore told the anxious notables that he relied on them to calm popular emotions, giving them more ground for hope than blame. The Wafdist tail went up, and stayed up. Some of their leaders would not speak to Dr. Nimr for many months.

We, in Chancery, felt much sympathy with Wingate, who never returned to Egypt or received another post. We were a little anxious about personal relations with our new High Commissioner. General Allenby had a well-earned reputation for violent temper, and none of us wished to retire to the A.D.C.'s room after an interview, as had been the fate of some of his generals in Jerusalem, in order to vomit. On the evening of his arrival on March 25, 1919, John Cecil took in some papers for him to sign. Something displeased Allenby, and Cecil was all but blasted out of the room. He stood his ground: 'I don't like your tone, Sir!' he said. 'This is a Foreign Office Mission, not a camp. We are not used to being blackguarded in this room!' A very great man apologised, and his relations with his staff were instantly courteous, and soon affectionate.

As so often, an intervention by Lord Curzon had immediate unhappy results. He made a speech describing the Egyptian revolt as 'predatory rather than political' and praising the 'loyalty' of some Egyptian officials. All Egyptian officials immediately went on strike in protest at the insult.

Less than a week after his arrival, Allenby shook London by recommending that Zaghlul and his fellow-exiles should be released from Malta and allowed to go freely to Europe. Wingate was consulted in London, and replied that, in the circumstances of the moment, this proposal looked like inadmissible weakness. But having so recently appointed a prestigious figure to succeed Wingate, London felt unable to reject his first advice. Passports were issued to the Malta martyrs. They were joined in Paris by a number of other Wafdist leaders, and there, with happy and assiduous help from French journalists, they began publicising the claims of Egypt and the Wafd. Ismail Sidqi Pasha's activities in the night-life of Paris were reported as establishing various records, some of which may still stand.

The British Government's *volte-face* was not entirely beneficent, for its timing appeared to put a premium on violence. With hindsight, and some experience of Egyptian behaviour, I believe that a firmer handling of the immediate post-revolt situation and of 'extremism'—by which I mean the use of murder and violence as methods of intimidation—might have been better for both sides. I have no doubt that it would have been locally accepted without shock or surprise.

The Egyptian man in the street is very quick to recognise the facts of power; he does not have to be blown out of cannons, or even harshly treated, to conform. He will support long years of humiliation and, indeed, of ill-treatment, buoyed up by the golden certainty that somewhere along the road lies a banana-skin on which the object of his dislike is bound one day to put his heel. Arabic is one of the few languages which have an equivalent for the German word *Schadenfreude*; it is *shamata*, and the Egyptian variety is unique in its patient expectation of the moment of truth. When this comes, joy is unrestrained, and it has all been well worth while. This national Egyptian sport is known as the *khazouq*.

I believe that we might usefully have excluded the extremists from the political arena, and that our confrontation with the other leaders would then have enabled liberal intentions to be implemented in an atmosphere of reason and give-and-take. Moderation cannot make itself heard unless extremism is silenced. Sooner or later, of course, whatever the colour of Egyptian governments, the moment of truth and the banana-peel had to come. Countless thousands in the Nile Valley must have rolled with laughter in their graves when the long wait was ended at last, and the year 1956 brought Suez as a monumental *khazouq* for Britain.

6

The Armistice brought welcome abrogation of the British rule forbidding women to travel through the Mediterranean, and after years of arrested development our Cairo ladies could now see for themselves what was being worn, or not worn. A major bombshell burst in Shepheards' ballroom when Jack Gordon's new sister-in-law, Lady Idina, danced there on her way to Kenya. She represented to us the spirit of a New Age. Hers was the first bobbed hair we saw; hers the first foot-long cigarette-holder; hers the first scent we could locate, eyes shut, from any corner of the ballroom. Hardly less dazzling, but not otherwise to be confused, was Amy Nimr, later Lady Smart, fresh from the Bohemian disciplines of the Slade, already brilliant as a painter and stimulating as a critic of *Ulysses* and the French *avant-garde*. The Eton crop soon became a commonplace. I personally always resented this enforced reduction of great physical wealth and penury to one uniform mediocrity; but the milliners won: Lady Godiva could not have come to terms with a cloche hat.

Another relaxation of rules in 1919 abolished the means test for Foreign Office and Diplomatic Service examination candidates. Many bright young officers went home to try their luck, and my Cairo friends, John Loder and Francis Rodd, were very early successes. Both resigned, as did others, when a reshuffle in order of age (made necessary by a mixed list of entrants of ages varying from 22 to 29 years) slumped them down some seventy places on the promotion list. Lord Rennell later governed Morgan Grenfell in London, and Lord Wakehurst governed Northern Ireland, and the Foreign Office lost two first-class brains.

Mervyn Herbert, then Head of Chancery, had suggested that I

should sit for the Diplomatic Service examination, and I applied, armed with a most generous personal recommendation from the High Commissioner. I received a cable in reply from the Private Secretary, telling me that I was to take the July examination. Within a week of getting home, my diplomatic hopes were shattered. The Private Secretary informed me that he had not understood that I was not just another military officer: I could not be permitted to sit for the examination. A fortnight later I was told that Lord Allenby required my presence in Egypt immediately. So much for my three months home-leave. I hurried across France and had a most uncomfortable crossing in the P. & O. steamer *Assaye*, adapted to troopship-conditions in which sanitary arrangements had been overlooked.

The Residency had already moved to Ramleh for the summer, and my urgent recall from leave was not due to any discovery of misdemeanour on my part. There had been a number of staff changes as the result of normal transfers and promotions, and during the winter of 1918–19 one young secretary had become involved, to the point of a proposal of marriage, with a familiar ornament of Levantine society who bore a Greco-Polish name and styled herself 'Princess'. The Greek half of her name came from her father, a bank-clerk in Rome; the Polish half from a diplomat in Rome whose great and good friend her mother had been. When dying, this gentleman sent for his lady and told her that, having no money to leave her, he would adopt her husband as his son. Hence the 'Princess'.

The powers-that-be in London decided that this marriage must not take place, and my colleague, after manly protests, was authoritatively persuaded to decamp. The lady heard of this the same night, at dinner in the Summer Palace Hotel, when Charles Markham sent her an ungentlemanly little note, scribbled on the menu, which read: 'Ha! Ha! The bird has flown!'; this brought her fainting to the floor. I had been whistled back from leave to stop the gap in the aviary left by the bird in question, whose later somewhat erratic flights ended in his nesting in a handsome gilded cage.

The legacy was an uncomfortable one, for it included material for the Residency accounts of no less than six past quarters, long overdue, for which Whitehall was clamouring. My colleague offered to take this mass of bills, receipts, cheque-books and bank statements with him on his ship to France, and to return them in good order from Marseilles. This was highly irregular, and I told seven lies a week to our new Head of Chancery, who insisted daily on the production of the finished accounts. When the papers did reach me, they cast no light that was not lurid on our financial position, and it was a matter of months before everything was tidied up.

Our new colleague has been immortalised under another name by Harold Nicolson; it would be an impertinence to attempt further evaluation. He was not an easy Head of Chancery, being tremulously fussy.

The admirable Tommy Loyd left our War Trade Department to head the new Egyptian Department in the Foreign Office, before inheriting great estates and becoming Lord-Lieutenant of Berkshire. He was succeeded by a remarkable and gifted man, who was to be a major figure in the Residency for many years.

Robin Furness, a scholar of King's College, Cambridge, had been accepted for the Egyptian Civil Service and posted, not to the secretariat-type of job which he would instantly have adorned, but to the Alexandria city police. There I first met him; bespectacled, spidery and very long in the leg, looking like a cerebral and ruffled heron. He was improbable when in control of traffic. This enforced contact with life outside the ivory tower was very good for him, toughening his attitudes and compelling alternative interests to the mere carving of cherry-stones.

He had exquisite literary taste, and there was no more accomplished drafter of despatches in Foreign Office service. His tastes on other levels were comprehensively catholic, and we shared some strange excursions. Years of devotion to a rather surprising Egeria were followed by a long period of intimate frustrations before he finally became a husband and father. To him I owed my introduction to the works of Proust and to the acquaintance of Cavafy. Also to the more obscure 'curiosa' of the Greek Anthology. He abused his official position in the name of culture by having his translations of these printed, in parallel Greek and English, by the Alexandria police press.

Later, when he was Oriental Secretary to the High Commissioner, I was delighted to be appointed to assist him.

Another department of the High Commissioner's duties was hived off at this time. Allenby remained *ex officio* Minister of Foreign Affairs, but to handle those affairs, he set up an Egyptian Ministry, and jobs were soon made for all the Cabinet's nephews. There was, as yet, no Egyptian representation abroad; Egyptian interests were in British hands. But we had a cheerful bottle-nosed Turk, Ibrahim Waguih Bey, as Under-Secretary, and the new *Chef de Protocole* was Mahmoud Seddik Bey, a tiny man with thick pebble-glasses, who seemed to sleep and breakfast in his frock-coat. He was the posthumous son of the notorious Ismail Seddik Pasha 'Al-Mufattish', the main instrument of Ismail Pasha's extortions, who died, almost certainly murdered, leaving over two million pounds for his master to confiscate. There had to be a British director of the new ministry, and the first was Sir Robert Greg, formerly our Minister in Siam, who brought with him his new wife, Julia.

The Gregs survived, in various incarnations, many years of life in Cairo, always busily hospitable. They built a beautiful place around an already charming house on the Nile and filled it with lovely museum-pieces, for both had fine taste and Julia had the wherewithal to display it. I found an invitation to luncheon there rather an ordeal; conversation at table, however few the guests, was never allowed to become general. While Julia held one guest in polite talk, Robert boomed like a bittern at the other guest, and conversation became a shouting-match.

In this period, from early 1918 to late 1920, I learned a good deal about Chancery routines and about Egyptian affairs. We were still rather old-fashioned. We still corresponded with some Egyptian government departments, and with all our diplomatic colleagues, including the Americans, in French, which I still think better than English for diplomacy and treaties. It has the essential precision, and every word has a known connotation, whereas in English words tend to be blurred at the edges, and matters of life and death can be variously decided by conflicting interpretations of a phrase. We still used ciphers unacceptable by today's standards of security. We sent a telegram once to Somaliland in a cipher which Berbera did not hold. John Cecil, who was there shooting with Sir Geoffrey Archer, was able from long familiarity to interpret its meaning and to send us a coded reply. We were still living and working in a British Protectorate; but rough winds were soon to shake our little world.

7

The release from Malta of Zaghlul Pasha and his party had lost us many friends in Egypt among moderate and independent thinkers, and the foreign communities and the Turf Club were, of course, appalled that violence and bloodshed should so blatantly succeed. Allenby was strong enough to take a decision which he knew would be criticised (as I have dared to criticise) because he saw no future for Anglo-Egyptian relations in the measures of repression and retaliation which he had the power to impose. He recognised and respected the basic sincerity of emotion which had exploded into violence and revolution. The razor-edge between wise conciliation and ill-advised surrender was here most acutely evident.

His Majesty's Government, now implicitly convinced that Wingate had been right and Curzon wrong, followed up their concession of passports for the Malta exiles with the announcement, in mid-May 1919, that Lord Milner would lead a special mission to Egypt, to enquire into the causes of recent disorders, and to report on the form of constitution which, 'under the Protectorate' might best promote peace and prosperity, the development of self-governing institutions and the protection of foreign interests. Had this Mission come out immediately, and preferably while Zaghlul and friends were still in Malta, it might have worked miracles. Unfortunately, for this or that reason, and probably to some extent because 'director's weather' was desired, it did not come to Egypt until December. In the seven months of delay, positions were taken up and opinions hardened. Zaghlul and the Wafd refused to meet a mission charged with the continuance of the Protectorate and with a British concoction of constitutions, and they ordered a boycott. The terms of reference of the mission thus debarred the very elements it was designed to help from any contact with it.

The mission was a distinguished one. Lord Milner, a cabinet minister and elder statesman, had served under Cromer; so had Sir Rennell Rodd, later our ambassador in Rome. Mr. J. A. Spender represented the Liberal, Sir Owen Thomas the Labour, point of view. Sir John Maxwell had been a popular G.O.C. in Egypt at the beginning of the war. Sir Cecil Hurst provided the legal brains. In a minor ancillary role, I saw a good deal of these heavyweights and attended many a banquet in their honour. But the Egyptian boycott was apparently complete. Its reasons would have been better expressed frankly in personal interviews, and officially recorded; but terrorist methods frightened even well-wishing moderates from meeting the mission. It was, however, able to collect valuable material from official memoranda and from some clandestine interviews, and it left for England, after a three months' stay, in March 1920.

Its conclusions were surprisingly liberal, and Lord Lloyd (in his book, *Egypt since Cromer*) damned them all, jointly and separately. The delegates found, contrary to Cromer's own view, that the British protectorate had never made Egypt a part of the British empire. They ignored, as the British government had ignored, an interesting suggestion made by Lord Allenby in March 1920, that our treaty of peace with Turkey should include provision for a Turkish cession to His Majesty's Government of the prerogatives and authority of the sultan as suzerain of Egypt. This might well have eased the task of Milner and his friends. They recommended an Anglo-Egyptian treaty, recognising Egyptian independence, and an alliance providing for British defence of Egyptian territory. The necessary British troops, to be stationed at some place to be agreed, were not to be considered as an army of occupation. Egypt was to conduct her own foreign relations. The Egyptian government would be free to retain or to dispense with the services of foreign officials, except that a financial and a judicial adviser would remain, with supervising responsibility for the interests of foreigners: we had to carry French and other foreign opinion with us in these concessions. Egypt was to assist Britain in time of war. The Sudan was excluded from consideration, but Egypt's claim to Nile waters was recognised.

These recommendations went far beyond the mission's terms of reference. They may not unreasonably be considered as generous in the circumstances of the time.

But the assumptions of nationalist co-operation and goodwill explicit in the memorandum were still fantastically optimistic. The word 'independence' has strong overtones which make all limiting factors unacceptable. Further minor concessions were made during discussions in England with Zaghlul, whom Adly Pasha's finger had beckoned from Paris; and no undertakings were asked or given that the copy of the mission's note communicated to Zaghlul would be either accepted or recommended by him to the Egyptian public. Lord Milner was, perhaps, over-persuaded by his own sense of generosity.

No concession availed to convince the Wafdist leader of his responsibility as a statesman. He insisted that his own programme was an irrevocable mandate, to which no amendment was possible. Finally, however, he consented to send a party to Cairo to sound out Egyptian reactions to the Mission's proposals, which had still not been considered by the British cabinet. This party came out and, after research, reported that of the remaining members of the pre-war General Assembly, 47 out of 49 approved the proposals. One word of encouragement from Zaghlul would have then ensured their general welcome. The essential thing was a lead, but Zaghlul remained firmly non-committal. When the mission refused to reopen discussions, their memorandum became the not very welcome object of official approval in London, endorsed in parliamentary debate. On February 22, 1921, British policy towards Egypt became that recommended by Lord Milner and his colleagues.

There was serious opposition to the proposals in Egypt from non-Wafdist quarters, anxious not to see so complete a surrender to nationalist forces. Mohammed Sa'id Pasha, the Prime Minister, and some of the princes, were urgent in condemning the alleged inadequacy of the concessions made, hoping to frustrate them. Even the proverbially pro-British newspaper *Al Moqattam* adopted an extreme nationalist line of criticism. These antics were recognised for what they were and they cut no ice. The really condemnable attitude was, alas!, Zaghlul's.

When Wingate was High Commissioner, the clash had been complete between pre-1914 thinking in London and post-1918 thinking in Cairo. President Wilson's fireworks had illuminated wide fields of abstraction known as 'nationalism' and 'self-determination', and of the scene suddenly displayed Egyptians could see only the light and London only the darkness. In 1919, while Egypt was hailing a new truth, London had had forty years close experience of Egyptian behaviour and was thereby inhibited from accepting any new ideas without long inspection and analysis. But from March 1919 onwards, it was always easier for Egypt to accept 'rather-less-to-be-going-on-with' than for England to offer 'rather-more'. King Faisal and Nuri Pasha in Iraq played it the gradual way, taking all offers and then using them as springboard: Iraq was fully independent five years before Egypt. Congress in India did not despise and reject mere provincial autonomy. Zaghlul and his successor chose to remain prisoners of a perfectionist slogan which they themselves had drafted: *Al-Istiqlal-el-tam* or Complete Independence. It was one thing for Hafez Ramadan Bey, the attractively decadent leader of the shadowy Watanist Party, to stroll through Egyptian politics under the parasol of 'No Negotiations before Evacuation!' That was a bluff that would never be called. But for Zaghlul Pasha to prefer, in and out of office, the politician's slogan to the statesman's grasp of opportunity, and to fight tooth and nail any rival who looked like accepting less than himself, was a betrayal of his country's hopes.

An Egyptian is generally most reluctant to give offence where this may be resented; reluctant to anger a critic; reluctant to risk making an enemy. He dislikes saying: 'No', preferring to say: *'Insha'llah'* and to leave the petitioner some hope, if only in God. This is less piety than a flaw in moral courage. In Zaghlul, this innate urge not to displease led to excessive consideration for the real or anticipated criticism of rebels in his own ranks. He must have known that his own authority in Egypt was unique. For the masses, he was the shadow of God on earth. Had he wished to extinguish opposition from his colleagues, he could have done so with a flick of his fly-whisk. He seemed to lack the courage of his own convictions.

How otherwise can we judge his behaviour during his talks with Lord Milner in England? An Egyptian journalist friend of mine, Mahmoud Azmy Bey 'Al-Mutabarnat', whose respect for Zaghlul rules out any suggestion of insincerity, told me that when the Pasha gave him an interview in England at that time, off the record, he asked what Zaghlul thought of the mission's proposals. Zaghlul replied, knowing that he would not be quoted in the Cairo newspapers: 'As an Egyptian, I am surprised and delighted. As President of the Wafd, I find the recommendations unacceptable.'

I saw much in later years of that dark, high-cheeked Mongolian face, which seemed to carry such infinite authority. If Zaghlul had acted according to his instincts as an Egyptian, Egypt would have been better served.

8

In the early days of the Allenby dispensation, our social life was intensive, and we rarely went to bed on the day we got up. If I now had to work at a desk for seventy and more hours a week, the rest of my time would be spent in conspicuous inactivity; but for the under-thirties living in Cairo between the wars twenty-four hours were too few for a day. Most of our evenings were spent dancing, for that was the accepted thing to do after a dinner-party, and one could dance in one hotel or another every night of the week. When the lights were firmly turned off by an exhausted Hotel manager, Alan ('I'll walk beside you') Murray, then with his regiment in Cairo, took over the piano and played for us till morning-light.

Music sang to us from two grand pianos in Jack Gordon's

drawing-room, and at all Lucy de Kramer's parties. Ronald Storrs, on leave from Jerusalem, would improvise for hours, whistling like a bird to his own accompaniment. And Bruce-Ottley, then a neophyte in some tobacco firm, gave a new dimension to Arabic music. This, having quarter-tones and no chords, is rather an acquired taste. Long listening is, for the uninitiated, a strain. Bruce-Ottley, himself a gifted pianist, had studied seven or eight native airs and had woven round them a variety of accompaniments. Some were a matter of great chords; others were Mozartian in flow and light. All were so composed that no piano-note coincided with a quarter-tone in the native music. A little old man with a white beard from the Mousky played for us on the *rebáb*, a sort of one-stringed fiddle, and Bruce-Ottley accompanied him on the piano. The result was a surprise and a delight; it gave a new depth to the harmonic line, and one's ear was never shocked by discord. For the first time, I found Arab music instantly palatable. I have often wished that this technique might have been adapted by its inventor to the score of a light opera, based on some specifically Egyptian theme such as Marmaduke Pickthall's *Sa'id the Fisherman*; for this, I am sure, would have united East and West in happy appreciation.

The French colony in Cairo was traditionally headed by the Suez Canal representative, and, no less traditionally, Count de Sérionne, like his successors, did not flaunt the extreme anglophobia of the little *imperium in imperio* whose headquarters were Ismailia. No glimmer of the Entente Cordiale penetrated there, and nineteenth-century attitudes, inflamed by some sense of frustration at failure to share in the occupation and at thoughts of Fashoda, were *de rigueur* in office, mess and club. De Sérionne limped through Cairo drawing-rooms like a wounded lion, and was very popular. The Greek and Italian colonies of Cairo were not represented in the top-drawer, where their place was taken by Jews and Christian Syrians and Lebanese and, of course, Copts. Moslem Egyptians were still inclined to stay at home.

This was a world I came to know very well, and one which I would happily commemorate, name by name and face by face, were such indulgence acceptable. In a more uninhibited version of this record, compiled for family consumption, some justice is done to many claims of gratitude.

To the normal contacts of Cairo society, I added, wherever possible, Turkish and Egyptian friendships; and these, happily for me, were continually expanding.

My first visit to one charming old lady, Princess Iffet, was memorable. She lived in an old-fashioned palace at Shoubra, and there tea and sweet cakes were served by three Circassian girls. I properly averted my eyes from their Moslem femininity. It was a *tête-à-tête* occasion, and my hostess said: 'You do not seem to like my little Circassians, Monsieur Grafftey.' I told her that the effort of not looking at them was extreme. 'But do not be ridiculous!' she exclaimed, 'you are one of us'—which I thought flattering:'*Rincez-vous l'oeil!*' This I proceeded to do. They wore diaphanous baggy trouserines, and curly *babouches* on their naked feet; soft scarlet caps with swinging gold tassels, and scarlet and gold boleros over transparent gauze bodices. They were provocatively nubile at the age of sixteen. She used to import them from Constantinople, and marry them off after three years' service. Nothing comparable was visible at the Gezira Sporting Club.

After Lord Allenby's appointment as High Commissioner, one important change was made in social practice. It had hitherto been policy to limit the social obligations of the High Commissioner to a select few. A hundred might sign his Visitor's Book, and duly receive the acknowledgment of a card in return, but, outside the European colony and Egyptian officialdom, only five or six of these would ever get inside the house. This sounds old-fashioned, but it had advantages. It spared the British Representative the embarrassment of selection in a mass of potential guests, for he could not possibly entertain them all, and it insulated him from the pressures of local and Levantine intrigue. Where His Excellency dined out, and who dined with him, were matters of protocol; and everyone understood this. Under the influence, or so it seemed, of Lord Dalmeny, his Military Secretary, busily aided by Eric Waley, the Residency doors were opened much more widely, and many new names appeared on the place-cards. The Allenbys did not care what social reputations were established at their table; they were then numbed by the death in action of their only son. I personally was inclined to deplore this sudden extension of the High Commissioner's hospitality, with its invidious consequence of enhanced prestige for some of Cairo's *nouveaux-riches* but not for others. But it was not directly my business, and the quality of his luncheon guests was the least of Lord Allenby's preoccupations.

European and Levantine hospitality offered no monopoly of exotic fauna. We had our own British deviants from the British norm. Owen Pasha swung a Welsh kilt among the local *gallabiyyas*. Harry Farnall, a former Foreign Office personage who held for years the sinecure of British Commissioner on the Caisse de la Dette, dressed even more improbably, in a costume which memory insists began with a four-inch choker collar and proceeded by way of corset-tight white jackets to trousers wrapped round the leg like jodhpurs: always in spotless white. I saw nothing like it until Carnaby Street was hatched.

Sir William Willcocks, who had built the first Aswan Dam and hated doing it, was another eccentric who showed me much kindness. He combined a great reputation as a Civil Engineer with strong disapproval of any interference with Nature. He had prophesied, and how rightly, that the short-sighted interest of landowners, yearning to profit from the three crops a year made possible by perennial irrigation, would spell ruin for the Egyptian soil and the health of the Egyptian fellahin, once the pre-eminent peasantry of the world. Because the problem of drainage never seemed to enjoy the same priority as that of water-supply, large areas of the Delta became all but unfertile, with sub-soil water and a general salting-up bringing their harvest of disease and devastation. Only the three most southerly provinces were left to practise the old 'basin-irrigation' of Pharaonic times; there forty days of flood-water on the land leaves ten centimetres of rich silt and a benison of ten *kantars* crop to the acre (four *kantars* is a good crop elsewhere). Now the men of Keneh and Girga, who alone retain the strength and prowess of their ancestors, will be exposed to these same calamities and diseases, when the waters stored by the new great High Dam wash over their provinces in perennial irrigation.

Sir William held strong views on these and on many other matters, and was by way of being a religious fanatic. He translated the Gospels into Egyptian colloquial Arabic—never normally used in print—relying on his own memory for most of the words but referring tricky bits to his Nubian cook, for whom, also, Arabic was a precariously acquired skill. I had a set of these little volumes, published at the translator's expense. It was rather like reading the Bible in cockney and rhyming-slang; and I deciphered with some surprise the *ipsissima verba* of Our Lord, as filtered through such unexpected lips.

Poor Willcocks later lent his name and authority to a virulent campaign designed to prove that Sir Murdoch Macdonald, the Adviser to the Ministry of Public Works, had falsified essential data in his presentation of the facts of the Nile flood. This led to a libel suit, followed breathlessly by all Egyptians, to whom the Nile flood means life or death. In the event, Macdonald was fully exonerated, and Willcocks ruined. This temporary aberration in no way diminishes his stature in my memory. I have a series of his lectures, published as *From the Garden of Eden to the Red Sea*, in which he applies his vast expertise and lifetime's acquaintance with irrigation problems in Egypt and Iraq to the examination and technical explanation of events recorded in Genesis and Exodus: Where was Eden? What caused Noah's flood? What were the ten plagues? How did Joseph know the interpretation of Pharaoh's dreams? Where did the Israelites cross 'the Red Sea'? I still find this booklet fascinating.

9

In December 1920, I left Egypt for work in Arabia (separately recorded) and, later, in Constantinople, and returned in March 1925 to find much changed. In the winter of 1920, Lord Carnarvon and Howard Carter had still been probing the Valley of the Kings for an unopened tomb. Bicycles were still our accepted means of locomotion, stacked in their hundreds at the Gezira Sporting

Club by still unliquidated British officials. The Sphinx could still be seen mysteriously couched in the desert sand, for excavation had not then revealed those long, concretish and disproportionate legs. In the Egyptian museum, one could still gaze down through glass at the very features, dark and clear and millennia-old, of Rameses II himself, the Pharaoh of the Persecution who would not let God's people go. Egyptian sentiment later banished all the Pharaohs to basement seclusion.

In the world of Egyptian politics, the change had been dramatic. In December 1920, the British Government had still had hopes of negotiations for the Treaty and Alliance offered on the basis of the Milner proposals. These hopes were to be for long frustrated. The atmosphere in Egypt was not propitious, for Zaghlul Pasha now made the rain and the fine weather. He abandoned the non-committal attitude he had first adopted, once he had cause to fear that someone else might lead the team of Egyptian negotiators. From his hotel in Paris he issued, in early 1921, a series of impossible demands as conditions precedent to any negotiation. On April 5, 1921, Zaghlul returned from Europe to Egypt, giving his fellow-countrymen their first glimpse of him since his exile to Malta. His presence provoked a frenzy of popular enthusiasm, and a pattern of disorders, organised by the Wafd, began to shape. This was to be a tragically familiar pattern in the years to come.

There were sporadic, but frequent, murders of British soldiers and officials. In early May, Abdurrahman Bey Fahmi, a Wafdist lawyer, with twenty-one others, faced trial for the organisation of a murder-gang called the Society of Vengeance. The murders continued.

Fierce riots broke out in Tantah, where the police had to fire on the mob. They were officially rebuked for their firmness. Consequently, on May 23, 1921, when Alexandria went mad, the local police naturally did little or nothing. In all these disorders the real impulse was one of Egyptian party-politics, with the Wafd against the rest; but the flavour of murder was strongly xenophobe. The straw hat which was the badge of Levantine Alexandria's pride became a target for mayhem and mutilation. Tens of Europeans and Egyptians were killed and hundreds wounded, and the British military authorities had finally to assume administration of the town. This was one of the moments when, in my view, a severely strong hand with extremism might have paid political dividends; but Lord Allenby's communiqué explaining why he had had to intervene was moderately phrased. Lord Lloyd calls it 'appealing and apologetic'. The Turf Club wanted Allenby's blood. The foreign communities were furious. Against such a background of successful terrorism, Adly Pasha's attempt at negotiation in the autumn was only the first of many failures. He returned to Egypt in December, and a hectoring and ill-advised note which Curzon had instructed Allenby to send to the Sultan swept him into resignation on a wave of national resentment. With him disappeared the hopes of all the moderates in Egypt; the murder-campaign and terrorism were such that no ordinary man dared accept nomination as Premier.

Abdel Khaleq Sarwat Pasha, however, bravely promised Allenby that he would form a cabinet. After giving this assurance he left the Residency for the Mohammed Ali Club, and outside the entrance he was set upon by two drunken British soldiers, who knocked his *tarboush* from his head—a very grave insult—and stole his gold watch. He wrote to Lord Allenby from the club withdrawing his offer of collaboration.

This point of deadlock and the crackle of disturbance up and down the country persuaded Allenby that Zaghlul must be again removed from Egypt if Anglo-Egyptian relations were to return to relative normality. With four companions, Zaghlul was shipped off to Aden; but nothing was ready for them there and they continued their journey to a less arid exile in the Seychelles. In Egypt, calm, if not stability, was at once restored.

There was now no basis for that co-operation with the Egyptians which had been the secret of British rule since Cromer's time. The British Advisers needed Egyptian Ministers to take their advice, for they could themselves do nothing executive. In the absence of a cabinet, the administrative machine was grinding to a stop. Lord Allenby began conversations with Sarwat Pasha, who accepted all British concessions and rejected all British claims. At last, on January 12, 1922, the High Commissioner came up with a block-buster.

He proposed to his Government that H.M.G. should inform Sultan Fuad that they were prepared to abolish the Protectorate without waiting for a Treaty and, with the reservation of certain essentials to their own discretion, to recognise Egyptian sovereign independence. Martial Law would be abolished as soon as an Act of Indemnity was passed; and the creation of a Parliament to control the policy and administration of a constitutionally responsible Government would be favourably viewed. London, where Curzon was still Foreign Secretary, asked for further enlightenment and instructed that two Advisers be sent from Cairo to supply it; but Lord Allenby, whose tone throughout this correspondence was of an impatient urgency, insisted on prompt approval of the draft despatch containing his proposals. He said that their immediate acceptance would mean a lasting settlement with Egypt and that their refusal could only lead to a rule of repression driving us to annexation of the country, '. . . which would greatly increase our difficulties'. As not a few personalities at home had long favoured annexation, this despatch provoked some annoyance and a stern reply. Lord Allenby was charged with concealing his intentions while misleading his government as to the prospects of accommodation with Sarwat Pasha. An explanation was demanded of this 'violent metamorphosis', which involved the abandonment of positions long held sacrosanct. Consideration of the resignation which he had not failed to attach to his surprise-packet was refused until the two Advisers had been sent to explain things in London.

His Lordship rang for his Oriental Secretary. 'This,' he said, 'is a BOO telegram. Write a BOO-BOO despatch for me in reply.' Robin Furness took two days out of the office to draft the document required, in which he included a passage from Aeschylus in Gilbert Murray's translation: it was that sort of despatch. When reading the draft, the High Commissioner grunted in recognition of Aeschylus, and said: 'I think we might have this in the original Greek', which he proceeded to inscribe. He took this BOO-BOO despatch with him to London and left it at the Foreign Office on his way from the station to his hotel.

It had become apparent, when Lord Allenby received from Egyptians, British and foreign elements alike an enthusiastic send-off in Cairo and at stations along his route, that his dismissal, which may well have been considered, might not be easy. The details of his proposals were unknown in Cairo, but his thinking was known to many. Unexpectedly strong support for him came also from *The Times*, for Valentine Chirol, knowing the Cairo scene well, advised Lord Northcliffe, who was then passing through Egypt, to study the question on the spot, and Northcliffe's despatches were powerful. Curzon tried to persuade the High Commissioner to withdraw his resignation, but in vain.

Allenby's position was not, in fact, a weak one. For when he proposed that the conditions concerning our rights and interests, which had hitherto prevented agreement on the abolition of the Protectorate, should become 'reserved points', until such time as agreement could be reached on them, he realised that sea-power and our garrison in Egypt were pledges enough, and that these, and not any so-called Protectorate, were the basis of our position in Egypt. During the crucial interview with Lloyd-George the Prime Minister, Allenby (according to Lord Wavell) blew his top. 'I have waited five weeks for a decision,' he exclaimed; 'I can't wait any longer!' Lloyd-George put a hand on his arm. 'You have waited five weeks,' he replied, 'wait five minutes more!' He suggested a few insignificant amendments; and the policy enshrined in the Declaration of February 28, 1922 was approved and with it Lord Allenby's major contribution to Egyptian history.

The reserved points were four in number:

(a) The security of Imperial communications in Egypt.
(b) The defence of Egypt against foreign aggression.
(c) The protection of foreign interests in Egypt and the protection of minorities.
(d) The Sudan.

These matters His Majesty's Government reserved to their absolute discretion, pending later agreements by free discussion and friendly accommodation.

In Egypt nothing is sacred. Amin Yusuf Bey, a nephew of Madame Zaghlul and a persistent claimant of Residency interest in his various misfortunes, who used to weep in my office arm-chair once a week, soon became known to Cairo coffee-shops and the satirical press as 'the fifth reserved point'.

* * *

In the Seychelles, Zaghlul Pasha stubbornly refused to recognise the February 28 Declaration as having any validity whatsoever; because it was unilateral, he said, it had no binding effect on Egypt. This effectively hamstrung all attempts made during the next fourteen years to settle the 'reserved points' by negotiation, and British optimism proved vain. Logically there was point in the Egyptian argument that you cannot formally recognise a country's sovereign independence and insist on negotiating positions incompatible with that status. We had either given away too much or too little.

However, the climate changed for the better. Sarwat Pasha formed a cabinet on the day after the Declaration, and on March 15, 1922, the Sultan became His Majesty King Fuad of Egypt, and Lord Allenby handed over control of Egyptian Foreign Affairs to the Prime Minister. A commission under Rushdy Pasha drafted a constitution on the Belgian model, which Allenby had to fight hard to protect from Fuad's attacks; and this constitution produced the most constant cause of friction between the King and his ministers during the coming years. Yehya Ibrahim Pasha did a good job in finalising the constitution, passing the Indemnity Act enabling the abolition of martial law, and negotiating the liquidation of the many foreigners in Egyptian service.

This liquidation cost the Egyptians over £8 million, a lot of money at the time, and the compensation granted, calculated on a scale devised by Ernest Scott, Counsellor at the Residency, became more or less standard in similar operations later. Unfortunately, the maximum figure of £8,000 individual gratuity was worth a good deal more in 1922 than when the Indian civil service and Sudan civil service were liquidated in 1947 and 1953.

I personally watched, with emotion, the disappearance of all three of these proud fraternities.

Every established official in Egypt received compensation for a 'blasted career', though clerks and typists could cross the street and find a new job in ten minutes. Many remained on contract with the Egyptian Government. Within a few years, most of this new wealth had evaporated; I once met an ex-Inspector managing a tobacco-shop. I can only recall one who made good in the City; but one subordinate official in the railways, who had for years played the Stock Exhange on paper as others play crossword-puzzles, turned his £3000 into £80,000 in three years, and then died.

*　　*　　*

As expected, elections in the winter of 1923 gave Zaghlul, now back in Cairo, a huge majority, and on January 27, 1924, he became the first Prime Minister of independent Egypt. The schizophrenia inhibiting him from formal acceptance of the Milner recommendations which he personally welcomed was again apparent after his first audience with King Fuad as Prime Minister. He then told Reuter's correspondent that he had expected the King to be difficult, but not as impossible as he had found him. 'Egypt will need a strong arm to help her,' he said; and admitted that he meant a strong British arm. Yet when he went to London to negotiate with Ramsay MacDonald, he demanded, as a pre-condition, that Britain should evacuate all her troops and extinguish all interest in Egypt.

His premiership was a tragedy from the start. He never thought of condemning the murder-campaign which blackened political life, with liberals of Adly's new party now victims, with the British, of Wafdist assassination. As one of the reserved points, the Sudan began to attract Egyptian agitators, and there were violent disturbances and mutinies in Egyptian garrisons at Khartoum and Atbara. In May, 1924, Zaghlul reminded parliament bitterly that an Englishman was Governor-General of the Sudan and Sirdar of the Egyptian army. This, he declared, was inconsistent with national dignity. Anxious to frustrate the King's power to thwart him, he resigned, and organised a monster demonstration in his own honour, which shouted 'Saad or Revolution' for two hours outside Abdin Palace and made Zaghlul's audience with the King inaudible. He formally thanked and dismissed this mob on leaving the Palace.

Three days later, his tacit blessing for the violence of the past three years, and his specific attack on Sir Lee Stack, Governor-General of the Sudan, led to a careful blocking of Stack's car at the busy corner where the Sharia Kasr-el-Aini runs into the Midan Ismail Pasha, on its return from a visit to the Ministry of War. Many shots were fired and a bomb was thrown, but it did not explode. Campbell, the A.D.C., and Marsh, the chauffeur, were hit; Sir Lee Stack was mortally wounded. He was rushed to the Residency, where Asquith was a house guest at the time, and was lying on the sofa in Lord Allenby's study when Zaghlul called to enquire. He died in hospital the following night. Zaghlul spoke truly when he said that day to Reuter's correspondent: 'This is a death-blow for me!'

I am told—I was in Turkey at the time—that this tragedy struck the streets of Cairo to silence; people tiptoed about their business, apprehensive of they knew not what British retribution. The funeral service on November 22 was a very tense affair, for the last-minute decision of Zaghlul and his cabinet to attend the ceremony took the organisers by surprise, and only by an inspiration was appropriate seating accommodation found for them.

Parliament was due to meet that same day at 5 p.m., and Lord Allenby was determined that Zaghlul should not confront it and resign before feeling the full weight of British anger and outrage. I have seen the draft of the ultimatum which he informed H.M.G. he proposed to deliver to Zaghlul that afternoon. It was written in pencil, on the back of other notes, by Robin Furness as he and Clark-Kerr and Amos, the triumvirate of advisers acting as Allenby's brains trust, sat in Clark-Kerr's sitting-room after lunch on the day after the murder. The text of the ultimatum reflects something of this haphazard ambience.

After demanding ample apology, the identification and condign punishment of the criminals and a ban on all future political demonstrations, it imposed a fine of £500,000; the withdrawal of all Egyptian forces from the Sudan; and acceptance of the British point of view, hitherto resisted, on various matters affecting the European advisers and foreign officials. Finally, it stated that the Sudan would extend irrigation in the Gezira area to an unlimited extent, as need might arise. This last clause brought British vengeance into every smallholding in Egypt.

As Lord Allenby was on the point of leaving for his appointment at the Beit-el Umma, Pattman, the cipher officer, reported that the first of two parts of a long cipher message from London had come in. Allenby, anxious that the blow of the ultimatum should fall on Zaghlul and Zaghlul alone, felt unable to delay or to await news of Foreign Office reactions. He drove off, with a clattering escort of the 16th/5th, his old regiment, and read the ultimatum to Zaghlul in English, leaving him a copy in French. He returned to find that much of his Note had been strongly disapproved of by his Government.

A few weeks earlier, Fascist Italy had extracted £500,000 from Greece as compensation for the murder of General Tellini in Greek territory on August 23, 1923, while he was delimiting the Graeco-Albanian frontier. 'Is £500,000 the market-price of a Major General?' London enquired. The threat to Nile Water, Egypt's most sensitive nerve-complex, was condemned. The piling up on a dead man's body of a mass of material which the Residency had been unable to settle otherwise seemed improper and irrelevant to Whitehall. Lord Allenby's case was that the very severity of his terms enabled later concessions to whatever less anglophobe Prime Minister might succeed Zaghlul, who did, in fact, resign. There was also the chronological crisis of timing. But the grievance created by his action gave his critics in London ammunition which they did not hesistate to use.

These critics included not only a right-wing Tory element always inclined to put good administration above other considerations, which had never forgiven Allenby the Declaration of 1922, but also a powerful group inside and outside the Foreign Office, which saw in Archie Clark-Kerr, Allenby's First Secretary, the anti-Establishment hellhound, tempting the High Commissioner to one extravagance of concession after another, while remaining in the shelter of the magnificent puppet he manipulated. Any blow at Clark-Kerr would at once provoke the great Field Marshal to some gesture of menacing resignation. Much frustration was generated by this interpretation of events. Now that Austen Chamberlain was Foreign Secretary in a Conservative administration, the need for a change in Cairo staffing was felt to be inescapable. Without consulting the High Commissioner, he gave publicity to a new appointment, that of Nevile Henderson, then on leave from Constantinople, to be minister plenipotentiary 'while employed at the Residency in Cairo'. This was at once interpreted in Egypt as betokening a change from Allenby's policy. As Lord Wavell puts it, Henderson's appointment was equivalent to the supersession without warning of a general's chief staff officer during an important operation. Allenby took this as evidence of lack of confidence in himself and his staff and, after trying in vain to have Henderson's mission made into one of temporary liaison only, insisted that his offer of resignation, dating from a few days after the ultimatum incident, should be submitted to the King when the pressure of the crisis was past.

By now I was back in Cairo and I had some to-ing and fro-ing in these painful exchanges. One message from London had to be carried urgently to Lord Allenby, then fishing below the Aswan Dam. My journey from Luxor to Aswan, still a narrow-gauge railway of great discomfort, was a nightmare of heat in the Upper Egyptian May. I was not far from passing-out when Ralph Harari, Komombo-bound, heard that I was aboard and succoured me in his own compartment from an immense ice-box. The result of that message was that the High Commissioner, with the same stubborn determination that had earned him in the army the nickname of 'the Bull', pressed for the acceptance of his resignation. He asked specifically that he should have two days' notice of the date and hour of the announcement of his successor, and that this announcement should contain an assurance that no change of policy was intended by the change of personalities.

These requests were not favourably considered. Less than a week later, I had to take to Lord Allenby a Reuter's telegram baldly announcing the appointment of Sir George Lloyd as High Commissioner, to succeed him. He read this news item and rose to his feet, leaning his hands on his desk. He was rocking with emotion. In Spain, before the war, I had watched too many *corridas* not to recognise 'Death in the Afternoon'. He begged me to leave him, and it was certainly no scene for an audience.

* * *

Lord Allenby's send-off from Egypt was spectacular in its evidence of goodwill from all sections of the population. I travelled with him from Cairo to Port Said, to translate the many speeches made to him at stations along his route, and his own simple replies.

His proconsulship was memorable, and memorable for good. His position was one of great strength, and this strength he used first to extract Egyptian Independence from an unwilling British Government and then to extract a liberal Egyptian Constitution from a reactionary autocrat. At the same time he managed to maintain essential British interests without forfeiting the respect, indeed the admiration, of Egyptians, for as a race they recognise and look for good manners while also recognising strength.

Sir Reginald Wingate, ostensibly in imitation of a wartime abstinence in Buckingham Palace, had banned alcohol from the Residency table, and his butler, the formidable Mr. Jones, could offer guests only a choice of lemonade and barley-water, a process which he defined to me as prostituting his profession. Lord Allenby lived up to his reputation and his allowances and restored the hocks and burgundies, though preferring gin as his own staple refreshment. This endeared him to his staff, but it was not the only reason for our devotion. He was always courteous, always simple, always straightforward, and never really happy in a job where decision was so often frustrated by political cross-currents in London. If I believe that he was sometimes over-persuaded by his advisers, this is not to suggest that he was ever persuaded against his will; only that the death of his only son seemed to have removed some of the essence of his will.

He was a man of surprising erudition, and his interest in what interested others was constant. 'Mabel!' he would boom down a long dinner-table, 'listen to what Judge Pratt has been telling me about cannibalism in Kenya!' After the Sirdar's murder, Allenby was not allowed to take his early afternoon walk round 'little Gezira' alone; one of us, bulkily hip-pocketed with a large revolver, had to accompany him. I found these occasions, except for my unusual armament, delightful. The High Commissioner held forth on books, medicine, and of course birds, with authority and charm.

One may ask whether the problems which faced Lord Allenby would have the same treatment today. There was a measure of optimism fringing folly in that policy of concessions to moderate opinion while extremism was left the master of events; but the experience was then novel enough to justify experiment and error. It was then something new for Britain to abandon any area of her pride. Just as the British element in the Egyptian civil service was the first of its kind to be dismantled in the cause of self-determination and nationalism, so the liquidation of our imperial position in Egypt with retention of essential British interests was then a novelty in political exercises. Nowadays the operation would probably be more tidily, and certainly more rapidly, accomplished.

10

My work, after March 1925, was in the Oriental Secretariat of the Residency.

The Oriental Secretaries in Cairo and Tehran, like the dragomans of the embassy in Constantinople, became suspect as Turkey, Egypt and Persia became more independent of European influence; they knew too much to be welcome in the changed relationship. They existed to provide the head of the mission with full information on local politics and personalities and to advise him on the affairs of other Near and Middle Eastern countries.

They interpreted the vernacular press in all its manifestations, and the trends of local parliamentary debate. They also translated, when necessary, during interviews, and when their master made speeches on tour. They vetted the non-European candidates for interviews or for dinner-parties, and were responsible for all protocol matters concerning such social manifestations as calls and return-calls, greetings and condolence, table-placings, audiences with the monarch, embassy representation at funerals and at charitable, theatrical and similar *corvées*. They were also expected to minute with some expertise all incoming papers concerning their special subjects and to draft the necessary despatches or telegrams in reply. They were drawn, almost exclusively, from the Levant consular service, but the usual limited period of tour did not apply to them. They were apt to remain for many years on end in these specialist jobs and continuity of experience was thus assured.

As we were expected to know all that went on, and to report events almost before they occurred, we were allowed to neglect the British colony to some extent in our cultivation of local personalities. We belonged to the Turf Club but we rarely went there. Outside the Residency, the Mohamed Ali Club was our workshop. It was, in 1925, an island of civilised sophistication in a world of clamour. There were but few British members; most inmates were of the Turco-Egyptian caste soon to be obsolescent. On those billowing sofas, beneath those vast chandeliers, in conversations hushed by those velvet curtains and deep-piled carpets, discretion was so much a way of life that indiscretions were frequent. The hurly-burly of political strife was so alien to this *Troisième Empire* elegance that the most secretive pasha might be forgiven if, over his black coffee, he confided some humour of the day's events or some revealing judgment on his neighbours.

Our representative duties took us into many local backwaters: I followed many a coffin side by side with Zaghlul. In the fasting month of Ramadan, we paid three visits a night, four nights a week, to the leading Moslem divines, the *Ulamá*, and the judges of the Supreme Mohammedan law court. As an exercise in Arabic, this was valuable. I used to adapt the small-talk of the first of my *Ulamá* in conversation with the second; and the third hardly needed to speak, for I was by then full of eloquence. The price paid was high, because the food offered to callers during the Ramadan nights is the sweet and sticky stuff with which the Moslem fills in between his two lamplit meals; and politeness forbids any refusal. Tea with butter in it probably tastes better in a Tibetan climate than in Cairo. Our visits took us far afield, to Heliopolis and Heluan and to corners of Cairo and its suburbs far removed in spirit and space from Kasr-el-Doubara. The messenger who accompanied us had to explore the route well in advance. Driving through the ancient and hidden quarters of Cairo on these Ramadan journeys, when every minaret is illuminated, we might arrive at the great house of Sayed el-Bakri in Qoronfish, which was once Napoleon's headquarters. He was head of all the thirty-three sects of Sufism in Egypt, and in his great courtyard a different group of Sufi devotees would gather, each night of the month, to recite the Koran each in its individual *tariqa*, and to perform its own peculiar ceremony of the *zikr*. It was a privilege to watch these devotions. And somewhere, in most of the houses we visited, one or more blind dervishes would be chanting a recital of the Koran under the Ramadan moon.

Most of these *Ulamá* were worthy obscurantists like Sheikh Abu'l Uyun or the Grand Mufti of that day, holding to the original pattern of their thousand-year-old university. Rare exceptions like Sheikh Mustafa Abdel Razek, Paris-educated, who could quote Verlaine to prove a point, were not enough to inspire any process of renaissance. But gradually the influence of one of my closest friends, Sheikh Mohammed Mustafa el-Maraghi, worked upon the dry bones and created of Al-Azhar something alive and purposeful and exciting where only routine and tradition had prevailed. He trod in the footsteps of Sheikh Mohammed Abdu, and the present Azhar is their monument.

In 1925 it was still usual for the High Commissioner to entertain these religious leaders on one night of Ramadan with the sweetmeats and soft drinks proper to the occasion. This was an ordeal for all concerned. We had to collect as many Arabic-speaking

Englishmen as possible to help us out, and four or five of our honoured guests would always wander in, unwelcomed, two or three hours before the appointed time. Few enjoyed themselves; and when, by some dreadful slip-up, Residency invitations were once sent out for the Lailat-el-Qadr, the holiest night of the Mohammedan year, enough was enough, and the wise men were spared further entertainment.

After 1882, any Egyptian with a sense of grievance against the Government, or against another Egyptian, was liable to write to Lord Cromer or to his successors for redress, and this habit of 'petitions' long survived the period of effective intervention. In the bad old days, I had passed most of these petitions, with a compliments-slip 'for such action as you may think it deserves', to the competent British adviser, who sent it spiralling down the chain of British officialdom until it reached the inspector able to investigate and report, and to act. If, in fact, the pasha had installed too large a pump and was leaving those at the tail of the canal without water for their fields, Eric Parker read the riot act. If the Omda really had asked for a bribe, Dick Wellesley had him sacked. Our British inspectors were not related, and had no plans for being related, to the local bigwigs. Unlike some of their Egyptian successors, whose official attitudes reflected more subjective criteria, they saw all Egyptians as equal before Allah and the law, and their decisions were untainted by nepotism or fear. Cromer's large benevolent shade continued to protect the poor and help-less.

Long after all the alien Inspectors vanished—and the first to go were, of course, those in the Interior—petitions continued to flow into the Residency at the rate of over 4000 a year; but now I had to put them into the waste-paper basket. The man who said he was 'a Lieutenant in the Tramway Service, dismissed on sanitary grounds', could not be assisted. The woman who said that, thanks to a Greek grocer, her daughter had 'left the house Miss and come back Mrs', got no official sympathy from us. But one Egyptian spinster, who had a quarrel with her landlord, tore up my letter telling her that 'the High Commissioner could not intervene and that this correspondence must cease', but carefully kept the envelope, with its Residency franking-stamp, to show to her landlord, who collapsed instantly. She called to thank me for my assistance.

One of my pleasanter ways of collecting information and getting to know people was the ostensible inspection of British consular agencies in the provinces. British businessmen in the leading provincial towns received a small allowance for stationery and stamps and the title of consular agent in exchange for largely unspecified duties in relation to other British subjects in their districts, and some showing of the flag. They all, most kindly, accepted a purely nominal act of inspection by myself and made me their guest for days on end, arranging tours and visits and confrontations with local personalities, which were invaluable. I soon had a wide circle of acquaintance outside Cairo and Alexandria, and felt that what I heard or sensed in interviews, or during the immense Egyptian meals inflicted on a visitor, was of help in assessing political reactions elsewhere. Now, I suppose, Abu Zeid Bey Tantawi of Sennoures, Hussein Bey Zummur of Giza, Mansour Bey El-Gahami, and the countless others whose friendship I so deeply valued, have joined their forefathers. They are most affectionately remembered.

The attraction of the Egyptian scene has been a constant in my life, for it was a question of love at first sight. I have never been able to take the beauty of Egypt for granted. I am not now speaking of the wonders of 'package-tour' Egypt: tombs as large as houses, ageless in the sand; obelisks mirrored in a sacred lake, and a pyramid, black against the flame of sunset. I am thinking of the things of everyday life: of lateen-sailed boats, fluttering across the great river; of palm trees nodding at their own reflecttion in flood-water; of camels, an always surprising silhouette, yoked ignominiously to minute donkeys to plough a furrow, or splendid in their caparison of honour, bearing a returning *Hajji* on the last lap of his journey home from Mecca. Look where you will in that wide open landscape, there is always some fragment of an Old Testament frieze: a white-bearded old man riding his white donkey on a canal bank; little naked urchins serrated along the back of a water-buffalo; other buffaloes, antediluvian in Nile mud; a swarm of sacred white ibis, homing on the tree which their acrid droppings are killing, or the bright prism of a kingfisher flashing in an irrigation channel. And everywhere, grave women who walk like queens. These things and all that I saw in the course of my journeyings in the Egyptian countryside sealed for ever my happy capitulation to the East.

Egyptian hospitality is proverbial, and those provincial meals were indeed gargantuan. The notable who was to be my host usually summoned many friends to share in his welcome, and the long tables, laid out of doors in a shade of tamarisk, bore a heavy weight of food. All too often this had been displayed *en masse* in a whirlwind of flies long before we arrived, and nothing was oven-warm. Soup and Nile fish were followed by roast chickens, pigeons, a Fayoum turkey, roast lamb, and an assortment of *kebáb* (grilled meat) and *dolmas* (mincemeat and herbs in vine-leaves), with massive vegetable accompaniment of *bamia* (ladies' fingers), stuffed courgettes, *bedinján* (egg-plant), lentils and beans, onions and tomatoes, and mountains of saffron rice. Garlic was agreeably obtrusive. For this I was once blacklisted by all that evening's dancing-partners, and I walked vainly for hours in the Maadi desert wind, seeking purification. Throughout the meal, *laban zabádi* (or yoghourt) was there for the taking; also that tempting, highly flavoured version of mayonnaise known as *ta'miya*, in which one dips and dips again the coarse bread, pungent with fenugreek.

This menu, seemingly ample, was hospitably recurrent, for any pause in the proceedings provoked offers of more pigeons, more roast lamb, more roast chicken, more everything. I learned at last that the guest of honour is permitted, and probably expected, to call a halt when he has had enough. When I had had rather more than enough, I would announce to the host that a move towards the sweets and fruit was all but overdue. Those sweets! *Umm Ali*, a bread-and-butter pudding with cream and chopped nuts and sultanas; *kunafa*, equal parts of vermicelli and sugar; *aish serai*, butter-fried bread heavy with syrup and whipped cream; *bakláwa*, a flaky brick of gooey delight, and (especially in the month of *Moharrem*) the traditional *ashoura*, crushed wheat boiled in rose-water with spice and nuts, cinnamon and currants. There was a choice of up to ten kinds of fruit.

I eschewed all green salads and, above all, watercress. A slow but sure process of immunisation gradually defeated the effervescent dyspepsia which was built-in for any visiting tourist.

One unsophisticated neighbour at a tea-party helped himself repeatedly to jam with his hand, direct from jar to lips; later, having failed to light an unpierced cigar, he reversed it, stubbed out the charred ash and put that end in his mouth, in triumph. At another party, while some thirty of us were waiting, seated round our host's tiled hall, we were plied with pyramids of the tangerines which answer in Egypt to the name of *Yusuf Effendi*. We must have eaten ten apiece. My discreet movement of disposal was soon revealed as unfashionable. In an atmosphere of competitive endeavour we all practised explosive expectoration, and the floor was soon dancing with pips like a hailstorm in Piccadilly.

These were rural occasions. For some specialities one had to go to Hati's restaurant in Cairo: for that delicious treatment of green wheat in milk, for instance (*farîk*, or the coarser *burghul*); or for the bull's testicles which brought to those in need their sympathetic magic.

The finer flowers of the Byzantine *cuisine* were gathered in the dining-rooms of my Circassian friends. There one was offered *imam bayildi* (the name commemorates the Imam who swooned with delight at its flavour)—a simple dish of aubergines, sliced with onions and tomatoes, and heavily peppercorned, in oil, or *cherkessieh*, where the rich sauce of the roast chicken is made of crushed walnuts, or a *shish-kebâb* of fish spitted with vine-leaves in the Tunisian fashion. A lot of people prefer baked beans and sugared salad-dressing and tin-openers. How foolish I was to start this subject!

The ballroom of the Residency had long been inadequate for the needs of an expanding staff. Soon after my return from Constantinople to Egypt, we moved to a new Chancery (since abandoned) which the Office of Works had built on to the existing foundations of something the Rumanian government had begun to build in 1914 and had then abandoned. Their intentions had dictated its shape, which was starfish; but here we had room to work in comfort. Any exceptional Nile flood covered the basement, where the old archives were housed, with rich silt, reducing our records to complete illegibility, which was not without its advantages. Furness had his own room; I shared one with another assistant. I had managed to rescue, during the transfer, Lord Cromer's office-chair, which I hoped would ensure that I was sound on fundamentals. Nevile Henderson was Minister. Clark-Kerr was under punitive transfer as Counsellor to Tokyo, but powerful interventions procured him promotion as Minister to Guatemala instead, where he declared his intention of collecting blue butterflies and blue films. Arthur Wiggin, who had been many years in Cairo, was Head of Chancery.

I took over the flat and furniture of Dick Wellesley, in the rue Houaiyati, above the flat of a British official called Melville. This elderly and most respectable man, returning without his latch-key from a party, summoned our venerable *boab*, or doorkeeper, and bade him touch his toes, so that access to the fanlight might be acrobatically attained. The rejection of this posture by an octogenarian Nubian was immediate, categorical and unflattering to Melville's intentions. My own Nubian servant, cook and general factotum was Saleh Mohamed Ahmed, of Dibeira in the Sudan. He was old, but not as old as he looked, and he usefully enjoyed the respect of other Berberines. To watch him, laden with suit-cases, golf-clubs and other paraphernalia, attempting a burst of speed along a railway-platform was Laurel-and-Hardy entertainment. He was a crotchety little man, but completely honest, and not a bad cook. He had a son, of whom he was properly proud, at Gordon College, Khartoum, and he tried to act *in loco parentis* to me, also.

11

Ahmed Ziwer Pasha, who became Prime Minister when Zaghlul fell, 'to save what can be saved', was an old friend of mine; he had been Governor of Alexandria during my incarnation there. He was of immense bulk, and lifts flowered in every ministry in Cairo for which he was responsible. When sitting down in one of the large armchairs of the Mohammed Ali Club, he used to adjust one particular vertebra to the edge of the seat before collapsing backwards like a landslide in a frock-coat. When he came to my wedding, I reserved three chairs for him in church, which were really not enough. He liked his comforts, and slept for two hours every afternoon in his car on the Pyramids Road, maintaining a state of incommunicado which was the despair of his staff. His Jesuit education made him suspect to Egyptians, and he was alleged to have died a Catholic. He had total moral courage, much humour, and was basically very lazy indeed. He once told me that his worst enemy was a guide in Berlin in the bad days of 1919, who steered him into a cabaret where he found interest and promise in a blonde called Francesca. When this interest was about to become active, it was revealed that Francesca was really Franz. I know more than one Egyptian minister to whom this surprise would have been welcome, but Ziwer Pasha was not built either physically or morally for any *Petite Chaumière*.

When Lord Allenby left Egypt in mid-June 1925, he left behind him a situation of parliamentary deadlock. Elections held in March had given almost equal numbers to Ziwer and to the Wafd, and when Zaghlul was elected President of the Chamber, Ziwer, by royal decree, dissolved parliament, promising new elections in the autumn. His Government of Liberals, Independents and Ittehadists (Unionists) continued in a situation of relative calm, with palace intrigue as the main threat to its survival.

King Fuad's main instrument in these intrigues was his then *Chef de Cabinet*, Hassan Nashat Pasha, a very able and ambitious man. He was one of three young men who had soared up like rockets and become Pashas and objects of general jealousy shortly before the war. Saleh Enan Pasha, Under-Secretary of Public Works, was another; and the third was Hassan Anis Pasha, who had been Egypt's first airman. This man soon went shabby. Saleh Enan slipped up when he tried to alter a statement made to parliament while it was in print for the official journal; but the Tura Cement works later made him a millionaire. Nashat Pasha was at the top of things in 1925, making hay in the King's name; selling beyships and pashaships, with some help from the court poet Shawki, for Ittehad party funds, this being the new party of the 'King's Friends'; lording it everywhere. His origins were said to be of the simplest; but to see him entering the San Stefano hotel as someone's guest, young, dark, arrogant and charming; moving gracefully towards his hostess while gloves, ebony cane and silk cape were smoothly removed by a succession of underlings, was to know, by the time he was bowing over his hostess's hand, the enchantment of the theatre.

Furness's last words to me before he went on leave that summer were an injunction to ensure that nothing developed to break up the Liberal–Ittehadist coalition in the Cabinet. It was essential that the new High Commissioner, who was not arriving until October, should not find a situation distorted by King Fuad's manœuvres. I doubt whether Furness himself, had he been on the spot, could have achieved this. The Acting High Commissioner, Nevile Henderson, then as later, had no great sympathy with democratic processes. He seemed to fall at once under Nashat's spell; and the not unwelcome conviction that he was winning the confidence and goodwill of a king made him deaf to warnings that this might be a slippery slope. Lord Allenby, himself a mastiff, once remarked that Nevile Henderson had the head of a fox-terrier. It was more elegant than that. When at white heat, he was an enraged Borzoi, and white heat was generated by any opposition, however courteously phrased. He had—a rare thing in the Foreign Service—a savagely violent temper; when he said he wished he could flay a certain cipher officer with his own hands, he meant it. I was ordered out of the room at least once a week, and one cannot influence one's masters from the wrong side of the door. So I was distressed but not surprised when, in early September, Nashat's skilful provocation of Abdel Aziz Fahmy, the Liberal Minister of Justice, led to his resignation and to that of his Liberal colleagues. Ziwer was then in Vichy; he returned to find himself with an Ittehadist group running things the Palace way, with no comment from the Residency.

Sir George Lloyd, our new High Commissioner, was a person

of great nervous energy, an M.P. who had travelled widely in the Near and Middle East, and a former Cambridge cox and Governor of Bombay. He was darkly Welsh and a bright light of the Tory Party, well out on its right wing. When his appointment was announced, my Egyptian clerk heard one Egyptian say to another in the tram: 'I know Lloyd George, but who is this George Lloyd?' He was told that it was the same man . . . '*lakin yigi bi-tizoh* . . .', but he was coming arse-first. No wonder he was never popular with Egyptians.

He had all the virtues of a Tory imperialist and much impatience with what he called . . . 'the Western schoolman's theory, not the least fallacious and superficial of the series, of "self-determination" '; but his virtues were irrelevant to the Egyptian situation. Imperialism is enriched by a sense of mission, a sense of trusteeship, a sense of paternal interest in the emergent fledgling; and there was no room left for paternalism in Egypt, after 1922. This frustration of his instincts lent some futility to his actions. In an associated field of emotional activity, there is no more noisily futile an object than a frustrated broody hen.

He claims in his book to have accepted a mission not normally congenial—because of the political changes since 1919—only when he had satisfied his conscience that he could support the policy of the 1922 Declaration. By support he means the maintenance in meticulous rigidity of the four reserved points, with recognition of Egyptian independence outside their framework. There remained some elasticity in his own interpretation of the reserved points, and also the fact that he liked to impose himself as arbiter of everything, for he had no great sympathy with anyone else. As soon as any Egyptian Prime Minister looked like making a good job of it, it was time for Lord Lloyd to 'cut him down to size'. Almost his last words to me before going on leave in 1929 were to the effect that his first task on return would be to take Mohammed Mahmoud Pasha down a peg or two. But from that leave he did not return.

It had been understood that Lord Lloyd—he had been made a peer while waiting to take up his post—would start work by getting Hassan Nashat Pasha out of the Palace, but this operation had to be postponed until a tricky bit of Italo-Egyptian negotiating about Egypt's Western frontier was satisfactorily concluded. Sidqi Pasha was the Egyptian negotiator, and an advance copy of his report to the Cabinet somehow found its way into the Residency. This was a 14-page cyclostyled document, foolscap-size, of blurred Arabic typescript, single-spacing; and Lord Lloyd asked me at 6 p.m. how long it would take me to let him have a translation. As usual, he divided my answer by four and told me to present it before dinner. Only when arguments about the future of Sollum was out of the way could Nashat be winkled out of the Palace, to Egypt's great delight. He was sent to Spain as Ambassador and later became his country's Ambassador in London. Then he married an English girl, abandoned public life and settled down to grow the best mangoes in Egypt. His talents fitted him for the highest post.

Historically, there is a rhythm perceptible in Lord Lloyd's four years of office, reflecting the fact that April and May, the months when the sirocco *khamsin* wind blows, key nerves to straining-point. The fifteenth hole of the Gezira golf-course was then lovely with a long border of foaming jacaranda trees, and Lord Lloyd once said: 'When I see those jacarandas in bloom, I know it's time to send for a battleship!' After some fiddling about with the law, parliamentary elections were held in May 1926 which gave the Wafd a large majority. H.M.G. had never yet interfered in the working of the Egyptian Constitution, but on May 29, in full *khamsin* weather, the High Commissioner sent for Zaghlul and tried to persuade him to accept an Adly Cabinet, without success. The battleship was therefore sent for, and its advent advertised. The newly-elected deputies were anxious to taste the fruits of office and did not welcome a clash with H.M.G. which might lead to an early dissolution of parliament. At a banquet in Zaghlul's honour, they did Lord Lloyd's work for him, pleading with their leader not to strain his health with the burdens of office. Zaghlul was surprised and baffled, and collapsed. In his next interview at the Residency, he abdicated the premiership for himself and for his deputy, Nahas Pasha, also.

It was at this moment that the three-man court trying Ahmed

Maher, Nokrashi and other leading Wafdist politicians for complicity in murders leading up to Sir Lee Stack's death acquitted all but one of them. Judge Kershaw, the only British member of the Court, shocked local legal convention by publishing his own disagreement with the verdict in the case of Ahmed Maher, and resigning. It was generally assumed, perhaps unjustly, that this behaviour was prompted by the High Commissioner.

I did not attend this trial, but I had watched with interest the trial in 1925 of the gang involved in the Sirdar's murder, whom the police had most skilfully rounded up. They were an odd lot. To me the most sinister was Sheikh Ibrahim, an elderly carpenter, a devout member of one of the more fanatical Sufi sects. Tidy, respectable and impassive, he brought to murder the conviction of answered prayer. Two very young men, the brothers Enayat, were student *exaltés*, drugged by the flattery and authority of another prisoner, Shafik Mansour, a pince-nez'd Wafdist lawyer who had been a candidate for the office of Director-General of Public Security and only took to assassination when frustrated in this hope. There was brash young Ismail Effendi, and he, like Sheikh Ibrahim, behaved as if indifferent to the legal proceedings; but Ismail seemed genuinely assured of acquittal. I was told that he had been a protégé of Hassan Nashat Pasha, King Fuad's right-hand man, and my report in this sense earned me interrogation by Taher Pasha Nur, the public prosecutor. To have established such a link would have been political dynamite. In the event, all but the younger Enayat, who had talked, were hanged: Shafik Mansour abject; Sheikh Ibrahim calmly praying; Ismail Effendi, suddenly aware of some last-minute betrayal, frantic and expostulating.

As in the 1926 case, the key figures in this enquiry were Hassan Rifaat, the Director General of Public Security, and Ingram Bey. Three young Egyptian officials had been sent to European capitals before 1914 for instruction in advanced police methods: Hassan Rifaat brought his special skills from St. Petersburg. He was for long the implacable enemy of Wafdist extremism and the *alter ego* of Keown-Boyd in Public Security. Ingram Bey, head of the C.I.D., had been an N.C.O. in the British Army. He was a gentle man, one of the only two I have known capable of passing as Egyptian in disguise. His handling of the informant in this case was masterly, but it would be improper to particularise on that. The case only broke when the younger Enayat was discreetly persuaded to escape from Cairo, to be duly picked up in the Western desert where he began talking. Ingram's influence over criminals had something of a psychiatrist's 'identification'. Night after night, one or other of the prisoners would ask that he should come and talk to them, and bits of the jigsaw were then fitted into place. He was soon promoted to command the Alexandria city police and moved, against advice, into the commandant's official house; and there he, his wife and two children died of typhoid within weeks.

During Lord Lloyd's first year, the Residency was not a happy ship. The Oriental secretariat was by-passed completely when Arthur Wiggin, our Head of Chancery, hitched his waggon firmly to the new star by assuming also the functions of Private Secretary. Lord Lloyd had no prejudices favourable to Lord Allenby's Oriental Secretaries and was temperamentally happy to try unorthodox methods. During one crisis, he employed Georges Antonious, the Lebanese historian, in a most confidential capacity and wished him to be appointed in place of Furness when my immediate chief, embarrassed by a Foreign Office assumption that he was advising the High Commissioner in the devious courses adopted, offered his resignation. The Foreign Office at once proposed Furness for the lucrative post of British representative on the *Caisse de la Dette* in Cairo, but even this Lord Lloyd felt it essential to thwart. When a man is down, he must realise that he is down and why he is down. The appointment went to Sir Robert Greg. Walter Smart, our Oriental Secretary in Tehran, was nominated to succeed Furness; and I worked happily with and under him for the next nine years.

In the jacaranda season of 1927, a draft 'Army Act' laid before Parliament seemed to the High Commissioner to conflict with the sacred *status quo*, and strong measures were pressed on an unwilling British cabinet. H.M.G. preferred some *modus vivendi* to fit in with their policy of 'collaboration, not compulsion'. 'We must not ride the good horse 1922 to death!' they said. They would almost certainly have settled for the appointment of a British Military Mission, and Lord Lloyd did not make himself more loved by sending Wiggin, a mere First Secretary, to argue the issue with the Secretary of State. Zaghlul Pasha himself sent a message to Lord Lloyd at the time by Reuter's correspondent, to the effect that he would welcome a British military mission, provided it were headed by a general of high rank; but Mr. Delany's enquiries, later, revealed that his message had not been reported to London by H.M. High Commissioner.

Lord Lloyd was, indeed, inclined to conceal from the Foreign Office developments or trends conflicting with his own personal policy, and this tendency caused alarm in London. I had to invent a most wearisome chore, a 'Weekly Review of the Egyptian Press', and send home ten pages or so of press-analysis every Saturday, merely to ensure that material and comments not otherwise reported became known in London. I knew that Lord Lloyd would never plough through the massive enclosures to the brief covering despatch which he was asked to sign. Reports of Egyptian views expressed to me during my provincial tours served the same purpose of enlightenment. I confess to no sense of service disloyalty on considering these devices in retrospect.

The next few months were calm. Sarwat Pasha had succeeded Adly, and he and the Liberals began to gain some slight popularity because of the Wafdist deputies' intolerable interventions in administration and their well-earned reputation for nepotism and corruption. Unfortunately for Sarwat, who accompanied King Fuad on an official visit to England that summer, the Foreign Office 'enmeshed' him—the phrase is, of course, Lord Lloyd's—in negotiations for a treaty which he had no hope of imposing on Egyptian public opinion.

Sarwat's chances were made doubly dubious by the death, on August 23, 1927, of Zaghlul Pasha, who alone in Egypt could decide on the acceptability or futility of Treaty negotiations. Sarwat and he, long estranged, had latterly established friendly relations, and Zaghlul, gratified by Sarwat's consultation of him on the formation of his Cabinet, had been known to speak warmly of his old enemy. Zaghlul seems, indeed, to have mellowed quite remarkably towards the end, and he might conceivably have given his blessing to Sarwat's negotiations, had he lived. He sent a message to Lord Lloyd by the invaluable Mr. Gerald Delany, Reuter's correspondent, informing the High Commissioner that he need not worry his head any longer about Saad Zaghlul, who was no longer thinking about Lord Lloyd, but only of his Creator whom he was now preparing to meet. This message was received with a wry smile by one who did not like people not to think about him.

There was some criticism after Zaghlul's death of his devoted doctor, Neguib Iskander, who had permitted a minor surgical intervention of some risk to a diabetic. The Pasha's last word was an echo: *Intâha*, 'It is finished'. But it had really finished when the Sirdar was murdered.

Nevile Henderson, as Acting High Commissioner in Lord Lloyd's absence, took me with him from Alexandria to the Cairo funeral, and I confess that as we walked behind the gun-carriage, I felt a respect and a sense of regret not less sincere than the clamour of the mourners in the streets. Now Egypt has other heroes. That gawky bronze statue of Zaghlul overlooking the Nile, arm raised and fingers wide outstretched in an oratorical gesture, is part of history, like the obelisk in Station Square.

★   ★   ★

The Foreign Office tried hard to get their Treaty with Sarwat Pasha, and various concessions were made to his point of view; but the whole thing was unreal. He had to keep negotiating to survive, and once he revealed the fruits of his efforts, the Wafd (now led by Nahas Pasha) would torpedo him. On his return from London from November until February 1928 he argued and re-argued every comma, and then, showing his hand to the Wafd, was sunk without trace. He resigned, and in September 1928 he died. He was, I think, the bravest and one of the best of Egypt's political figures in the decade following the war.

Nahas and the Wafd had been busy during Sarwat's long drawn-out negotiations, and various measures designed to strengthen the Wafdist position were on their way to the Statute Book. A draft 'Omdas' Law' gave them control of the country's grass-roots. A draft 'Arms Law' abolished all executive control of dangerous weapons. An 'Assemblies Law' denied the police all right to control demonstrations, to disperse meetings or to inter-fere with public gatherings. The *khamsin* wind was blowing, but London failed to support Lord Lloyd's policy of strength and accepted equivocal assurances from Nahas Pasha. The Wafd were delighted; but King Fuad, seeing his particular enemies treated with such indulgence by H.M.G., decided to take a hand. He procured the resignation of Mohammed Mahmoud Pasha, the only Liberal left in the Cabinet; launched the story of a scandal affecting Nahas Pasha's professional integrity and dis-missed him summarily, appointing Mohammed Mahmoud to succeed him. Lord Allenby's constitution was now effectively hamstrung.

Mohammed Mahmoud Pasha, one of the originators of the 1918 Wafd and a fellow exile of Zaghlul in Malta, was a rich landowner from Assiout and a Balliol graduate. His Government did much that was useful in a quiet way and notably signed with Britain the terms of a Nile Water Agreement, treating an inflam-matory political subject as a practical 'working agreement'. As a result, plans were made for the raising of the Assouan Dam and the building of the Gebel Aulia Dam in the Sudan, to enable irrigation of another 700,000 acres. There was, however, constant evidence of the King's ambivalent attitude towards him, which kept the Wafd in optimistic expectation. They were also buoyed up by hopes of a Labour Party victory in the forthcoming British elections; and this, in fact, came to pass in June 1929. In April 1929, a slight *khamsin* breeze blew up between Lord Lloyd and Sir Austen Chamberlain which had later importance. Egypt asked Britain to consider four extensions in the limited taxation applied to British subjects under the Capitulations, and Sir Austen was sympathetic on all points. Lord Lloyd concurred in respect of two points; urged delay before acceptance of another, and objected firmly to the fourth. When Mr. Arthur Henderson became Labour's

Foreign Secretary in June, this reply by the High Commissioner was made one of his texts in a comminatory tirade.

The manner of Lord Lloyd's dismissal was strange; not because the Labour Government could have been expected to retain a man in whom they had no confidence, but because his alleged clashes with Sir Austen Chamberlain, and not with any Labour government, were adduced as proof of his '. . . turbulent, ungenerous and deliberately misinterpretative behaviour in regard to the instructions and views of his late chief . . .'. All this in a speech by Mr. Henderson to the House of Commons at a time when Sir Austen Chamberlain was out of the country. Anyway, Lord Lloyd's resignation was extracted from him, and Cairo saw him no more.

Mr. Arthur Henderson proceeded to open negotiations for a treaty with Mohammed Mahmoud Pasha, when they met in London; but he introduced what he called 'a change of procedure' by designing this treaty to be the instrument of a return to parliamentary life and an end to Palace rule. Mahmoud Pasha was told that it would have to be ratified by an Egyptian parliament to be acceptable. The Labour Party could not be comfortable in office while Nahas and the Wafd were denied their parliamentary majority; and, from then onwards, British intervention or non-intervention in Egyptian internal affairs became matters reflecting the prejudices of this or that British political party.

*   *   *

Lord Lloyd started off as the darling of the Turf Club, which welcomed a strong proconsul, but his popularity waned within a year. The attitudes of a former Governor of Bombay gave offence. All traffic in side-streets was held up when the High Commissioner drove through Cairo; this was viceregal stuff and had nothing to do with security. Guests for luncheon and dinner were received by the A.D.C.,s, dazzling at night with their Cambridge-blue lapels, and Lord and Lady Lloyd only joined their guests a brief moment before it was time to go in to table. Prime ministers and dukes and lesser mortals found this procedure discourteous.

Lady Lloyd was a superb ambassadress, and only this detail marred what was otherwise her impeccable relationship with Cairo society.

She revived a much appreciated custom of calling upon the princesses and wives of senior ministers. The organisation of these visits took me—but only by telephone—into the most exalted *harims*.

His staff viewed Lord Lloyd's behaviour with mixed feelings. None of us had ever before observed a politician in full action. For those concerned with the local political situation, his pursuit of a personal policy clashing with British government intentions was anathema, as were the rather labyrinthine methods of this pursuit. But if for some of us, as for most Egyptians, he was a *Shaitán*, there was some interest in watching the devil tick. He might be a disloyal servant, but he was a stimulating master. We were soon made aware that we had over us a ball of fire, anxious to keep us always on our toes, and up to all the tricks. From the first enquiry each morning: 'What do the papers say about me today?', we were under constant interrogation. We soon learnt that any answer was better than none, and that it was not prudent to correct his own pronouncements. Riding near the Pyramids one morning he waved a riding-crop at the landscape and observed that the *bersím* (a sort of lucerne) was coming along well. Dod Frankland, his A.D.C., concurred. The young British Police Officer riding with them whispered to Dod that there was no *bersím* in sight, and was told: 'If H.E. says it's *bersím*, old boy, it's *bersím*!' The later sight of tomatoes burgeoning green passed without comment.

The foreign representatives disliked him. The American Minister, an elderly gentleman whose wife, to the scandalisation of all Nubia, did her own marketing in Cairo, was jitteringly furious at the High Commissioner's pomp and circumstance, and always tried to push his way behind the British sentries outside the Residency wall and to have his own car parked where it might prevent the British Rolls-Royce from precedence after palace parties.

Interpreting for him once, when we were trying to persuade the venerable Amba Yoannes, the Coptic patriarch, to appoint an enlightened man as Coptic Bishop of Khartoum and not his own obscurantist preference, I asked Lord Lloyd to put on an act of rage when I gave the signal. The dialogue continued suavely and futilely, and I gave the sign. He jumped up from his chair and thumped the desk, patience obviously exhausted. The hundred-and somethingth successor of Saint Mark also jumped—indeed, he almost jumped out of his robes—and our Qommos Hanna Salama was appointed Bishop of Khartoum next morning.

He never ceased to surprise me. He struck the name of the Queen's father, Abdurrahim Sabry Pasha, a famous rose-grower, from the *Qurban Bairam* greetings-list, because he had sent Lady Lloyd a bouquet of roses with all stems pierced, allegedly so that she might not strike them. And when I asked him for the usual cheque for the High Commissioner's box at the Opera, he remembered that he was a director of Lloyds Bank. 'No!' he said, 'they can give me the two middle boxes in the balcony-row above. Tell them they will be able to charge double for all the other boxes in that row because I'm up there! I'm not a usurer in my spare time for nothing!'

So controversial a figure could not but attract antipathy. At least one Hymn of Hate was in active circulation at the time. I did not perpetrate this bit of malice. I did, however, write verses both for and to Lord Lloyd. He had seen something of mine in the local newspaper and bade me reply metrically to a broadside of poetic greeting written by the Headmaster of Eton, then spending Christmas with the Lloyds, with his pretty daughter.

But when he instructed me to represent him at a gazelle-hunt organised by the Tahawi family in the Eastern Desert—a splendid affair of swooping falcons, racing Saluqis and death—I had to minute his invitation in a rhythm of protest, in these terms:

ROUSPÉTANCE

When Death, serene or sinister, removes from public life
A Patriarch, a Minister, or some exalted wife;
Significantly labelled, top-hatted and ensabled,
Assistant Oriental Secs. mournfully represent His Ex.

Benevolent foundations by Ashkenazi Jews
Result in invitations not easy to refuse;
Among those crowding in agog to Hospital or Synagogue,
Assistant Oriental Secs. discreetly represent His Ex.

On these and like occasions, sebaceous glands in spate,
They venture no evasions of what Protocols dictate;
Prominent in processions, Requiems, Intercessions,
Assistant Oriental Secs. variedly represent His Ex.

But if these deputational exigencies include
Cavorting equitational across the bright *Nefud*;
If H.E. seeks vicarious delights with horse and hound,
Let someone less precarious as cavalier be found.

Suppose his vicar at the chase somersaults on the sands,
What black disgrace, what loss of face
In Oriental lands!
No! For the prestige of George Rex
I will not represent His Ex.

★　　★　　★

I did not see Lord Lloyd again until June 1940, when I was
briefly in London, between expulsion from Albania and a journey
round Africa to Suez. We met in Whitehall, and to my surprise
he insisted on my coming up to his office for a talk. He was the
newly appointed Colonial Secretary in Mr. Churchill's Government, and such congenial employment obviously delighted him.
I demurred and said something about his being a busy man.
He brushed this aside. 'I know you never approved of me,'
he said, 'but you can let me give you a cup of coffee!'

I spent a happy half-hour, listening to the chatter of a happy
man. Did I know that Winston was going to send him to Cairo,
as Minister of State in the Middle East? Did I realise the strategic
importance of Dakar? How did Miles and Farouq get along?
There was one peep of the old Adam. He said that Winston had
given him a 'liberalish' cabinet minute by Amery, the Secretary of
State for India, to tear to pieces for him.

The round peg was firmly in the round hole. Working with

Churchill, he could shed the insecurity that had diminished his Cairo service. All that immense vitality, energy and missionary faith was perfectly harnessed at last, to a supreme war-effort. But in February 1941 he died, of a neglected chill.

12

Fortunately for us, the observation of a politician at play in the unedifying setting of Egyptian politics was not our only interest. Egypt between the wars had much to offer that was pleasant. Every winter brought its quota of young lovelies, fresh from their débutante season, to distract the many eligible subalterns of various cavalry regiments from their gloomy preoccupation with 'mechanisation', then a dirty word in polo-playing circles. Not a few little craft in this attractive fishing-fleet sailed in choppy waters, favouring all too often for our comfort the company of very senior officers, whose heavy paternal gambits we watched with frustrated envy. Most of the young visitors brought mothers or aunts, for protection against local hazards; but, each season, some of our Cairo ladies revealed for our inspection young cousins and nieces whose names they had never heard the year before. One lady, whose charges left her every year with a new ring on their finger, must have had the specialist rating of a Michelin three-star hostelry.

The British in Egypt then assumed that the sun rose and set in their centre, and for most British visitors this circle offered world enough: parties, picnics, eligible escort and a Gezira Sporting Club where every game could be played. The few denizens of a non-British world who were observable there, playing bridge or mah-jongg in bad French and good pearls, merely served as a foil for Anglo-Saxon attitudes.

Acceptance and favour in this enclosed social garden was decided by feminine influence. Our matriarchs were of various ages but shared a common interest in the disciplines of tribal convention. They were not particularly fond of one another, but their joint displeasure was social death. Besides keeping an eye on general behaviour, they black-balled, or filtered through, alien and country-bred candidates for entry into the magic circle. Local British subjects like the Rolos, Casdaglis and Hararis, were not subject to veto, because their passports endorsed their intelligence and charm; but for the mass of the Levantine world the faces of our censors held no welcoming smile. Such elements were expected to go and play in their own backyard.

In that backyard I used to have fun, for I found there not only charming and attractive people but the informed interest in literature and the theatre which blossoms from a French education and culture. If some on the fringes were aggressively *nouveau-riche*, most of them could lend me the latest French novel, give parties for the visiting actress, artist and author, and discuss trends and modes unknown on the polo-field. Nor were the clouds of glory they trailed from Paquin and Cherhuit and Worth the least pleasant reminders of their spiritual home: I once claimed to recognise up to ten different French scents—a useful gambit, *faute de mieux*.

When entertaining on Saturday evenings at the Mohammed Ali Club I tried to mix these two worlds; as time went by, the insularity of the Heaven-born melted a bit at the edges.

There were other circles, separate and only rarely overlapping, in which I was privileged to move. With my Coptic friends, no difficulty of frequentation arose, for no *harîm* curtain hangs in a Coptic house. But with a large and ever-expanding circle of Moslem and mostly Turco-Egyptian friends, the conventions of centuries had to crumble before normal social relations became possible. The men were willing enough to accept invitations, alone; if they entertained me, it was in a club or hotel. But gradually the word got around that I was genuinely fond of Egyptians, genuinely interested in their affairs and sympathetic to their ideas and aspirations; above all, that I was discreet and would never advertise kindnesses which might embarrass my friends. One door opened after another, and soon I was a happy guest in rooms normally locked and barred. It was French that was spoken, or Arabic. Moonlight picnics in the desert, or at the Spouting Rocks at Sidi Bishr, were given piquancy by the knowledge, shared by all, that King Fuad must never know. I was sometimes the only non-Egyptian at parties of two or three hundred people. Years later, when Princess Shevikiar settled in Cairo and entertained all the world and his wife, such parties became commonplace; at the time each seemed a privileged occasion.

The highlights of each winter season were State visits, for these brought fabulous dinner-parties at Abdin Palace followed by performances in the private theatre, watched by the royal ladies from behind a gauze screen. A similar screen masked the Queen's box at the opera. The visit of King Amanullah of Afghanistan was a shambles from the start. His brother-in-law, the Afghan Minister of Foreign Affairs, who preceded the party to Cairo, refused to accept as habitable the palace prepared for them, because it contained no bidet. When Amanullah dined at the Residency, he mistook Mr. Jones, the butler, for his host. And when he went in state to say his Friday prayers at Al-Azhar Mosque, he was ridiculously unable to do so, because the brim of the Ascot-type grey top-hat which he insisted on flaunting came between his forehead and the prayer-mat. International congresses, also, of many different interests, found lavish hospitality in Cairo, and inspired a series of postage-stamps.

An unexpected visitor to my office in Lord Lloyd's time was Madame Aly Fahmy, who had put six shots into her husband in a Savoy Hotel corridor and, thanks to Marshall Hall, had been acquitted at the Old Bailey. She came out to Egypt to claim the widow's share of her late husband's great estate. I had to advise her that neither the Egyptian nor any other brand of Shari'a Law provided ladies who killed their husbands, even if white-washed at the Old Bailey, with an interest in their estate. That there had been the most agonising provocation, as Marshall Hall's display of photographs to the jury argued, was irrelevant.

In summer, 1929, when Rex Hoare had succeeded Nevile Henderson and was acting as High Commissioner, a visit by the Prince of Wales and the Duke of Gloucester brought some worries to his office. Lord Lloyd ordained, from London, that most of their stay *en route* to a shooting expedition in Kenya, should be spent in Cairo, with only one night's sojourn in Alexandria, and this was to be devoted to a reception for the British community. This ruling reflected an unwillingness to expose their Royal Highnesses to the temptations of Alexandria night-life, which was of a different quality from the more austere and circumscribed entertainment offered with Russell Pasha's permission in the capital.

Joan Hoare, pretty and birdlike and quite incalculable, decided that a *gulla-gulla* man was indicated for the diversion of her distinguished guests, and I tried in vain to interest her in alternative talents available in the local night-clubs. The Ramleh Residency did not really lend itself to outdoor parties, for the lawn sloped down behind the house like a railway embankment. On this slope, the local Britannics clustered, and watched a *gulla-gulla* man produce chickens from the royal ears and the royal fly, a spectacle I found distasteful.

I could write, pleasurably to myself, and at great length, about the friends of those days; but any attempt to condense years of kaleidoscopic whirl to readable proportions can result only in a catalogue of names and anecdotes: a nostalgic but unacceptable exercise. It occurs to me that a contemporary record, in the jargon of the time, may suggest the mood and perspective of those years. The letters of 'Topsy', as revealed to the readers of *Punch* by A. P. Herbert, inspired me to persuade her sister, 'Flopsy', to share with readers of the Cairo journal *The Sphinx*, some of her own letters about the Cairo scene. These letters were esoteric reading even in 1928–29, for the world under Flopsy's lens was a small and special one, and nobody's name was quite correctly remembered. When we have quoted her on the opening stages of a Palace party, and on her own way of spending the evening of a birthday, we can consider the trivialities of Cairo in the late twenties as adequately recorded, and pass on to more serious things.

. . .'Well, Trix, my heart's *meringue*, last week there was a large and most *international* Congress here, discussing how to grow *water-melons* of all things and, my dear, I am quite *irretrievably* committed to it because by some happy *slither* of a pen I was *commanded* with Susan and the Colonel to an evening of *cham-berings* and whatnot at the Palace in honour of the so-called delegations and of course I went and I haven't felt so un-ambiguously *carriage-class* for years. When you arrive, my dear, you're decanted into a swarm of Ruritanians in knee-breeches and white gloves who *whisk* your car away and *organise* you through a portal and you *process* along a red carpet and *stroll* a gauntlet of serried bodyguard who look as if they might throw a wedding *arch* of scimitars at the drop of a hat and when you're through them you're waved down a *tributary* arcade, where top-hats are parked and noses powdered and deep breath taken for the *excelsior* ascent of a vast staircase which has dark and *saracenesque* soldiery *mameluking* with lances on every step, quite too *petrified*, my dear, and Madame Tussaudish and for all I know recruited in *Pompeii* after the trouble there. At the top there are *battalions* of chamberlains with Nile-green lapels *sheepdogging* the delegates in to make their bow to Majesty and I wish you could have seen some of the visiting uniforms, *pendent* with stars, and a Lithuanian Admiral in front of me had forgotten to take the tissue *paper* off his back-buttons and as for most of the wives, either its a rule in Central Europe to let Nature take its *course* or the cultivation of water-melons pro-vokes *unrestrainedly* sympathetic physiological reactions. As the Rector of Al-Azhar said to me last week, some things have to be *sin* to be believed . . .

. . . Your ravished
Flopsy.

And now the closing hours of what had been a busy day:

My *onliest* and *ownest* Trix,
. . . Then Young Wilkinson and the surviving Something-Smythe threw a party for me and we began at Groppis, and among the most beautiful girls to be seen at Groppis was my darling Mr. Bowley, as usual, and the scene was a very *worthy* one, being Thursday, very *Rule Britannia* and white tie so we soon *waded* along to inspect the Pelote Basque which I had always been led to believe meant some sort of Spanish *embrace* but the

dictionary *lies*; it's another game altogether because *predatory* little men with Pyrenean faces and *gondoliers'* sashes round their middles answer to the most *unbalanced* names and *swoop* about like *pike* in a vast three-sided aquarium taking alternate *cracks* at the ball with a long *tendencious claw* thing strapped on to their arm and I can only say my dear that they catch the ball in this alleged *cesta* with the prehensile precision of a sea-lion and *wang* it back against the wall a hundred miles away as if David-and-Goliath and point-75 guns were mere *stages* in their development really it's too marvellous to watch them, and the public is just as *special*, because there you see jaded *saffron*-coloured men playing 'how-many-fingers-do-I-hold-up' over Turkish coffee-and-a-glass-of-water which is *their* way of selling house-property, and village headmen in striped *nightshirts* comparing news and hiccoughs and shiny young *secret* policemen in *emphatic* suitings and Army-issue boots and ladies *crooking* the little finger over their Amstel and watching the crowd through smoke-rings and two or three *stentorian* men, *hyde-parking* on tables to a crowd of experts, *giving* red at eighteen whatever that involves and *taking* blue at nineteen and doubtless shaking the betting world to the core only I just didn't grasp it and towards the end of the big game everyone gets all *het* up and men wriggle about on their chairs and if a *pelotero* misses a sitter which the betting makes it very easy to do he raises his *claw* in appeal to some inattentive Basque divinity and beats the wall with his forehead to register dissatisfaction and unless you have money to collect you have to decide where to go next.

We didn't stay long *poised* on the pavement, because the Facts of Life (Night) in Cairo are distressingly soon acquired so we took taxis and our last breath of real air and plunged down to the *Birdcage* which is where the women from the tourist-ships exchange notes about their new-found friends and report *progress*. It's rather like the Black Hole of Calcutta done in jazz because it's the sort of room your Mother keeps *apples* in at home and it's crowded out with fifty-seven *more* varieties of visitor than it was meant to hold and in the middle of the *clutter* of tables is an almost imperceptible space *just* too small for hopscotch and when the band digga-digga-doodles this little lung is invaded by *tribal* movements from every side with honeymoon and the world-well-lost couples *somnambulating* through dreams and tourists *unbuttoning* after the day's work with Tut and the Mosques and tight-waisted Syrian and Greek young men with blue-black hair and a *jungle* eye for any woman in an Assiout shawl, and submerged ladies *trampled* by *flushed* commercial travellers and master mariners, the real *authentic* salad, my dear. And if you sit near the band you have the big drum in your ear and the limelight bang in your eyes and you can't see Emmeline Novelli's corsage *burst* at the word of command, so don't.

Well, darling, we subsidised this *aviary* for a bit with the band being very titillatory and *hormone*, and at about 3 a.m. the local Baron started picking on some poor working-girl and had his ears boxed and his gang waved chairs by numbers and it looked *encouragingly* like a rough-house but we *tore* ourselves away and up to street-level again and you can say what you like, Trix, but air is what's best for breathing, even nowadays.

It was still *indecently* early for bed of course and we managed to *slough* off some of our party and the rest of us *purred* away to a very obscure place round a lot of corners and down the blackest streets *ever*, somewhere near the Mousky, and here you have to *hazard* yourself, my dear, into the real *Cimmerian* stuff feeling that at any moment some cut-throat may *firework* off at you or some invisible negro *whiteslave* you by the leg until Something-Smythe or whoever is dragomanning the party presses a mysterious *knob* high up on some wall and a red light glimmers out and a door in the wall swings *invitingly* open and really getting into the place is about all there is to do there because once you *are* inside you merely ascend some very un-washed stairs and eat *onion-soup* at a large table on a landing entirely *flanked* by most tendencious and *silent* doors which are assumed for publicity purposes to conceal *drug-addicts* in every *stage* of debauch but which *actually* I believe lead into a *police-station* or into the sleeping quarters and usual offices of the Coptic Patriarchate. Anyhow we melted away at last and all but a quatuor went home to bed but I'm sure it's unlucky to fall asleep on your birthday-night and we four were feeling markedly *hale* and *insomniac* so the question arose what next?

The night was magically warm, my dear, and full of blossom so we collected *swaddlings* of rugs and cushions from Something-Smythe's flat and chose one of those long *feluccas* that bob their lanterns in the ripples below the Semiramis and when the man had *planked* in a sort of *slumber*-deck and *dowsed* the lantern and torn down the tenting between us and the stars we composed ourselves for philosophic converse and *slid* out into midstream and there we lay, my dear, for the rest of the night when we weren't *languishing* up and down between the bridges, with a *Charonic* old man crouching *immobile* behind us at the tiller and a speck of a boy doing the Childhood of Raleigh forrard and I'm sure young Wilkinson and Dolly went sound asleep because we heard the most *indicative* noises from their side of the deck but *my* boy-friend and I just lay and *drenched* ourselves in starlight and watched the palmtrees grow up out of their own reflections and *feather* the moon and listened to the *gloop* and *ripple* of the water on our bows and talked only when we had some *really* beautiful and profound thought that generally sounded rather *drowsy* in words but what did *that* matter until suddenly, my dear, there was a *flutter* of light down in the East and the blacks became grey and the greys became luminous and saffron, and dawn came through like a violin-note, clean and inevitable and lovely and that made a day, and taking one thing with *another* my Trix that rounded off as full a birthday as your adoring Flopsy has ever had since she was first *born* to *be* your adoring

Flopsy.

13

After an Indian political officer, a highly political General, a non-political Field-Marshal and a Tory politician, H.M.G. played for safety and eschewed further experiment. As their fifth High Commissioner they appointed a career ambassador, Sir Percy

Loraine, who had already made a reputation in Persia and in Greece and was the horse all of us hoped to draw in our Chancery sweepstake. He was a model of ambassadorial skills and manner; a handsome baronet of large private means, with a tall and handsome wife who brought a new, warm grace into the Residency drawing room. Loraine's cold, glaucous eye was misleading; he was a most human person, with a marked taste for late hours.

His professional technique consisted in attracting to himself the highest thing in sight. This was to yield remarkable results later in Ankara, where he and Mustafa Kemal became blood-brothers. Unfortunately, for most of Loraine's tour in Cairo, the highest thing in sight outside Abdin Palace, was Ismail Sidqi Pasha, a brilliant intelligence, but Prime Minister of a detested, unconstitutional government, relying on the support of a most unpopular monarch. There was no honey there for Sir Percy.

By then Egyptian politics were becoming repetitive and relatively unexciting. Our own role in the unceasing internecine strife of party against party became that of an Aunt Sally for every party in opposition, who accused us of favouring the government of the day; there was no longer a direct and full Anglo-Egyptian confrontation. What began in Cairo as an *Union sacrée* had degenerated into a long Egyptian dog-fight: the Wafd striving for hegemony; the Liberals for some gradual and assured progress; both fighting the Palace for democratic objectives threatened by King Fuad's ambitions. The list of the original members of the Wafd, all twenty of them, was good for a laugh in any coffee-shop, so tenaciously were they now at loggerheads. Outside the various party headquarters, disillusion became a habit of thought.

This disillusion fed on the disgust with which decent people watched deputies interfering in every corner of the administration, in furtherance of their personal interests. Some politicians made too much money out of the sale of their influence.

Our now officially defined interests rarely had to be defended. We intervened politically only when Wafdist excesses or Palace behaviour became intolerable. The army of occupation, once an object of ideological obloquy, became hardly more than a grievance of politicians out of office. These constantly pointed out that, if we wished to upset this or that government, we had the military means to do this; because we did not use these means, we were unpardonably partial. I never heard these complaints from anyone in office, only from others wanting to get there. The exception to our self-denying ordinance about intervention was the case in which some Egyptian, persecuted by the Wafd for earlier assistance to us, could not be denied discreet protection. Such cases did not cover the misfortunes of politicians, who had known what they were risking, but those of smaller folk, unable to look out for themselves.

When Sir Percy Loraine took over the Residency, Mohammed Mahmoud's treaty was being revealed (inevitably) as yet another non-starter. Nahas Pasha succeeded him and tried his hand at negotiations, which brought some goodwill but yielded no other result, beyond giving London a sight of Madame Nahas Pasha's many-splendoured laundry, draped over the balcony of her hotel room. Nahas had married late in life, and his wife used her new influence indefatigably.

It is worth looking at the Henderson-Nahas negotiations, since these were the last to be conducted before success was reached in 1936, and the first under Wafdist leadership since Zaghlul's fiasco of 1923. Most of the clauses earlier agreed with Mohammed Mahmoud Pasha were now accepted by Nahas, and this consecrated agreement on the establishment of an alliance, the termination of the military occupation, the abolition of the Capitulations and British support for Egypt's candidature to membership of the League of Nations. Two Wafdist demands about the Sudan alone led to the abandonment of talks, and Nahas and Henderson parted on friendly terms.

King Fuad thereupon dismissed Nahas and appointed Ismail Sidqi Pasha, to govern without Parliament for three years. For most of Loraine's time, political life stood still.

The régime was administratively fruitful but unpopular.

A minor crisis of some embarrassment arose when the British firm of contractors engaged on raising the level of the Aswan Dam, whose tender had been surprisingly low, announced that lack of funds prevented further progress. The annual phenomenon of the Nile flood was due in a few months, and this lent extreme urgency to the situation. Sidqi Pasha refused to consider any financial aid to the contractors, whom he sternly condemned, and was able to find an alternative firm, this time Italian, to complete the work.

Depending solely on King Fuad for support, Ismail Sidqi Pasha turned a blind eye to many deplorable Palace initiatives and himself suggested others. I personally regretted, though others did not, the construction of the Corniche Road in Alexandria, linking the royal palace of Ras-el-Tin, on the harbour, with the royal palace of Montaza, many miles to the west. The official pressures on Ahmed Seddik Pasha, Director General of the Alexandria municipality, were such as to ensure shoddy work; and after a mighty scandal, most of the road, which transformed Alexandria, had to be built all over again.

Montaza Palace—now (I believe) a museum—had been built by the Khedive Abbas Hilmy in Cromer's time. I learnt that there were some things in Egypt of which not even Lord Cromer was aware, when sitting next to King Fuad's Italian architect and general go-between, Verrucci Bey, at an Abdin palace dinner. He told me that some structural repairs he was making at Montaza had revealed three skeletons, those of two women and a man, walled up in one of the palace corridors.

*　　*　　*

In 1929, promotion to the rank of Consul and a salary-scale of £800–1,000 a year, brought welcome relief to my overdraft. It also brought an awareness that I might at last consider marriage without too unrealistic a prospect of acceptance. I was already thirty-seven years old, and the pretty child who accepted me was half my age. We were married in April 1930, in the little church built at Stanley Bay, outside Alexandria, by her father's father, old Sir George Alderson. We sailed next day in a cruise-ship, full of Mrs. Ronald Greville, for Monte Carlo, where I was informed at the Sporting Club that my daughter was too young for admittance.

I parted with my servant Saleh, with my little flat, and with many other bits and pieces of bachelor life, and we took a pleasant 8-roomed flat in Garden City, in the rue Nabatát. There we lived happily for some years. Roger was born in April 1931, and Jeremy in October 1934.

We entertained as best we could, mostly in the circles of British officialdom and junior foreign diplomatists; but a small Oriental secretariat fund enabled me to entertain Egyptians more often than my salary permitted. I used to take a box at the Opera House for this or that visiting season and take there the interesting people who would not have been amused by a dance-floor. Those were the salad-days of Frank Roberts and George Labouchere, of Louis Scheyven, Rives Childs, Abdel Qader al-Gailani (who always came to dinner in a top-hat) and Alphonse and Gaby Bentinck—but this is not a *Bottin Mondain* of the early thirties. As painters we had Amy Nimr and Hamzeh Carr, both of whom have pictures hanging on the walls of the 'Beit-el-Kritly', the lovely Cairo house in which Colonel Gayer-Anderson's treasures survive him. Lucy de Kramer made music, and we heard a beautiful contralto-voice belonging to Céleste Shoucair. Robert Graves, was, all too briefly, Professor of English Literature at the University; he was followed by Bonamy Dobrée and his wise and lovely wife. We were all slightly alarmed by the lecturer in English, then a young man of twenty-four, who seemed to be a beatnik ahead of his time and scorned the social trivialities which absorbed us. We thought a spell in Moscow might be good for him—and it was! Today, when Malcolm Muggeridge comes on the screen, I sit at his feet.

Another apparition from the future B.B.C. was Stephen King-Hall, then Intelligence Officer, *Queen Elizabeth*, or whatever the flagship then was. The Mediterranean Fleet paid annual visits to Alexandria in the late summer, which brought much entertainment on both sides; and he dined with us at San Stefano when the British community threw a party. One of our table was an attractive Lebanese girl, whose education Stephen took in hand. Long after the others had gone home to bed, he was offering instruction in the art of tobogganing head-first on a tea-tray down the hotel stairs, which calls for nippy succour at the bottom. He left a note in my room next morning, before leaving for Cairo, bidding me ensure the presence of this young woman as his guest at a naval party two days later; but knowing, as he did not, that she was not only married but well under her husband's thumb, I sent him a telegram in Cairo; 'Have filtered your message through stop no luck stop. Feel must warn you I know no case in modern history where appearances more deceptive.' His reply was immediate: 'Thanks for storm signal. Sailors don't care!'

The hospitality we received, like that we offered, was still on a junior diplomatic level, except for the Germans; even minor dogsbodies were invited to the German minister's dinner table. Herr von Stohrer, who had a beautiful wife, actively cultivated everyone in sight, and was especially good with Egyptians who had been on courses, or simply on holidays, in Nazi Germany. In those days of the early thirties very little was heard of concentration camps, and I was impolite enough to quote to my neighbour at his table the little jingle: *Du lieber Gott! Ach, mach' mich fromm, dass ich nicht zu Auschwitz komm'!* without myself knowing just what horrors it hinted at. For a long time, the German Legation tried to find out from whom I had heard this.

*   *   *

When the King appointed Sidqi Pasha as Prime Minister and suspended Parliament, Sidqi's first aim was to change the electoral law. The 1923 constitution had provided for a two-degree system of election as being that most suitable to an electorate roughly 90 per cent illiterate: groups of thirty electors on adult suffrage each elected one delegate possessed of certain qualifications, and these in turn elected deputies to parliament. Zaghlul, to ensure the mob-vote for the Wafd, instituted the direct system of election in 1924. The elections under the new/old indirect system were held in May 1931, and were boycotted not only by the Wafd but also by the Liberals under Mohammed Mahmoud Pasha. The King's party of Ittehadists, and Sidqi Pasha with a new group he had formed called the Shaab (or People's) Party of Reform, had to prove that they, with such odds and ends of help as they could pick up, could produce a respectable majority of voters at the polls to refute the loud opposition claim that they represented nobody but themselves.

It was an unedifying spectacle. Every device of administrative authority was used to produce voters at the polls. Groups of unhappy men were led from polling booth to polling booth to make their mark. Sir Robert Greg recognised his gardener in one such gang and learned that he had voted ten or eleven times already that morning, always under different names. Anyone identified as spoiling a ballot paper, or voting for the Wafd, was patted amicably on the back by the policeman in the booth, and the chalk-marks thus left on his *gallabiya* earned him a severe beating-up by the policeman outside. There were over fifty deaths. As I heard it, the first provincial results of electorate-polling were unconvincing: Keneh, 97 per cent; Girga, 98 per cent; Aswan, 105 per cent! With a parliament of stooges, government had nothing to fear for years.

In September 1933 Sidqi Pasha had a stroke, and was succeeded as Prime Minister by Abdel Fattah Yehya Pasha, a gentle and gentlemanly nonentity. For a year King Fuad really made hay, using as his instrument a most able man, the Director of the Royal Waqfs, Zaki el-Ibrashi Pasha. The fellahin on the royal estates at Inshass were said to be paid one piastre a day; rich properties all over Egypt tumbled into the royal domain; the régime stank.

Sir Percy Loraine had unfortunately given the British community in Cairo and Sir John Wardlaw-Milne M.P. in London, some grounds for displeasure; and he received what he considered an Irish promotion, sweetened with a Privy Councillorship, to Turkey. With him, Egypt lost his two honorary attachés who had acted as A.D.C.s and earned local fame as 'the Dolly Sisters'.

Lord Allenby had had good, soldierly A.D.Cs; Hobbs and Kimmins. Lord Lloyd had the best there were: Jack Aird (who went as equerry to the Prince of Wales), Harry Floyd (who went to the Duke of Gloucester), Dod Frankland and Colin Cadell of the R.A.F. It is true that Floyd had trouble with the lock of a lavatory in Montaza Palace during Lord Lloyd's audience and had to be assisted from the window in full regimentals, complete with sword, by Tewfik Nessim Pasha—then, appropriately, the King's *Chef de Cabinet*. It is also true that Floyd and Frankland were reported for dancing in an upper room in the Was'a at 4 a.m., after Furness's goodbye party, shouting 'Haha! the A.D.C.s!' But these leisure-time extravagances were no blot on their impeccable official performance. A good A.D.C. is never noticed; a bad one is pure poison to his master.

I assume that H.M.G., reacting against the Lloyd régime, may have slashed credits and allowances; we saw no more military A.D.Cs. The two bright young men whom the Loraines brought from Athens had great fun. They placed divorced couples, each ignorant of the other's presence in Cairo, next to each other at dinner. They played leap-frog on the Residency lawn. They had shrill quarrels in the A.D.C.s room about their very particular friends. They had a ship in a bottle on their mantelpiece, and you were always wrong about it. If you thought it ugly, they sneered; if you thought it quaint they sneered more loudly. They went to a fancy dress party as tramps, with convincing syphilitic sores; in 1933 this was a novelty.

But only Allah is All-Seeing. A former colonel of the Scots Guards, in which the elder Dolly Sister served during the war, told me recently that this was one of the bravest men he had ever known.

Another young man, Nat Allgood, who acted for some time in an A.D.C. capacity to the Loraines, marked up an all-time high in ADC-manship. Charged with ensuring that a visiting peer, who was more often in liquor than not, caught his boat-train to Port Said, Nat woke him up from the billiard-table and escorted him to the station. There his Lordship firmly refused to entrain unless a dirty book was produced for his entertainment *en route*. Nat sped to the bookstall and sped back, with the first book he found, from which he surreptitiously read an alleged extract to the traveller: '. . . Seizing the trembling child, he tore off her flimsy clothing with one rough gesture. Then, pulling her towards him . . .' and so on. This got the Loraines' guest safely into his reserved seat; and he must have been some way along his road before he realised that he was reading Russell Pasha's illustrated *Handbook of Egyptian Birds*.

★ ★ ★

Sir Percy's dazzling success in Turkey was followed by an appointment to Rome which brought him less joy. It seems to have been expected rather than hoped that means would be found of keeping Italy out of the war, and Loraine was to be the wizard who achieved this. His skills brought him within sight of success, but he was never able to exercise these skills on Mussolini himself, who remained fettered to his Axis partner.

14

One of my duties as Assistant Oriental Secretary was to stand beside the High Commissioner and his Lady and name to them the guests arriving at their garden-parties. Of these there were often more than fifteen hundred. The exercise required an assured acquaintance with all the non-Egyptian elements and occasional recourse to the refinements of Debrett; also, the recognition of a wide range of local personalities and experience of their own hierarchy of address. The Turkish conventions of style and title then prevailing gave many versions of a Pasha's Excellency, if he was a past or present Cabinet Minister, a past or present Prime Minister, or whatever. Moslem religious divines also had a selection of honorifics, as did other Church dignitaries. The Coptic Patriarch's Beatitude was not shared by Porphyrios, Archbishop of Mount Sinai, or by the Grand Rabbi. I was not expected to ask for a name, and I do not remember any slip-up. Indeed, I look back upon myself in that distant role with some admiration, for I find it difficult now to remember the names of my colleagues on a rural district council.

This reference to a Residency garden-party, when so many Egyptian friends were the High Commissioner's guests, encourages me to pause, for recognition of some of those who spoke for Egypt in those days, only a few of whom have so far been mentioned in this record. No study of 'Egypt and the High Commissioners' can be complete without this Egyptian name-dropping, and those in whom these ghosts evoke no sympathy or interest must excuse me, and pass on.

The establishment of a constitutional parliamentary régime for which the foundations were laid in 1923–24 brought radical change to the character of Egyptian political representation. This, on the higher levels, had been something of a Turco-Egyptian monopoly. Now men of the old *élite* might still play their part, but they were no longer taken for granted. Names famous in Egypt through the nineteenth century gradually survived only in the narrow field of Palace flunkeydom, with a sinecure as Chamberlain the last remaining toe-hold on power.

The first flood of native-born Egyptians into the chamber of deputies, the senate and the cabinet was typical of all that followed: there were far too many lawyers, and rather a lot of Copts. A Coptic lawyer, William Makram Obeid, the Balliol-trained Secretary of the Wafd, sat in the Cabinet with his lawyer father-in-law, Morcos Hanna Pasha, an unhumorous and starched personage who endeared himself to me by always sending me tit-bits of *meloukhiya* from his garden when we shared a hotel dining-room. *Meloukhiya* is the classical Egyptian delicacy: it makes a soup that looks like glutinous grass and tastes pleasantly rank. Tewfik Doss Pasha, son of an itinerant bible-colporteur in Assiout, was also both Copt and lawyer, and there were many others. Not all remained loyal to the Wafd.

The original 'Wafd' (delegation) consisted of the twenty men of whom Saad Zaghlul Pasha planned to be the leader in arguing the cause of Egyptian independence, after the Armistice of 1918. They soon splintered into warring factions and some retired from the arena. Two men, Ahmed Maher and Nokrashi Pashas, who had stood trial for political murder as members of the Wafd, later became Prime Ministers, in a different uniform. There were other less controversial schismatics. Ali Shamsy Pasha, whirlwind activity and considerable intelligence incarnate in a pint-sized frame, was one of the eight rebels who, because of his dimensions, were always referred to as 'the seven and a half'. When he was later Chairman of the Board of the National Bank of Egypt, and Sir Frederick Leith-Ross its Governor, the Bank of England recommended my brother Tony for the vacant post of Sub-Governor. Ali Pasha informed me, over coffee in the Club, that he could not oblige: he considered one Grafftey-Smith as much as Egypt should be expected to put up with at any given moment. This rebuff proved to be fortunate for the future Sir Anthony. Another of that splinter-group, Abdurrahman Azzam, generally labelled as 'the attractive young fanatic', was of Arab stock and had fought the Italians in Cyrenaica. Azzam's xenophobe impulses have latterly been harnessed to the congenial role of spokesman for the Saudi Arabian Government in its dispute with Britain over the ownership of the Buraimi Oasis, which we claim for Oman.

Prominent among the Wafdist orthodox was Mustafa Nahas Pasha, who succeeded Zaghlul as President of the party. This was an unlikely but very successful demagogue. Tall and balding, he walked stiffly, head thrown back; his shoulders always pivoted with his head, which gave an impression of much dignity combined with much self-satisfaction. He had two floating eyes, and one never knew where he was focusing. Zaghlul's uncle, Fathallah Barakat Pasha, the organiser and disciplinarian of the Wafdist machine, and Hamdi Seif-el-Nasr, a political bruiser and built like an all-in wrestler, were loyal Wafdists who died before the day of victory. Hamdi was an army colonel; perhaps he was born too soon. Very picturesque was Hamed el-Bassel Pasha, one of Zaghlul's companions in Malta exile. He was a Beduin Arab of a family long settled in Minia province, and he always wore the flowing robes and soft long-tasselled fez of his class. When he made his first visit to England, during one Wafdist administration, we had unfortunately forgotten to take his name off an official black list; after some research, a minor official at Dover asked him triumphantly: 'Do you know a man called Wafd?' Hamed Pasha, unconvincingly dressed for Britain in frock coat and top hat, was escorted back to his channel steamer, and he told me he was sick all the way to Calais.

The Wafd were traditionally unco-operative; many of the

members vaunted a record of political terrorism, and all were
opposed to any British presence in Egypt. It was difficult,
therefore, for us to meet them, except when their party was in
office. Easier and rather more congenial friends were the Constitutional Liberals, a relatively moderate group founded by the
noble Adly Yeghen Pasha. He was succeeded as the party's
leader by Mohammed Mahmoud Pasha, who had been another of
Zaghlul Pasha's three companions in Malta. The legend, common
in those Eastern countries with which England had imperial
connexions, of the pro-British native paragon whose heart was
changed on the day an English subaltern hailed him as 'bloody
wog'! and demanded his removal from a railway-carriage, was
related to me in Egypt as authentic in the case of two notable
Egyptian personalities. One was Prince Omar Toussoun, who
never had an anglophile thought in his life; the other was Mohammed Mahmoud Pasha. In his case the story was, at least sym-
bolically, *ben trovato*. It is probably true that the shock to a sensitive
young Egyptian aristocrat and Balliol scholar of finding, on his
return to Cairo from the egalitarian liberties of Oxford, what
Cromerism really meant to an Egyptian, was extreme. The legend,
I may say, probably derives from a novel by A. E. W. Mason, *The
Broken Road*.

Mohammed Mahmoud was dark-skinned, and as Egyptian as
Zaghlul; but more pragmatically wise. He lacked all demagogic
appeal, and, with great estates in Upper Egypt, he might have
lived fatly without making an enemy. Instead, he shared Zaghlul's
exile and gave his life to the pursuit, along unpopular paths of
moderation, of his country's independence. He had a tiresome
brother, Hifny, and few close friends. A cultivated reserve
dictated all his reactions, but he was a widely respected and
completely honest man.

His ablest lieutenant was Abdel Aziz Fahmy, whom Curzon
had unwisely vetoed for Cabinet rank in 1917. He had a look of a
stage-solicitor, pince-nez'd and pernickety, and his usefulness
was diminished by rather doctrinaire attitudes and a petulant
impatience with circumstance. Had he been less perfectionist,
he might have made a good Prime Minister.

A very gentle person, Mohammed Ali Allouba, who purred like a cat, and two doctors, Mohammed Haikal and Hafez Afifi, figured prominently in Liberal counsels. Hafez Afifi, after holding the London Embassy, succeeded the redoubtable Talaat Harb Pasha as Governor of Banque Misr, which was nationalist Egypt's answer to British economic imperialism. There he made rather too much money. I glimpsed him in April, 1956, shrunken and shaking, creeping along a club corridor; scarred for life by experience of an Aswan concentration-camp.

The perennial Liberal Minister of Agriculture, Rashwan Mahfouz, was typical of all Egyptian ministers of that portfolio: not because he was always more than overweight and bluffly cheerful behind a huge handlebar moustache, but because he was selected from the large landed families of Upper Egypt and the Delta who supplied all parties with men and finance. Most of these families were careful to hedge their bets; the Tawils and the Wakils, the Ghazalis and the Shurbaguis, delegated cousins to bring their influence and the votes of their peasantry to more than one political group. The powerful Abazas, who had fielded a football XI of brothers, had an honourable place from the first in both the main warring parties.

I spent pleasant evenings in Liberal company. Their group had enlisted the great Egyptian singer Umm-el-Kalthoum as its especial nightingale, and she used to sing to us for hours, while her chaperone, a bearded old gentleman called Shaikh Ibrahim, sipped his coffee with us and bowed to our applause. Wafdist gatherings were made melodious by her rival, Munira el-Mahdieh. I once followed an extraordinary cacophony through the palm-trees of the Winter Palace garden in Luxor, and discovered Umm-el-Kalthoum and Dr. Hafez Afifi lying side by side under a bougainvillea, carolling independently to the African sky.

The third Egyptian party, the Ittehadists, or Unionists, came into existence in 1924, when King Fuad felt the need of a political group of friends to defend him against new democratic pressures. Their first President was Yehya Ibrahim Pasha, a relic of Rushdy's 1914 Government, who served his master well. Popular rumour gave him a Coptic ancestry and a near relative in ownership of the main restaurant of Ezbekieh Square. Men like tiny Tewfik Rifaat, or Hilmy Issa (the name means Gentle Jesus) who rallied to their monarch's defence, were not of the highest calibre, but their uniform lent them considerable authority.

The Prime Minister most useful to King Fuad was not an Ittehadist. Ismail Sidqi Pasha was a lone wolf of great intelligence. He was always worth watching and he always needed watching. He played Egyptian politics with ruthless amusement, as a game he must win. If his opponents needed a bad image, he would arrange for the necessary number of bomb-outrages to blame them for. He once sent a group of Wafdist leaders on a long day's excursion, round and round Cairo, by deviating the train that was taking them to make trouble in Tantah. His amours were the staple of Cairo gossip. One Residency secretary became happily involved with a young married woman whom the Pasha favoured. Highly confidential representations flowed between the *Présidence du Conseil* and the High Commissioner before our man abdicated further interest. One of Sidqi's daughters married Prince Ismail Daud, which cannot have been much fun. Another son-in-law made history in his college boat by throwing his oar from him when near a bump, with the cry: 'I am exhaust. I can no more.'

Typical of the old aristocracy in office was Aziz Izzet Pasha, Sandhurst-trained, *schneidig* in corset and monocle, impeccably courteous. A different aristocrat was the philosopher of Egyptian nationalism, Lutfi el-Sayed, who translated Aristotle into Arabic. He was a valued friend; always accepting stoically the accidents of circumstance; always fixing his eyes on the ideal; always willing to interrupt those interminable games of backgammon to give me some good advice.

Another strain in cabinet composition came by promotion from the Civil Service. Ahmed Abdul Wahhab left the Finance, Abdul Hamid Soliman the Railways and Hussein Sirry the Public Works for ministerial rank. Sirry, a graduate of Cooper's Hill, became a Prime Minister, and he married the brilliant daughter of another Prime Minister, Mohammed Sa'íd Pasha, who had been a very skilled operator in his day. When King Fuad dismissed Mohammed Sa'íd Pasha from the lucrative post of *nazir*, or

Sir Henry McMahon

Lord Allenby

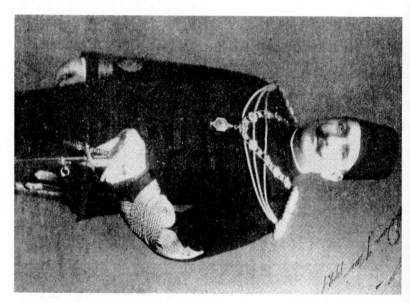

Sir Reginald Wingate

Sultan (later King) Fuad of Egypt

manager, of Prince Seifeddin's vast estates in order to take the pickings himself, most people thought that the Pasha was finished. But, as I was able to inform the Foreign Office, it is difficult to hamstring a centipede.

I have mentioned the political insurance-policies taken out by the large landed families in their discreetly varied allegiance. Another and even more vulnerable group of deputies and senators held men of great wealth but without family protection: Bedrawi Ashour Pasha, for instance, whose 22,000 acres in the Delta gave him an annual income of over a quarter of a million pounds and a captive constituency. If he offended any government, he risked being crushed like a slug. Or Ahmed Abboud Pasha, for long a name to conjure with in the City of London. Having no family influence at all, and being owner of the monopoly *Sucreries d'Egypte*, the Khedivial Mail Line and many other plums, he had to bow down in various Houses of Rimmon. These two tycoons were able to insure against every eventuality except a military socialist *coup d'état*. In the Egyptian Government's very comprehensive 'List of Sequestrated Properties' of 1961, I find the name of Ahmed Abboud and the names of no less than twenty-seven individual descendants of Badrawi Ashour.

The *jeunesse dorée* of Egypt was, of course, well represented at Residency garden-parties, and marriage within this group brought to Cairo two famous French actresses, Gabrielle Dorziat and Gaby Morlay. Those young men were attractive, and obsolescent; wealthy, and therefore doomed. But we are drifting into a world of the decorative, and these ornaments need not detain us.

There are still parties at the Embassy in Kasr-el-Doubara, with other guests than those I knew. I should find myself a stranger there, for death and Gamal Abdel Nasser have left very few Egyptians to whom I might wave to-day in affectionate *salaam*.

15

Sir Percy Loraine was succeeded by Sir Miles Lampson, from Pekin, who was to be the last of the High Commissioners. He was then a widower, and his daughter Mary acted as his hostess; but in the summer of 1934 his niece Betty Lampson came out to stay, bringing her pretty friend Jacqueline Castellani, and she, as Lady Lampson and later Lady Killearn, reigned for many years in Kasr-el-Doubara.

My own great privilege of those years in Cairo was to work with Walter Smart, the Oriental Secretary. Before coming to Egypt in 1926, he had been Oriental Secretary in Persia; and his effortless command of two such highly specialised posts marked him as an outstanding counsellor to his diplomatic chiefs. He had gone while still a schoolboy from Clifton to a French Lycée, and this formation gave to his thinking a cutting edge of logic and an unsentimental realism peculiarly French, invaluable in the appraisal of diplomatic documents and diplomatic crises. He had a keen and precise sense, extremely rare in Middle East experts, of what the Foreign Office and the Cabinet would think of any particular embassy representation. He never endorsed the pursuit of ends which from the angle of Cairo seemed all-important, if he thought (and he was generally right) that the Embassy's masters in London would be unsympathetic.

He was invariably courteous and considerate, but his friendship was never demonstrative. The fine neo-Platonist texture of his mind imposed, in day-to-day relations, a certain reserve. This had not always been obtrusive, if his own stories of years gone by are any evidence. One of these related his frustration at a minor orgy organised in Tehran by the then Imperial Russian First Secretary, in the Imperial Russian Embassy Chancery. After the preliminaries all were invited to bed down on the carpeted floor, but the host had forgotten to provide pillows or cushions of any sort. Hastily he opened the safe and distributed large volumes of Russian cipher and code-books to remedy this carelessness. Smart was torn between the mood of the moment and a longing to eavesdrop on secret Russian communications.

Later, when the French actress Eve Lavallière and the comedian Morton were in London at the same time, they dined with Smart, who left the evening's entertainment to their choice. They elected to visit an opium-den. Smart duly led the way to Limehouse, asked a few discreet questions and knocked on a dark door.

There was no reply. A police-constable came up and said: 'Was you looking for an opium-'ell, Sir?' He then hammered on the door, calling on the timid owner to open up. That evening ended with Eve Lavallière sweeping into the Savoy Hotel after this experience and being sick on their best hall-carpet.

In our service, Smart had been famous for years as the vice-consul who received £1,000 compensation for a bullet in the buttock, acquired when riding with an international commission interested in Bakhtiari affairs. After that date, consular officers on horseback were alleged to adopt a characteristic and provocative posture.

He allowed his wife to divorce him shortly after arriving in Cairo, and, regrettably, this circumstance barred him from the high promotion and ambassadorial honours which were natural for him. He was blessed in finding in Amy Nimr, when he married again, a companion whose gifts of character and culture illumined and enriched their life together.

Smart was on leave, as was the High Commissioner, in the summer of 1934, and I was acting Oriental Secretary to Maurice Peterson, an old Cairo hand, who had been sent out as Acting High Commissioner. In August, King Fuad was reported to be dangerously ill. In fact, three European specialists who came to Cairo separately to examine him, all assured us that this illness would end in death in a few weeks time. Farouq was still a minor, and the composition of the necessary regency council was only known to the King, who had selected it. It would certainly prove to reflect King Fuad's own attitudes and ideas.

It seemed to me that we must secure a change of government before the King died, for otherwise, if the same detested régime survived King Fuad, there would inevitably be an outburst of popular resentment; Farouq would have a very rough ride, and British troops might have to be called in to restore law and order. The first essential was to get Zaki el-Ibrashi Pasha out of the Palace. I advised accordingly, and Peterson recommended this action to London, where it was approved. Peterson left a strong Note in that sense at the Palace and he requested the Prime Minister to ensure that Ibrashi disappeared. The Prime Minister took his time.

It now sounds very old-fashioned, but in those dark days any firmly expressed and official British request required acceptance; or, it would be better to say, had never been refused acceptance. The British cabinet, then a coalition, were not, however, worried by our rebuff and instructed us to let the matter ride. The Ramsay MacDonald part of the coalition was perhaps happy not to appear to interefere in another country's affairs; the Hailsham element was perhaps happy not to appear to humiliate a king. By a remarkable accident of circumstance, there was no official then working in the Foreign Office building with any first-hand experience of Egyptian affairs. Our clamour for support received only a dusty answer.

The Residency *démarche* about Zaki el-Ibrashi Pasha's dismissal had, of course, become locally known and Egypt waited to see whether the weakest Prime Minister in her history would tell us to go to hell, as he could easily have done at any moment. Ahmed Abboud Pasha in England, then wearing an Ittehadist uniform, cabled daily to his friends, insisting that London was not behind the Residency; and journalists thronged my room, asking for precision and news. I had to bluff for a week, suggesting constantly that grave results might follow the Prime Minister's inaction. Some suitably tendentious telegrams to *The Times*, drafted in collusion with my good friend Mr. Lumby, were echoed back in London press-messages to the Egyptian papers and these helped to maintain in Cairo an atmosphere of hesitation and doubt. Finally, after a stimulating week, Abdel Fattah Yehya Pasha cracked. He extricated Ibrashi from the Palace, and then himself resigned. A respectable constitutionalist, Tewfik Nessim Pasha, succeeded him as Prime Minister, and Maurice Peterson was loudly cheered in the Cairo streets on his way to pay his first official call.

Unfortunately for me, King Fuad recovered from his illness and lived for another eighteen months. He not unnaturally rallied from his sick-bed with a fair measure of animosity towards myself, and my punitive transfer was decreed.

Sir Miles Lampson retained me in Cairo until the autumn of 1935, and I went with him on a tour of the Sudan in the spring of that year. Normally, the High Commissioner was privileged, when visiting the Sudan, to tour either the wild west of Kordofan and Darfur, or the remote and romantic pagan south. But Sir Stewart Symes, then Governor-General in Khartoum, had himself visited neither of these show-territories in his official capacity, and we were bundled into sleeping-cars and sent round the cotton-growing areas of Kassala and the Gezira. Henry Hopkinson and I, with an A.D.C., accompanied the Lampsons and Mary, and had a most enjoyable holiday, with stops at Luxor and Wadi Halfa on the way down, and visits to Sennar, where Lady Lampson caught a Nile perch much bigger than herself, Gedaref, Aroma and the Mekali Wells, Erkowit, Kassala and, from Port Sudan, Suakin. For me the only cloud in the sky was the necessity of bumping from Cairo to Khartoum and back in a lurching Hannibal aircraft, very sick-making; but I did not actually disgrace myself until we were safely home on Cairo airstrip, taxi-ing towards the red carpet.

Then it was time to go. I was already in North Iraq when Italy invaded Ethiopia later in 1935. This was a development of decisive importance; with such a war on their frontiers all Egyptian leaders saw a bright red light; all were eager to crowd round one conference table. On December 12, 1935, an Egyptian 'United Front' formally requested the reopening of treaty negotiations. An Egyptian delegation of seven Wafdists, headed by Nahas Pasha, and six anti-Wafdists had universal blessing. On August 26, 1936, a treaty was signed, covering all the points of difference which had pricked so many earlier balloons of hope. This treaty granted to Britain the right to station a maximum of 12,000 troops 'temporarily' in an agreed zone of the Canal; the military occupation of Egypt was ended, and Cairo and Alexandria were to be evacuated. Training-flights by the R.A.F. were also conceded. Wide provision was made for mutual assistance in time of war.

On May 26, 1937, Britain sponsored Egypt for membership of the League of Nations, and in October of that year the Convention of Montreux ended the long scandal of the Capitulations.

I am as sorry not to have been among those present at such moments as I am glad that the dreary inter-party tug-of-war that followed, over this or that constitution, and the street-clashes between the Wafdist 'Blue-Shirts' and Palace 'Green-Shirts' under Ahmed Hussein, are not covered by my title.

If I personally regret that Sir Miles Lampson remained in Cairo as Britain's first Ambassador, it is because some manifest change at Kasr-el-Doubara was essential to mark the change in post-treaty relations. He was physically and temperamentally incapable of giving any convincing impression of change, and this had unhappy consequences.

It is no disparagement of our last High Commissioner's gifts and achievements to say that, whatever his predecessors had or did not have, he had luck. Extraneous circumstance, Mussolini's rape of Ethiopia, enabled him to bring to a close a long, uneasy period of tensions and ambiguities, of British protectorate and sternly qualified independence; and to ring up the curtain on a new scene in Cairo, in which British High Commissioners had no part to play.

Chapter Three

Arabia Infelix

1

Sixty years before I sailed from Suez, the Khedive Ismail's private yacht had known splendour and great company; but in 1920, as the Khedivial Mail Company's s.s. *Dakahlieh*, only cockroaches, and no ghosts of de Lesseps and the Empress Eugénie, haunted its creaking cabins. The master was a flamboyant Maltese called Tagliaferro. The only other first-class passenger was a cloak-and-dagger Italian businessman, Pastori, equivocally active in Ethiopia and bound for Jibouti. I disbelieved most of his stories, though now I should be less incredulous. The wind blew, luckily, from the south. Lawrence speaks of '. . . the delightful Red Sea climate, never too hot while the ship was moving . . .'. If the ship is moving with the wind behind her, there is nothing delightful about the Red Sea climate, as many a wretched stoker, flinging himself overboard in madness, has died to prove.

At Wejh, I took their Christmas dinner from Cairo to a bearded Canadian team, prospecting for oil. Oil lay around them in pools on the sand; but this was only one of Nature's jokes; no oil has ever been produced there. They were brushing a sand-storm off their new supplies as I left them. After a vist to Yembo, we reached Jedda on Christmas morning.

Two years after the 1918 armistice, Jedda had changed not at all from the 'white town, hung between the blazing sky and its reflection in the mirage' which Lawrence had seen two years before the armistice, when Arab hopes were high.

The pilot threaded us through jagged reefs to our anchorage: even the skilled navigation officers of our Red Sea sloops found the approach to Jedda a minor nightmare. A flight of lateen-sailed *sambouks* was already winging towards us from the water-gate, and soon we were packed in with a heaving, grinding mass of dhows and hoarse shouting men, clamouring to attract passengers for the shore. The swell made the transfer from ship to *sambouk* perilous. I went ashore in the Agency launch to my new home.

Lawrence might have been with me, and indeed with every other new arrival in that strange silent town: '. . . We walked past the white masonry of the water-gate and through the oppressive alley of the food-market on our way to the Consulate. In the air, from the men to the dates and back to the men, squadrons of flies like particles of dust danced up and down the sun-shafts which stabbed into the darkest corners of the booths through torn places in the wood and sackcloth awnings overhead. The atmosphere was like a bath. . . .' Coming out again from the *suq* (market) into the glare and dust of the road running inside Jedda's high city wall, I saw the dome of a small secretive building with immense barred gates on the left; this was the prison. On the right were white, pink and yellow coral houses, some of three or four storeys, with huge carved teak doorways and a bloom of lovely *mushrabia* (lattice-work) casements protruding over the highway. At the end of the road, near the Medina Gate, stood one of the largest of these buildings, which was to be my own personal prison for the next three and a half years.

The Hejaz, now my consular district, survived solely by exploitation of the annual pilgrimage to Mecca and Medina, and its possession of these two Holy Places (the *Haramain*) made it, in Moslem eyes, a Holy Land. Europeans and other non-Moslems were, strictly speaking, not suffered to enter it, and, if seen at large by a Bedu, were liable to be shot without question. The Arab Revolt had brought many infidels in British army khaki to Hejaz ports and inland, but they paid for their presence with packing-cases full of sovereigns. The prospectors at Wejh had been welcomed because advantage was expected from their labours. Now that the war was over, the only exception to the rule was revived; only in Jedda were non-Moslems permitted to reside, and only by especial favour were they allowed to walk a few hundred yards outside the Medina Gate of Jedda. They might follow the shore of a pale-blue lagoon, to a point where a group of foreign consuls had been shot at, killed and wounded, not many years before; or they might visit the long concrete worm-cast where *Ummuna Hawa*, our Mother Eve, lay buried in the desert sand. She is reported to have continued to add many inches to her stature even after burial; hence the elongated tomb. Her shrine, much patronised by Arab women in search of fertility, was the first to be demolished and scattered, with her tomb, to the winds by the iconoclast Wahhabi troops, when King Hussein and his dynasty were themselves swept from the Hejaz landscape.

One major concession had been extracted from the Sherif in Mecca by the British Agent in 1915: a scratch 9-hole golf-course had been improvised in the desert beyond the lagoon and its use authorised because at no point was it out of view of the *Qishla*, or barracks, standing on high ground outside the town. This golf-course kept us sane, and saved our lives with our reason. It enabled some sort of exercise; we took the same walk every day, but it was at least varied and entertained by our adventures with niblicks and jerboa-holes. Beduin swooped and looted our green-flags and stole the cigarette-tins which lined the holes. These could always be replaced. Our caddies were among the *élite* of Jedda children by virtue of their office. Mine was one of the better ones, but at the age of eleven he disgraced himself in public with a goat, and was thereby disqualified from carrying my clubs.

There was no electricity in the Hejaz, except for one small Delco-set, lighting the mosque in Mecca; and no water-supply other than a broken-down condenser, standing in the shallows, which oozed out one ton a day of briny, seaweed-stinking liquid. The few tins of this that we were allowed to buy was used only for washing the floors. For drinking, cooking and baths we depended entirely on water from Egypt, which we collected from Khedivial Mail steamers every five days or so, on their south or northbound visits. The Agency launch regularly took out two large demi-johns to be replenished, and on these we lived. Our water was rarely better than tepid, for the intense humidity of the air pre-vented any evaporation, and the porous *zirs* (earthenware pots), which in a dry heat yield an ice-cold drink, were for us merely containers. We became so used to tepid water and soda-water that a really cold drink on board a visiting ship was a debauch, spoiling us for Jedda conditions for weeks afterwards.

From mid-December until the end of January, there was a chance of gusty, cooler weather, and even of rain. When it rained every Jeddawi hurried out to his own catchpit, cunningly hollowed and sloped in the desert, and collected into goat-skins the sand-thick rainwater, which he emptied into a *sahrij*—a small cellar reservoir—under his house. In time, the sand settled, leaving something for him to mix with the filth from the town-condenser. I have seen four-gallon petrol-tins of this mixture sold for six shillings in pilgrimage-time.

Five miles inland, and on across to Iraq and the Persian Gulf, a dry, parching heat rules Arabia. Eggs are quickly baked in the desert sand. But where the Red Sea air meets this throbbing vibration of heat, a special and local climate exists. The temperature rarely rises above 95° Fahrenheit; indeed, a rise to 115° is welcome, for this means that the wind is blowing off the land. Normal humidity is in the neighbourhood of 96 to 98 per cent, and there it stays, at midnight as at noon. No flapping *punkah* relieved the oppression of this sodden air.

When I returned to Jedda twenty-five years later, as Minister, I found electric light and fans, refrigerators, even some air-conditioning. My staff, but not I, then found life in Jedda intolerably uncomfortable. It was certainly not comfortable in 1920, with no electricity or ice and next to no water; when we were confined for thirty months on end to one small excursion of perhaps half a mile from our office-door.

I learned then how not to behave when unable to sleep: to toss about is fatal, and some sort of rest can generally be had merely by lying motionless and hating it. The humidity and its reflection in the eruption of constant prickly-heat were the worst of our troubles. If I touched the mosquito-net with my hand during the night, I could hear the patter of drops on the tiled floor, for every hole in the net became a water-drop because of the extreme condensation. However vigorously one might towel oneself after a tub, one was streaming wet before the first bit of clothing went on. In that damp air the normal, invisible, processes of perspiration, which go on continuously without our noticing them, were inhibited from evaporation; and it was this phenomenon, and not a mere sweating from heat, that kept us under water for the duration of our stay in the Hejaz. How many sheets of despatches, typed and ready for signature, have I had to destroy and type over again, because of the stain laid across them by a dripping forearm.

★　　★　　★

Christmas Dinner, 1920, was my first meal in Jedda, and it enabled me to meet all the Europeans in the Hejaz. Major Batten of the Indian Army, who was acting British agent, was the host, and his British, French, Italian and Dutch guests, the total European community of the country, numbered eighteen around the table. Batten, and a Captain Barnes who assisted him, and Major Pinder, an Army doctor responsible for our agency dispensary, were in uniform: I was the first British civilian in the agency-consulate since summer 1914. The French Consul-General was M. Léon Krajewski, one of many French officials of Polish origin. His wife was a daughter of picturesque Colonel Churchill, who had settled in Damascus and married a local beauty. There were two grown-up sons, who helped their father in the office while growing beards, and an attractive daughter, Farida. She was engaged to a British vice-consul—now an ex-ambassador—and needed all her good sense and an insistent engagement ring to fight off the bees swarming round a honey-pot. Gobee, the Dutch Consul, and his wife were a plain, bony, melancholy couple. For him, the war years had been one long exercise in cautious neutrality, and this made everyone and everything suspect to him. There was a chirpy little Italian Consul, who caused scandal by indenting for a series of *cioccolate*—Eritrean 'house-keepers', who were expected to be maids of all work. These females were replaced every three months or so from Italian Headquarters in Asmara. Two ex-N.C.O. clerical staff, Borrodell and Lambie, completed the British official contingent, and two young men from Gellatly, Hankey & Co.'s office, made up the rest of the British community. A large florid Dutch merchant, Arthur Van der Poll, had recently become a Moslem, in hopes of doing business in Mecca, but had been forbidden to enter the Holy City for at least one year after his operation. He shared our Christian plum-pudding, as did another European Moslem, Commandant Depui, known as Sayed Ibrahim, of the French Consulate. This was a waspish veteran of Morocco, who had fought with the Emir Faisal outside Medina, under Pisani. He affected great Moslem piety, and claimed to have *la main de Fatma*. He acted for the French Consul-General from time to time, but seemed unable to inspire confidence either in Moslems or in Christians. He never joined in our representations about the slave-trade, because his own elderly negress-housekeeper had been bought and not hired.

I soon realised that the very discomforts of Jedda had created not only a classless society, in which typists and consul-generals were at familiar ease out of the office, but a genuine *esprit de corps* among all the Europeans in the town. It was understood by all that there was to be no grumbling at what could not be cured, and that any anti-social behaviour, such as drinking too much, or attempting advances to the Jeddawi womenfolk, was, by convention, taboo. Partly for comfort, partly for morale, everyone changed into 'Red Sea kit' after the evening tub; black or white trousers, a black cummerbund, and a white shirt with open collar. In this easy uniform, we met at each other's houses for parties to which all were invited. This practice of comprehensive entertainment, essential if someone here or there was not to go under in lonely despair, persisted for another twenty-five years. Then the swollen numbers of American invaders made selection inevitable. With the change, something unusual and good went out of Jedda life.

The mood and shape and secret of the town as I found it have been so exactly captured by Lawrence's pen that it would be impertinent in me not to quote him. He describes a Jedda that I grew to love:

'It was indeed a remarkable town. The streets were alleys, wood-roofed in the main bazaar, but elsewhere open to the sky in the little gap between the tops of the lofty white-walled houses. . . . Every storey jutted, every window leaned one way or other; often the very walls sloped. The lattices and wall-returns deadened all reverberation of voice. There were no carts, no shod animals, no bustle anywhere. Everything was hushed, strained, even furtive. The doors of houses shut softly as we passed. . . . The atmosphere was oppressive, deadly. There seemed no life in it. It was not burning hot, but held a moisture and sense of great age and exhaustion such as seemed to belong to no other place . . . a feeling of long use, of the exhalations of many people, of continued bath-heat and sweat. One would say that Jedda had not been swept through by a firm breeze: that its streets kept their air from years end to years end, from the day they were built for as long as the houses should endure.'

This is so truly evocative that I can hardly quote it without nostalgia. Lawrence never liked Jedda: why should he? I had some correspondence with him about one of his scallywags who came claiming a pound or two arrears of pay; and in a letter to me Lawrence said that the one and only thing he liked in Jedda was the carved teak-wood doors. He asked me to pay the Bedu what he claimed.

*   *   *

Until 1914, Great Britain was represented in the Hejaz by a Levant Service Consul, to render aid and assistance to British pilgrims; the title of 'British Agent' (*Mu'tamad*) was a war-time improvisation of Colonel Cyril Wilson, who came to Jedda on secondment from Governorship of the Red Sea Province of the Sudan. For years, he was an admirable spokesman for British policy in the endless, and often futile, arguments raised by King Hussein. He was a courtierly, politically-minded soldier, and in him and his like the Sudan Government in its early days had recruited the salt of the earth.

Hussein's unwelcome and unilateral assumption of the title of

'King of the Arabs' had caused instant offence and resentment outside the Hejaz, and great embarrassment to His Majesty's Government, who never gave their blessing to the ambitions implicit in this claim, but accepted the *fait accompli* with polite distaste. It added nothing to Hussein's dignity as Emir and Sherif of Mecca and a descendent of the Prophet.

Wilson was succeeded by Colonel Vickery, a Gunner, who was more forthright, and sometimes rather brutal, with our ally. At one interview King Hussein announced, not for the first or the last time, that death was better than dishonour, and that he was all but irresistibly tempted to throw himself from the office-window. Vickery rose from his chair and walked slowly to the window, where he stood for a moment, as if calculating the exact height from the street. Then he gave one loud, contemptuous sniff, and returned to his desk. His Hashemite Majesty would have had about fourteen feet to travel along the suicide's road. Major Batten, of the Indian Army, was now in charge, while London decided whom to appoint as Vickery's successor. I was anxious to know who was coming, because Batten and I were too much of an age for an easy hierarchical relationship.

The Board of Trade occasionally addressed to 'Jedda, Palestine', or to 'Jedda, Egypt', requests for information about trade affairs; but most of our work was concerned either with the pilgrimage or with the flocks of chickens coming home to roost in the aftermath of the Arab Revolt.

The British share of the annual pilgrimage to Mecca was a large one. British subjects from the sub-continent of India, from Nigeria, Malaya, East Africa and even South Africa (where there was a colony of Moslems all called Smith), were joined by British Protected persons from the Persian Gulf and Trucial States, from Aden, Egypt and the Sudan. Their troubles were many and various.

★　　★　　★

The *Haj*, or Moslem pilgrimage to Mecca and Medina, was a closely organised event. At the Hejaz end, after the necessary screen of quarantine precautions, there was an impenetrable

network of official guides, each specialising in one or other town
or district of the Moslem world. They were responsible to the
Hejaz Government for the various fees then paid by the pilgrims,
and for their supervision, control and welfare. In return, they
steered their little flocks through the preliminary formalities,
attended to their needs, and brought them finally to the ecstatic
moments of Muna and Arafat, from which their new title of
'Hajji' would derive.

The first of the preliminary duties is the circumambulation of
the Ka'aba in Mecca. This is the *tawáf* and those who guide the
pilgrim in this duty are called *mutawwifin*. Some are very good;
some, alas, are rogues. They all have to live, and look to their
pilgrims for their livelihood.

Any adventurer considering a swoop in disguise on Mecca
during the pilgrimage season should think again. On arrival, he
will be asked to say where he comes from. Whatever corner of
the Moslem world he chooses—from Algiers to Indonesia—
he will be handed over to the mutawwif specialising in pilgrims
from that town or district, and so will find himself in a group of
those best able to expose his pretence. A brother of Lord Wavell
made the Haj in disguise, but he had with him three or four Moslem accomplices, who acted as lightning-conductors; and, being
an official in British East Africa, he had the ability to talk both
Arabic and Swahili. When asked a question in Arabic, he explained that Swahili was really his language, and *vice versa*.
Even so, he was lucky.

We often wished that British authorities in the pilgrims'
home-countries would exercise a comparable control. Our most
incessant troubles came from the Government of India's unwillingness to admit any administrative responsibility in pilgrimage matters.

There is a case for helping a Moslem to make the Haj, for this is
one of the five *fara'id* of Islam: the 'special excellencies' obligatory
upon every true believer. Some make the pilgrimage year after
year; others scrape and save for a lifetime in order to come; others
again buy merit by sending substitutes in their place on a '*badal
haj*', or 'pilgrimage by replacement'. Millions can never hope to

see Mecca or observe a duty prescribed when Islam was still only a name outside Arabia.

What we came to think of as 'good' Governments, such as the Egyptians, and the Dutch in the Netherlands East Indies, saw that it was in their pilgrims' own interest to be assured of a return home, and they imposed return-tickets to the Hejaz. They imposed also certain means tests, to enable their people to provide for themselves on the way to Mecca and back. This was their reading of the limitation of the Koranic injunction of pilgrimage to *man istata'a ileihi sabilan* ('to them that can make their way thither'), which otherwise would be an incitement to mendicancy. Dutch and Egyptian measures for the welfare of their pilgrims were administratively excellent.

The Government of India on the other hand, always super-sensitive to Moslem prejudices, refused to impose any control on Indians leaving for the pilgrimage. If a man could beg, borrow or steal thirty rupees for his single passage to Jedda, good luck to him. We had to extract from New Delhi tens of thousands of rupees every year to pay for the return passages of destitute Indian Moslems, and part of this was presumably paid for by Hindu taxpayers. The unpopularity of Indian pilgrims in the eyes of the Hejaz authorities was, of course, extreme. Where others came responsibly and respectably on pilgrimage, up to fifty per cent of Indian pilgrims cadged their way from the ship's side in Jedda harbour to Arafat and back home again to India. I remember the s.s. *Shustar* bringing 1,200 pilgrims from Bombay, 800 of whom did not have the sixpence required to pay for their lighterage to the shore.

On their way to Mecca, fraternal charity in others, and their desire to earn merit while pilgrimage-bound, kept them in alms; but once the last stones had been thrown at the *Shaitan*, there was a general stampede to get out of the country, and there was no more charity. We had a crowd of 6,000 Indians, men, women and children, camped outside our office in Jedda for six weeks, waiting for Indian Government approval for their repatriation at official expense, and then for ships to come from India to fetch them. We saw births and deaths and murders, and the stench around the

The Sûq, Jedda, 1921

British Consulate, Mosul, 1935

Forecourt of Yezidi Shrine, Sheikh Adi

British Agency, Jedda, 1923

house was intolerable; to come or go meant battle with gaunt and desperate women and men.

The Government of India had a pilgrimage officer in our office, whose task no one envied. They also financed the near-by agency dispensary, for the seasonal needs of their pilgrims, and this was kept open, as good propaganda, all the year round. In those days most Jeddawis preferred to come to Major Pinder or his Indian successor, or to the equivalent dispensary run by the Dutch Consul, rather than go to the Government 'hospital', which was an ante-room to the grave. Pinder refused to treat cases which he considered unethical; the Arab who enquired about a cure for enuresis was interesting until it transpired that the cure was for a newly acquired Sudanese boy, priced at £40 gold, who wet the Arab's bed every night. This always seemed to me an extreme example of 'buying a pup'.

There was a steady traffic in slaves, and many pilgrims ended up in slavery. I once saw a pitiful caravan of Ethiopian children, boys and girls of about ten to twelve years of age, filing through the bazaar to the slave-market which we could never find. A boy then sold for £20 gold and a girl for £30 gold. Some of these imports allegedly came from the French adventurer and author, Henri de Montfried, who was rumoured to have teams out collecting them for shipment from Obok and Tajura in French Somaliland. Some were tricked by so-called missionaries from Mecca, who converted Ethiopian villagers to Islam, led them to the Hejaz on pilgrimage, and cashed in. Some were sold by their Fellata or Fulfulde parents, who had walked for three years across Africa from Nigeria or French West Africa to pay their religious duty.

These people, generically called *Takrunis*, were a constant problem. They drifted across Africa on foot, with no papers or proof of nationality or identity. At the great cross-roads of Sennar, they were taken in charge by Shaikh Maiwurni, a regal figure from their own country, who waxed fat on their passage. They normally spent one season, and sometimes more, picking cotton for the Gezira cotton plantations, in which the Sudan government had an interest.

I invoked the Nigerian Government's interest in their plight, and they proposed a rough system of control, with metal tabs as identification discs, and a general speeding up of the pilgrimage process. That excellent administrator Sir Harold MacMichael, then in Khartoum, wrote me a pontifical despatch about the 'undesirability of interference with the age-old habits of pilgrimage', and I knew that we were sunk. The casual labour these *Takrunis* provided on the Gezira estates was indispensable to the Sudan government. The Nigerian scheme was not put into effect.

As a legacy of the war, we still had a small police-guard of a corporal and three men, supplied by the Sudan Government from Port Sudan, and it was arranged that this should be composed of men speaking the various *Takruni* dialects. They were invaluable, for they heard all the news from other Fellata or Fulfulde elements in Jedda. There was a beehive-hut village south of the town, called Nakutu, where many hundreds of these people settled, for they supplied much of the unskilled labour of the town. Thanks to our policemen, I was able to rescue not a few Nigerians from the ranks of the Hejazi Army, into which they had been press-ganged on landing. (This rather motley force was referred to by King Hussein in one letter as 'Drinkers of the Milk of War!') One Takruni giant was no loss to the force, for he displayed a habit, when given a word of command (which he did not understand, knowing no Arabic) of squatting down on his hunkers and registering excretal contempt.

They were always destitute, and all rules about fees and quarantine-dues were suspended in their favour. They made the Haj, including the visit to Medina, on foot and often alone: no *mutawwif* bothered about destitutes. I found one, late at night, moaning on the floor of the office entrance-hall; he was bleeding from the groin, and I sent for our Indian doctor to attend to him. The poor fellow had been set upon by Beduin on the Medina road, and they had believed him to be hiding a bag of money between his legs. They slashed at it with their knives. This was, in fact, a brutal but effective operation for advanced hydrocele, and the pilgrim made a good recovery.

As the *Takrunis* rarely had enough money to pay the full fare for the steamer-crossing from Suakin to Jedda, they sometimes bargained with dhow-owners along the Sudan coast to run them across for a lesser fee. Only too often, the skipper would land them in the wilds, a hundred miles and more south of Jedda, and leave them to die there, telling them that Jedda was but a mile or two away.

Nowadays, when jet aircraft bring Pakistanis from Dacca and Karachi in a day, and motor-transport is everywhere available, it is relatively rare to see a caravan of camels loading up for the journey to Mecca. In those days, there was no alternative transport, and caravans of a thousand camels filed through the Mecca gate in the sunset, lurching under their *shugduf* or camel-litter, in which two pilgrims balanced each other right and left. It would be hard to find a hundred camels in the Hejaz today, I expect; the camel-men have become lorry-drivers or own taxis. The journey to Riyadh then, across the desert to Ibn Saud's capital, took twenty-eight days. I was to fly it in an old Dakota in three hours. It was good to see the pilgrimage as it was in the Prophet's time, and indeed in pre-Islamic times; the soft, snarling shuffle of an endless caravan, carrying weary and ecstatic men and women along their road to Paradise.

2

The work reflecting our responsibility for tens of thousands of pilgrims was a year-in year-out burden, but our political problems were no less intractable. King Hussein was obsessed by anxiety about the implementation of British promises made to him in 1915, to encourage his revolt against the Ottoman Sultan and Caliph; these assurances we could not discuss without bearing in mind two other and later British commitments, mutually conflicting, which overlaid and made nonsense of the promises of 1915. At the heart of this tangle of twisted policies lay Palestine, the much-Promised Land.

Frederick the Great, in *Dialogue des morts*, says: '*Sachez, monsieur le philosophe, qu'il ne faut pas avoir la conscience étroite quand on gouverne le monde.*' He was developing the thesis that '. . . *les coups d'Etat ne sont pas des crimes.'* The toad beneath the harrow knows, among other things, that this thesis is disputable.

The latest and glossiest of our three commitments was the Balfour Declaration of November 1917, which stated that His Majesty's Government '. . . view with favour the establishment in Palestine of a National Home for the Jewish people and will use their best endeavours to facilitate the achievement of this object. . . .' If this has now been accomplished, it has been at the expense of the remainder of the Declaration, which continues '. . . it being clearly understood that nothing shall be done which may prejudice the civil and religious rights of existing non-Jewish communities in Palestine and the rights and political status enjoyed by Jews in any other country.'

Palestine was, in 1917, an integral part of Arab territory in the Ottoman Empire, inhabited by Arabs and by a few scattered Zionist settlers: the wickedly dwarfing words '. . . existing non-Jewish communities', which shocked and alarmed the Moslems of the world, referred to a population percentage of 8 per cent Jews and 92 per cent Arabs. One definition of *'suggestio falsi'* is 'Positive misrepresentation not involving direct lie but going beyond concealment of the truth.'

The Arab and Moslem world, dimly aware of what the future held, resented the importation of an alien element, however small. They suspected that Britain was paying a debt of some kind with Arab money. Possibly because he realised the shock to Moslems in India, Mr. Edwin Montagu, the only Jew in the Cabinet and Secretary of State for India, opposed the Declaration. He also, as a Jew, feared the effect of the policy enshrined in the Declaration upon Jews settled and assimilated outside the 'National Home'.

One of the more ardent propagandists of this policy was Sir Mark Sykes, to whose great personal charm I had succumbed at Cambridge. He had played a leading part also in the second, preceding, commitment, the Sykes–Picot Agreement of 1916. This bit of old-fashioned secret diplomacy in effect divided up the bearskin of the Ottoman Empire between France, Britain and Russia. Sir Edward Grey's letter of May 16, 1916, to the French

Ambassador established French and British rights of direct or indirect administration or control, as they might see fit to arrange these with any Arab State, with priority rights of enterprise and the supply of advisers in specified areas: area (a), area (b), 'the blue area', 'the red area', embraced Arab territory from Syria to Iraq, and these largely dictated the shape of the mandatory régimes which were later set up as vehicles of French and British administration.

There was also provision for a 'brown area': Palestine. The Sykes–Picot Agreement provided that Palestine should be under international administration or control, subject to consultation with Russia and the Allies, and with representatives of the Sherif of Mecca.

This Agreement was, not surprisingly, a secret—even our High Commissioner in Cairo, responsible for the political side of the Arab Revolt, only heard of it later, and casually. It became known when the Bolshevists found the text in Russian archives and published it, to show the world what imperialism looked like. King Hussein was then informed of it by his Turkish enemies, and no explanations given him by British emissaries availed to make it acceptable to him.

For he had been the beneficiary of the earliest and first of these British commitments, in October 1915. In order to persuade the Sherif of Mecca to rise against his liege-lord the Caliph of Islam, a promise of British support for the cause of Arab independence was necessary. The known interest of France in the matter of Syria and the Lebanon, later endorsed by the Sykes–Picot Agreement, prevented any precise British commitment in that area of the Arab world; but the definition of our support for Arab independence was otherwise geographically comprehensive.

Sir Henry McMahon, British High Commissioner in Egypt, who signed the historic letter of October 24, 1915, had followed a brief laid down by Sir Edward Grey, whose fairly specific instructions nevertheless left him some latitude. Palestine was not mentioned. Certain areas included in Mecca demands were denied to the Sherif: 'the two districts of Mersin and Alexandretta and portions of Syria lying to the west of the districts of Damascus,

Homs, Hama and Aleppo, cannot be said to be purely Arab, and should be excluded from the limits demanded.' Otherwise Hussein's definitions were accepted. But Britain's recognition and support for the independence of the Arabs was carefully limited to 'those regions lying within those frontiers wherein Britain is free to act without detriment to the interests of her ally France'. On October 26, McMahon wrote to Sir Edward Grey explaining that he had, by this reservation, 'endeavoured to provide for possible French pretensions to those places'.

Working forwards from October 1915 to May 1916 and on to November 1917, one can see that Hussein had some reason to object to the establishment of a National Home for the Jews in Palestine. I am aware that there are administrative ambiguities in the language of the McMahon letter; also that authoritative support has been forthcoming for the argument, later advanced, that the Damascus-Aleppo line mentioned was intended to include Palestine in the area reserved for discussions with the French. I can only say that this was not the understanding of Commander Hogarth of the Arab Bureau in Cairo, the main instrument of British policy in the Arab Revolt. Had it been desired to keep Palestine available as a present to world-Jewry or for any other purpose, some point of reference more southerly than Damascus— the Turkish Sanjak of Jerusalem, for instance—might usefully have been selected. In any case, what about the International Administration of Palestine, accepted by Britain in the Sykes–Picot agreement?

The troubles of the Emir Faisal in Damascus and his ejection from Syria by the French were, during my stay in the Hejaz, grievances as keen as any provoked by Lord Balfour; but those events did not leave scars as enduring as the wound of Palestine. Books have been written about every comma in the Balfour Declaration; few subjects are more intensely controversial. If I have discussed the matter at length; if I confess to a prejudice against that particular reflection of British policy, it is partly because I grew up with the McMahon letter as the sole background to my thinking about post-war planning in the Arab world, and partly because my own working life, like that of most of my Levant

Service colleagues, was distressingly affected, was indeed poisoned
by Moslem reactions to our support for political Zionism. For
all but two of the last thirty-five years of my service, I worked
in Moslem areas, and I was continuously handicapped by the
keen hostility to my country which our Palestine policy provoked.

The task of the Agency in Jedda was, therefore, an invidious
one. We had to listen, dead-pan, to King Hussein's requests for
the support he thought we had promised, knowing that it would
be useless even to report his claims once more to our masters in
London, who were weary of his asking for something they had
decided not to give. We could hold out no hope to Hussein, yet
we could not deny, in terms, McMahon's letter. Things were not
made easier by the unfortunate fact that no copy of the Arabic
version of McMahon's letter, sent to Hussein and kept by him,
could be traced in Cairo or elsewhere. It was essential to dis-
abuse Hussein urgently of any genuine misconceptions—the
truth was bad enough—but, although we knew what Storrs
and his Bahai translator Ruhi had meant to write, we could not
be certain that their Arabic pen had not slipped. The King's
pretensions became each year more personal and fantastic; we
could never get a peep at the precious Arabic document he held.
Before chapter and verse could be quoted to him, his illusions
had become an article of faith; and when, four years after Storr's
departure from Cairo, Keown-Boyd found the missing Arabic
draft caught up on the back of a drawer in Storr's desk in Cairo,
it no longer mattered that it confirmed our own and not the
King's interpretation.

As Vice-Consul and No. 2 on the staff, I was not, of course,
responsible for the execution of Agency policy. But between
appointments, and during the absence of a superior on home-
leave, I was in charge of the office for various periods totalling
about twelve months. It was during these intervals of brief
authority that I saw most of King Hussein.

He was then in his sixties; a small, neat old gentleman of great
dignity and, when he liked, great charm. He usually wore a black
thob, an ankle-length gown, but at night, relaxing, he would wear

white, with a white *kuffiya* (a head-scarf) loose on his head. Otherwise he wore the high, picturesque skull-cap of coloured plaited straw which was the head-dress of the Hejazi notable, with a tightly-wound white turban round it. He smiled rarely, and his smile had no warmth. His eyes were grey, lustrous and cold. He had beautiful hands.

To him, I was always Al-Mister Grift. Our prehistoric telephone would ring, and the high voice would call from Mecca: 'Al-Mister Grift?' and proceed to answer some trivial enquiry I had made, five minutes before, of the *Qaimmaqam* (his Governor) in Jedda or of the Officer Commanding Troops. No one dared answer any question without reference to his Majesty in Mecca. I never tried it, but I am sure it is the King who would have rung up to tell me the time, had I asked the local governor to set my watch right.

His mental processes were Turkish rather than Arab. The dignity of Sherif of Mecca lay between two rival branches of the family, and the Sultan Caliph liked to play one off against the other, and to have both within reach of his hand. For many years, Hussein had been virtually a prisoner in Constantinople, always manœuvring to escape the Sultan's anger or to win his smile. His Arabic, as spoken to me, was of almost kitchen-simplicity. As written in the long articles which he dictated for the Mecca newspaper, *Umm-al-Qurra*, it was a translation of Turkish complexities, which favour immense Proust-like gerundial clauses and leave the question whether a thing is, or is not, for the last two words of a column of newspaper. I used to plough through these articles with Ismail Effendi, our Egyptian (Bahai) translator, but neither of us was ever sure what the King was trying to say.

He had a violent temper, but I only watched it once. I was not present, though Lawrence was, when he threw an ink-pot at his charming eldest son, the Emir Ali, during the unsuccessful discussions of an Anglo-Arab Treaty which Lawrence had been sent from Cairo in July 1921 to negotiate. Later, when hostilities between King Hussein and Ibn Saud's Wahhabis had already caused the Emir Abdullah, later King of Jordan, to cut his way out of his tent and escape across the sands in his night-attire, the British government were most anxious to re-establish peace between the rivals. They proposed a mixed commission of three, to delimit the boundary near Khurma and Taraba, towns then in dispute between Nejd and the Hejaz. Ibn Saud had agreed to appoint a delegate; London agreed to appoint the neutral chairman; it only remained for King Hussein to agree to appoint his man. I was instructed to persuade him to do so.

I spent a little over five hours on end with him, *tête-à-tête*, and did my best. The reasonableness of the proposal, and its advantage to the King, who had nothing to oppose to Ibn Saud's fiery '*Ikhwan*' (Brethren), gave me some eloquence. But it was a *dialogue de sourds*. Hussein's hatred of Ibn Saud had historical and sectarian as well as, more recently, personal grounds. Finally, Hussein took up a quill pen and a small sheet of paper torn from a note-book, and drew a little map of the Arabian Peninsula, with stabbing, spluttering strokes. Recalling the long and impoverished exile in Kuwait of Ibn Saud and his father, before the recapture from Ibn Rashid of the Saudi stronghold of Riyadh, he made one final stab at Kuwait on his map and said: 'Let him go back there, where he belongs; when he is in Kuwait again, I will consider arbitration.' A year or so later Ibn Saud was in Mecca, and Hussein an exile.

On any subject but politics I enjoyed listening to him; he was pleasantly encyclopaedic about Arabia. I tried to lead him away from his grievances and embitterment, to talk of tribal feuds, or birds, or the nursery-lore of the desert. He often asked me, when in Jedda, to breakfast with him, alone. He himself ate little or nothing: he was accustomed to eat once a day only, and the rigours of Ramadan fasting did not affect him. He used to feed me, sometimes with his own hand, as if he were stuffing a turkey, until my eyes felt like starting from my head. This was probably part of a strong streak of sadism which marked him.

In Mecca, below his Palace, was an underground dungeon called the *Qabu*, into which he threw peccant officials or other notables or businessmen whom he feared or disliked. They were herded like beasts, and were only allowed up into the sunlight for thirty minutes each day. Some spent years there. When the impulse seized him, the King would take a great club and go down into this den, with a slave to carry the lantern, and there he would belabour one or other of his victims until he wearied. Some who had been there told me of the horror of these scenes. No one knew whether to risk an appeal for mercy, lest by speaking they might attract Hussein's attention and the club.

The only motor-cars in the Hejaz were the King's car, one belonging to an Indian merchant of Jedda and, of course, one or two owned by the foreign consular missions. Khandwani, the Indian, unwisely took his car to Mecca and set out in it for the Jebel Arafat, on pilgrimage. The King personally demolished it on the road with an iron bar, and if Khandwani had not escaped, he would have been demolished too.

I can certify to the vicious nature of this cruelty. After dinner one night, as we were sitting on the flat roof of the barracks, a negro slave came to us with a huge ape on a chain. The King ordered him to chase Sayed Ahmed, one of the guests, with it. This man, a minor official of good family, had a reputation for cowardice which he certainly deserved. He ran screaming around the roof, stumbling over chairs and people, and was about to throw himself in desperation over the edge when the King called to stop the fun. I was watching the King during this painful scene and I saw how his eyes shone and the thin drool of saliva at the corners of his mouth.

It was while I was with the King, in the little two-storeyed house he used when in Jedda, where stairways and ante-rooms were crowded with a press of secretaries and slaves, that I first saw the Emir Faisal, his third son. As usual when a Hejazi returns home after an absence abroad, he was wearing the pilgrim garb of *ihrám*: a white cloth round his loins and another white cloth draped across his shoulders. He had just disembarked, and had hastened to salute his father. I saw him often in later years, when as King of Iraq he passed through Alexandria on his way to Europe, summer after summer; growing yearly more shrunken, more old and more ill; but I shall never forget the beauty of that young head or the antique and timeless simplicity of his appearance.

He was soon to leave for Baghdad, where, thanks to Mr. Winston Churchill's imaginative sense of history, his royal destiny awaited him.

The Emir Abdullah, Hussein's second son, was at the same time carving himself out a kingdom east of the Jordan. I only met him twice in the Hejaz, before this happened. He asked me if I played chess, but I could not oblige him. He was very fond of winning at chess.

The eldest son, the Emir Ali, was an older, shorter version of Faisal. He was, of all the sons, the one most dutifully sensitive to his father's commands, and a strain of gentleness prevented him from pre-eminence in a world of feuds and rivalries. All the three elder sons had an Arab mother, and there was something birdlike about them; something mercurial in their thought. Abdullah was the most solid of the three. The fourth and youngest son, the Emir Zaid, was different. His mother was a Turk, the sister-in-law of Hussein Rushdy Pasha, Prime Minister of Egypt, and Zaid had something heavier than desert sand in his veins. He was hardly more than a youth when I first met him, openly impatient of parental discipline, excited by the memory of wild days in Damascus, when Faisal had ruled there. His brother sent for Zaid to join him in Baghdad, after his election as King, and the captain of the ship which carried him from Jedda to Basrah told me that the young prince had thrown off his Arab clothes and put on a pair of trousers before the ship was clear of the Jedda reefs.

Zaid became Iraqi ambassador in London; but that was long after we had spent some evenings together, with the Iraqi Consul in Egypt and a couple of dancing-girls, in a cabin on an Alexandria beach. Disparity of numbers made the party relatively respectable as well as amusing.

In 1925, after his father had fled the country, the Emir Ali became king for a day; but Ibn Saud's advance drove him, too, into exile, and he spent the last days of his life with Faisal in Iraq. His daughter was the mother of little King Faisal, and his son, Abdulillah, was murdered with young Faisal in the revolutionary explosion of July, 1958.

One thing that surprised me in my conversations with King Hussein was that he never once mentioned the name of Lawrence. Nor, indeed, did I ever hear Lawrence spoken of, while I was in the Hejaz, by any Arab, except for the one Bedu who came claiming arrears of pay. I had come to the Hejaz expecting to find a legend, and there was only silence. Two years after his entry with Faisal into Damascus, Lawrence was not a subject for conversation.

In July 1920, I had had to listen, night after night, to appeals on the telephone by Emir Faisal in Damascus to Lord Allenby in Cairo for help against the French, who were determined to evict him. Lord Allenby's silence then echoed in the conspiracy of silence that now shrouded Lawrence's name in the land of his legend.

★   ★   ★

The problems of slavery were often discussed between King Hussein and the British Agency, for slavery was endemic in the Hejaz. Every well-to-do Arab had his household of men and women slaves, inherited or acquired, whom it would have been no great kindness to release. Having cost him money, they were given the care of an expensive possession; they were generally the current representatives of a long line and they had inherited no sense of enterprise or independent decision. We had an understanding that any slave claiming British origins might take refuge in the Agency, and that we might then manumit him or her and repatriate them. This happened very seldom.

The slave-trade, bringing new material in from across the Red Sea, was a different thing altogether; abominable and unforgiveable. Our Red Sea sloops fought this beastliness.

One morning, a tidy middle-aged man in a dark blue *thob* (or gown) asked to see me. He told me that his wife had been stolen from the fields outside Omdurman twenty years before, leaving her baby near the well, and that he had had no news of her until the last pilgrimage. One of his neighbours had then been hailed from a Jedda casement-window and charged to tell him that his wife was a slave in that house. I must recover her at once, for she was the mother of his son.

I was disturbed to learn that the woman was of the household of Ahmed el-Hazzáz, a leading merchant of the town and a brother-in-law of the *Qaimaqám*, or Governor, of Jedda. I asked the *Qaimaqám* to produce the woman immediately.

Hajji Abdullah Ali Reza was in my office in five minutes with a financial problem. The woman had cost his brother-in-law sixty pounds gold; only if her husband, or I, could find this sum, would she be set free.

I made a short speech about the evils of the slave-trade, which cut no ice. I pointed out that there was no slavery in the Sudan, where the woman came from. He said I was telling him what he already knew. With a lucky flash of memory, I reminded him that Ahmed el-Hazzáz was at the moment on a visit to Port Sudan. He nodded. I then reminded him, also, that his brother-in-law had been accompanied to the Sudan by at least four servants, whose names were endorsed on the back of his passport, and said that I should cable to the Governor of the Red Sea province of the Sudan to investigate the status of these men; if they were slaves, they would be released in Port Sudan. This cable would not be sent if the woman was produced to me within ten minutes. It did not take ten minutes to produce her.

Her husband was standing by my side, very dignified in his fine blue gown, when she came through the door and hesitated, dazzled. There was no rush into each others' arms. She threw back her head-dress, shuffled towards him, and bowed her head, seizing his hands and holding them against her forehead. She was only in her late thirties, but she looked twice her age; a wrinkled old woman, worn out by life like an old shoe. But her eyes were shining, and they walked proudly together from the room.

I found this reunion very moving. I was to feel the same emotion years later, when for a long day I watched raped and mutilated girls from East Punjab and the Sikh States reunited with the fathers they had expected to disown them, after the horrors of the Punjab partition.

★   ★   ★

Not all our visitors were petitioners. British authorities overseas recommended to us their notables, when bound for Mecca,
for preferential treatment, and many colourful pilgrims passed
through our dining-room. There was generally at least one Indian
prince a year, travelling with a great retinue, and the top-brass of
the Indian government, or congressmen, who showed much
contempt for the Hejazi administration. The Emir of Sokoto,
in Nigeria, made himself unpopular with the stewards of the
Khedivial Mail Line by keeping his luggage on his first-class
bunk, sleeping on the floor, and using the wash basin for a toilet.

One dinner-guest was Lord Headley, then the leading U.K.
Moslem. He had been converted to Islam while a civil engineer
in India, by the industrious Khwaja Kamaleddin, who informed
him, when he expressed distaste for his strict evangelical childhood, that he was a Moslem in the bud. Lord Headley, whose
reactions were simple, promptly became one officially. I sent
David Lambie out with the Agency launch to help him ashore.
All did not go well. South-bound pilgrims from Suez assume the
ihrám or pilgrim dress when their ship passes Rabegh, and Lord
Headley was already rosy in a couple of towels when his ship
anchored. At the top of the steep gangway, a non-Moslem nail
caught the lower towel and held it, without his noticing this; and
his descent of the next few steps was spectacular. At dinner, we
threw many flies over him, about the tenets of Islam, but Khwaja
Kamaleddin, who accompanied him on the Haj, took care of all
the answers. Lord Headley was in buoyant form in his towelling,
throwing back whiskies, obviously delighted with the hero's
welcome he had been given in Egypt. I agreed with him when he
supposed that he was the first peer to come on the pilgrimage, and
I did not add that he was probably also the first peer to display
his bottom to a large crowd of Arab boatmen.

He made the Haj in great comfort, for King Hussein allowed
him to wear his own shoes, to carry a parasol throughout the
ceremonies, and to ride in the royal car. We thought this rather
invidious.

Another and better-known English pilgrim arrived in Jedda in
July 1921, while I was absent on leave in England. Rosita Forbes,

who had already a great reputation as an intrepid explorer and chronicler of wild places, had not had the complete personal success and satisfaction she expected from her expedition, with Ahmed Hassanein Bey, to the *Lost Oases* of Arkenu and Oweinát in the Western Desert. Her beauty enabled her to enlist most distinguished sympathies in Damascus, both English and Arab, and she planned a hazardous and daring adventure: a visit, alone and in disguise, to the Mecca pilgrimage. She sailed from Suez with other Egyptian pilgrims, under the name of Fatma bint Something and in Egyptian dress; and, in a first class cabin, which she rarely left, she made the journey safely to Jedda.

Her beauty matched her courage, but it was not at all an Egyptian type of beauty, though she might have passed for a Circassian. She had a fair and luminous skin, and eyes remarkable for their change of shade from light to slate-blue with her mood. She spoke fluent but not very convincing Arabic. She was unlucky enough, while transferring from the ship to the heaving, bumping *sambouk*, to be jolted by another woman, and her shawl-headdress, the *hábara*, fell back from her head. The woman stared at her. 'You are extremely fair', she said. As the lighter ran and luffed and gybed through the reefs, Rosita Forbes had time to wonder if she were not on the brink of exposure.

By unhappy coincidence, that particular shipload of pilgrims had not been given one of the necessary inoculations before leaving Suez, and Major Pinder and his staff were waiting on the quay to inoculate the passengers as they landed. Rosita Forbes decided that the needles were not being adequately sterilised after each injection, and she felt unable to share a needle with the possibly syphilitic peasant standing in front of her in the line. When her turn came, she whispered in English to Major Pinder that she was an Englishwoman and asked to be spared the inoculation. He went through the gestures, only, of treating her.

At lunch in the Agency, at which Lawrence (on his vain treaty-mission) was present, Pinder began telling this story; but Marshall, the Agent, kicked him hard under the table before too much had been said. If Lawrence had heard of any attempt to forge a pilgrimage, he would probably have informed the Hejazis at once.

That evening, Rosita Forbes came, still in Egyptian dress, to the Agency and informed Marshall that she must abandon her adventure. She was convinced that she had been identified as an impostor and that she would be murdered between Jedda and Mecca. High-level arrangements for her pilgrimage, once she reached Mecca, had been made; but the night-ride to Mecca appeared too perilous a risk. She left Jedda for Egypt by the first ship.

I know of no Mecca pilgrimage by a European woman in disguise. Had she been able to go through with it, she would have made journalistic history. Personally, I am not in favour of pilgrimages in disguise; I prefer Holy Places to remain Holy Places.

Rosita Forbes paid a later visit to Jedda, while I was there, on her way back to Egypt from Hodeida, in the Asir. Her plan had been to plunge into the then untraversed *Rub' el Khali*, the 'Empty Quarter', and to effect a dramatic meeting with H. St. John Philby halfway across this terrifying desert. The authorities in the Sudan, where she made her final arrangements, tried to frustrate the expedition, and she and the Egyptian railway-clerk who was travelling in the role of her husband had trouble in finding a dhow to take them to Hodeida. When they did, the journey was an ordeal of tempestuous high seas and corkscrew tossings. It lasted for fourteen days; long before it was over, she and the Egyptian were prostrate on the planks of the dhow. The Egyptian—and all who have been sea-sick will sympathise—moaned that he was dying but was glad to die. Rosita Forbes, herself a sodden wreck, told him not to be stupid but to drink the brandy which he would find in her bag. He emptied the bottle and soon felt himself a new man. She was furious when she discovered that the brandy-flask was intact, but that her flacon of expensive French scent was drained dry.

Who's Who speaks of an 'expedition to unknown Asir, 1922–23', but the expedition from which she was returning when I met her was not very long-lived, for someone in Hodeida had recognised walnut-juice, and after some revealing conversations in a local harem, she gave up, took ship to Jedda and stayed with us. The conversation at and after dinner was hair-raising. Rosita

Forbes had stories about every kind of crucifixion, mutilation and mayhem, as observed during her travels, and we had most of them. On going to bed, she explained that she was a bad sleeper, as a result of these harrowing experiences, and she did, in fact, have a nightmare. She asked me next morning if I had not heard her cries, but I had to confess that I was a very sound sleeper, and apologised.

At the other end of the scale, I had most unwelcome visitors to Jedda in two separate missionary invasions. There was a gentleman's agreement between the Foreign Office and the principal British missionary societies, under which they refrained from any proselytising activity in the Hejaz, which was the Holy Country of so many million British subjects. But Sandy Buxton's 'Heart of Africa' Mission, based on the Congo, refused this self-denying ordinance, and I was embarrassed one morning to hear that a British missionary, travelling hatless and barefoot as a deck-passenger on the steamer, had landed with the declared intention of proceeding to Medina, to spread the Gospel there. He was a tall, gaunt man, a former tea-planter in Ceylon, who had lost his wife the year before and, with her, most of his reason. I tried to dissuade him from his journey to Medina, but he insisted on going; indeed, his impending martyrdom seemed more important and urgent to him than any saving of Arab souls. I found that his passport was not in perfect order and used this to effect his deportation from Jedda by the Hejazi authorities.

Another couple, who lived in a tent near the Medina Gate with a Coptic servant whom they had converted to Methodism, took longer to evict. They distributed Gospels and tracts up and down the bazaar, and the port near the water-gate was awash with this literature which the police confiscated at sight. They, too, were at last got rid of.

As the son of missionaries, all this was rather painful for me, and I was worried lest my parents, in some missionary magazine, might read of their son's despotic action. But I never had any doubt that what I did was right. Were it to be known in India and beyond that Christian missionaries were active in the very port of pilgrimage, and striving to turn the Holy Country from Islam to

Christianity, the lives of our missionaries all over the Moslem world would be in jeopardy. To deny one poor fanatic his desired martyrdom was to save many as worthy as he from butchery.

There was no missionary impulse behind the visit of a large sailing-brig called the *Asia*—not to be confused with the French pilgrim-ship of the same name which burned to a wreck in Jedda harbour. This ship carried a number of young American enthusiasts, led by an editor of the *National Geographic Magazine*, who were looking at interesting bits of geography for themselves. Two of them, Merriam Cooper and Frank Shoedsack, were taking cinema-pictures, and Shoedsack made a daring flight over the town in one of King Hussein's packing-case planes. The couple did better when they made *King-Kong* a few years later.

The last Sultan of Turkey, Mohamed VI, Vahideddin, went to Egypt when he escaped from Constantinople, but King Fuad had no intention of letting him stay there, and wished him on to King Hussein. When I called on him, he was pitiful. He still didn't know what had hit him, and kept asking for his *a'ila* or family. This was a euphemism for his harem, but I didn't get the point for some time. He went to live in Mecca, where I hope his family joined him.

He had shared a steamer to Jedda with Mr. Charles Crane, a former American Ambassador in Tokyo, who had become the darling of the Arab world for his share in the King–Crane Report, which denied the French any standing in Syria or the Lebanon and favoured national Arab governments in these countries. For this, he was under sentence of death in Damascus, and was a more welcome guest in Jedda than the ex-Sultan. I saw a lot of him, as also later in Egypt and in Turkey, and liked him very much. The King laid on an evening's entertainment for him in the desert, some way along the Mecca road, where we had the ritual sheep's-eye, and rolled rice too hot to handle into balls which had to be thrown from a distance into one's mouth. The roast lamb had the texture of junket and was perfection. Before sunset there was a fantasia of racing horses and camels. After dinner, Beduin dancers twirled and stamped for hours, or so it seemed. 'What do these people do for exercise?' Mr. Crane asked.

Before becoming an Ambassador, he had made a fortune in plumbing, and Crane basins and lavatory-cisterns and baths adorned the advertisement-pages of the best American magazines. By way of a bread-and-butter letter, after leaving the Hejaz, Mr. Crane sent to King Hussein one of the most beautiful and exciting of these bath-tubs, rose-pink in colour and fitted with about sixteen different taps and gadgets to ensure 'wave', 'shower', 'hose' and various other refinements of ablution. As there was no possible way of using this bath in waterless Jedda, it was hoisted on to the roof of the King's little villa, and there it caught such rainwater as it could, during perhaps one week of each year.

The more usual, but always picturesque, form of entertainment on a large scale by King Hussein, was a dinner, called a *sumât*, at which a minimum of fifty guests sat down at a long horseshoe table laden with food, which was served to them by servants walking about on the table among the dishes. Bare-footed Arab men are not my taste: the formula would be better served by diaphanous-skirted waitresses. After we had eaten our fill, there was a second service for minor officials and businessmen, and then a third service, for the servants. After dinner, we could only pray not to be kept too long. When a visiting Italian governor, making conversation, asked King Hussein how many words there were for 'lion' in Arabic, we were there till two in the morning. A safer gambit was to ask the King to recite his own pedigree, which he enjoyed doing, back to Adam.

I recall one more visitor, a Scot called MacAndrew. He had inherited a famous collection of shells from his grandfather, and this he was continuing and enlarging, at considerable expense. He had a large motor-yacht, equipped with the latest gear for dredging, and the shells he collected in the Red Sea were things of great beauty. Local fishermen used to bring strange monsters ashore; I have seen more than one 'mermaid', such as was shown to tourists in Aden, and unidentifiable fish of every rainbow colour. But the MacAndrew shells were lovelier than any fish or any coral; and I hope they still exist to be admired.

Maharajahs and explorers, Sultans and pilgrims, might come and go. For those resident in Jedda, the conditions of life remained unrelievedly grim. But the peculiar philosophy which conditioned our reactions mercifully anaesthetised our discomfort.

Major W. E. Marshall, R.A.M.C., became British Agent and Consul in 1921, and he and I lived together, with a small fox-terrier called Emily and a Saluqi called Laila, in the flat over our office during his stay in the Hejaz.

His was an unexpected appointment. He was a bacteriologist by calling and he had no particular flair for political affairs. But he had accompanied Lawrence and the Emir Faisal in the Arab drive north '. . . things were always safe to go well', Lawrence says, 'where Marshall, the capable soul, directed them with a cultivated humour which was not so much riotous as persistent . . .', and the Foreign Office still cherished the illusion that anyone who had served with Faisal must be *persona gratissima* with Faisal's royal father. It was hoped that Marshall would extract a treaty from King Hussein; but no angel from Heaven, if holding a British passport, could have done this.

He was a friendly man, balding and careful; a keen player of piquet and a good golfer. He dreamed of some opportunity to grapple with the mysteries of a disease called *kala-azar*, and our day-to-day preoccupations interested him not at all. He was good enough to lay down the rule that we should all drink some alcohol every evening at 6 p.m., to replace the energies lost to prickly heat; and this was the easier to remember because we already set our watches and clocks to 6 p.m. every evening at sunset. We kept 'Jedda time'. For the Hejazis, sunset and its green ray meant 12 o'clock and the beginning of a new 'day'. We lopped six hours off this convention, and dined two hours after sunset, at 8 p.m. When one of the Royal Navy 'Little Flower Class' sloops in the Red Sea wired us her expected time of arrival in Jedda in terms of Greenwich Mean Time, confusion was extreme. We had to consult our pocket-diaries for the London lighting-up times, and do sums.

Marshall had a close call when putting on his evening trousers one night, for two scorpions, hiding in the leg, reacted with hostility. He was in great pain, and we had to flog him with morphia. It was, of course, routine-drill always to shake out dressing-gown sleeves and bedroom-slippers before use. The only other emotion I remember him displaying was mild irritation at my purist objection to his use of the word 'contra-indicated' in a despatch to London. As a rule, he gave me my head in the drafting of all despatches and telegrams.

One small item in our weekly review of the local press has been reported, but distorted, in James Morris's book, *The Hashemite Kings*. I had found in the Mecca *Umm-al-Qurra* an official notice warning pilgrims not to be misled by bad men offering them beetles as an aphrodisiac, because these beetles might well be bogus. As an illumination of the hazards of the Haj, this detail seemed worth passing on to London. For months after the despatch had been given the usual interdepartmental circulation in Whitehall, it brought me discreet enquiries from unexpectedly high quarters and requests that I should procure and send home by the diplomatic pouch specimens of the genuine beetles. James Morris has a story of King Hussein administering a monopoly of aphrodisiac lizards, and this, if not authentic, is at least *ben trovato*. It is a rare privilege to fault him.

The staff of Gellatly, Hankey & Co., the only other U.K. residents in the Hejaz, lived in a fine Arab house nearer the main town. Their firm, which boasted the first Lord Inchcape among its alumni, engaged youngsters of eighteen or so and sent them for spells of three years to the Red Sea ports and the Sudan, with a salary of £300 a year, but paying also all their mess-bills and living-expenses. They were infinitely better off financially than I was. My own salary of £300 a year, later £350, was supplemented by no allowances and could only be drawn in Egyptian currency. Gold was the local standard, and all prices were based on the gold sovereign; this meant a loss on exchange for me varying from five to over forty per cent, according to pilgrimage-pressures on the rate of exchange. No claim for compensation was ever considered. Officers of the Agency before my time had been paid in gold; I had only the paper that no Arab would touch.

Fortunately there was not much to spend money on. There was, of course, no theatre or cinema or other entertainment in the country. I was able to take my young brother Tony in charge, when he left school, and send him to France and Spain to learn the languages. I was also able to acquire some souvenirs, offered in the local bazaars.

One did not have to visit the *suq* to make a purchase, for every day runners from the merchants called at our houses with a variety of objects for sale, asking for a bid. If your bid was high enough, you got the object. There were Persian and Afghan rugs and carpets of all sizes; watches; exotic women's underwear; one surprising harmonium, and the loot from many a murdered pilgrim; all brought into our office for display. I bought a total of thirty-seven prayer-rugs and carpets, each one vegetable-dyed and lovely, for a few pounds each. What they would be worth today, I cannot guess. I had to leave them behind, with all my other possessions, when I was thrown out of Albania during the second World War. There was a steady supply of good rugs, because pilgrims unable to pay their *mutawwif*'s fees would leave their prayer-rugs in settlement of their debt.

One day I noticed that Lambie was flaunting a handsome gold repeater-watch, and I asked the office-messenger if he could match it for me. Within ten minutes he was back, with eight gold repeater-watches on a tray: presumably representing eight murdered pilgrims. Mine cost me £7 gold, and it still strikes the minutes and shows every conceivable unit of time.

It was a happy day when the dour Dutch consul was succeeded by Van der Plas, a real charmer with an Irish wife. The formation of the Dutch consuls in Jedda was thorough and most effective. They were selected from the younger government officials in the Netherlands East Indies and sent to Leyden University for three years, to study Arabic and Mohammedan practice under the redoubtable Professor Schnouk-Kurgronje, who had lived as a Moslem in Mecca. After three or four years spent in the Hejaz in the service of the Javanese pilgrims—of all pilgrims the most disciplined and affluent—they returned to Java or Sumatra and served in the Moslem areas of the islands. Charles Van der Plas was a cultured and actively intelligent man, and did much to protect us from mental decay.

Mrs. Van der Plas was on holiday in Merano with their little boy when she was stricken with some sort of brain-fever, the long-delayed consequence of an old toboggan-accident. The cable summoning her husband to Europe arrived as the Khedivial Mail steamer was sailing, and he had to wait for ten days for another opportunity to leave. Even then, owing to an unscheduled call at Wejh on the way north, his ship brought him to Suez a little too late to catch his onward transport to Europe. When first he had been warned, his wife had been given a bare week to live; it was over three weeks before he reached Merano, and as he came into her room, she sat up, smiled at him, and died.

Such tragedies of our slow communications were all too common. Life then held no wireless and no civil aviation. It could happen that a cable containing tragic news was followed, mail after weekly mail, by letters written before the event, with most poignant effect.

The most active, and by far the most affluent member of our European community was the Dutch shipping-agent, Van de Poll. He was indefatigably energetic as agent of all the shipping lines serving the Far East, thus handling the affairs of over 50,000 pilgrims from Java and Singapore every year. His £1 gold commission per head was added to the profits of a booming import-export business, and he retired, in his thirties, with half-a-million in the bank, after marrying the sister of his Abyssinian launchman. The 1939–45 War was to lose him all his money and bring him back to Jedda to start again on the lowest rung. It was also to make his daughter, then a student in France, one of the heroines of the Resistance.

He was as pink and white as a Glaxo advertisement and had the skin of a rhinoceros. Few liked him.

*　　*　　*

When King Hussein was persuaded to buy, for a great price, some decrepit military aeroplanes offered by the Italian Disposals

Board, he engaged some hardly less decrepit White Russian aviators to fly them, expecting them to load heavy cargo on to the wings. This influx gave us three or four more males and two females to look at.

The oppresive humidity and our constant battle with mosquitoes and scorpions, and, in defence of carpets or photographs, with 'silverfish', were obvious discomforts in Jedda life. No less distressing was our monastic isolation: it was an event to see a woman's face. Mrs. Bullard and Mrs. Van der Plas both spent brief winters in the Hejaz; but for most of the time, once the Krajewski ladies had left, there were no European women in the country. It was to be many years before the Americans came.

The native women were, perhaps fortunately, unidentifiable. They did not wear the revealing and all but notional *yashmak* veil of the Turks, or the obscurer veil of the Egyptians, but were enveloped from head to foot in a billowing hood, rather like the uniform-dress of the Klu-Klux Klan, except that the customary eye-holes were replaced by a little panel of closely latticed stuff. This garment covered everything but the hands and ankles and imposed a deterrently shapeless outline on the most willowy figure. The only women to dispense with conventional propriety were the local washerwomen, negress harridans of surprising inelegance, who wore only a short brown shift. By an unexpected play of priorities, they always chastely raised the skirt of this shift to cover their mouths when passing an unbeliever.

The Russian wives were hardly less lethal than their husbands' aircraft. Little Madame X., all collarbone and china teeth, steered straight for the trenches which still scarred the desert near the town, if taken for a walk. She also advertised a musical background which was *sui generis* by asking new acquaintances whether they had ever done it on a grand piano.

Madame Y. was more enigmatic. When I called at her flat on business with her husband, she flung the door wide open and levelled a large pistol at whoever was outside, in this case, me. She may have been expecting another White Russian. She did not care for men, and soon left her husband for a specialist life in Cairo. I found her there three years later, when she already owned an expensive milliner's shop and knew everyone behind the curtains of Cairo harims.

A Polish refugee spent an unhappy year pulling teeth in Jedda, but he caught the eye of the Emir Ali and accompanied him to Iraq; and when I met Dr. Makowsky in Bagdad fifteen years later, he was the Court Physician.

This, with the Italian Consul, was the roll-call of the European community as we knew it, and there were times when we numbered fewer than ten all told. On January 1, 1923, the Personal Column of *The Times* carried a message: 'All four Britons in the Hejaz wish the rest of the world a Happy New Year and themselves a cool one.' I had had some hope that this moan might bring me a number of pen-pals. The only reply came, after Easter, from El Fasher, the capital of Sudan's Darfur, where a junior official wrote to inform us that he was as uncomfortable as we were.

Apart from golf (which in my case should carry inverted commas) our only pleasure was bathing. Because of sharks, we dared not venture out of our depth and splashed in the near shallows of the Quarantine Islands, some miles south by launch. Picnicking after our bathe, we often saw the shadow of a shark where we had been splashing. Barnes and I were once carrying Farida Krajewski on our crossed hands through the shallow water covering a very jagged stretch of reef when we saw, racing towards us, a billiard-table, broadside-on. This was the largest giant sting-ray I ever met, and anyone stung by it would not have recovered. We stood still, petrified. Fortunately it was more frightened of us (for practical purposes) than we of it, for it veered away when some ten yards from us.

The sharks were frightening. When we went out to lunch with the masters of visiting pilgrim-ships, we watched shoals of them, circling the ship. These ships lay at anchor for weeks off Jedda during the period before and after the pilgrimage, and gay regattas were organised. Crossing the narrow gangway separating his ship from another, one young officer fell sideways, crashing on to the side of his own ship, then swinging in the swell. When the two ships swung apart, the sharks already knew of this. He was lost at sea.

For other casualties we had a non-Moslem cemetery, in the
desert beyond Nakutu village. This was a grisly place, always
haunted by pariah-dogs, and the *bedu* were said to raid it for
knuckle-bones used in one of their games. There German oriental-
ists and Chinese mess-boys lay side by side, awaiting the Resurrec-
tion. We had an understanding with each other that, if we died in
the Hejaz, the sea, and not this horrid place, should have our
bones.

I came near to testing this in August, 1923, when the Agency
launch broke down in the harbour on its way back from a pilgrim-
ship which I had had to measure—a tedious job, involving exact
calculations of areas and cubic space per pilgrim embarked. For
about two hours, we tossed in the swell, dowsed with big waves,
while the launchmen struggled with the engine. The soaking was
a refreshment in the steamy August heat, but that evening I started
a temperature, which I assumed to be due to dengue fever. I was
then living in *Beit Thani*, and there our Indian sub-assistant
surgeon, who had taken Dr. Pinder's place, put me to bed. After
various tests, he told everyone else, but not me, that I had pneu-
monia, and was on no account to know of this. I cannot imagine a
more stupid decision. I should not have been alarmed, had I
known: in those days I had great confidence in doctors. In any
case, I should certainly have had the sense to remain quiet. I was
informed that I had a fever, which I knew, and that I should not
get up 'more than necessary'.

I spent a most uncomfortable ten days, with a temperature of
104°, and was delirious for most of the time. Not being aware of
the real danger of activity, I used to get up and plod to the
lavatory, until I started fainting whenever I sat up in bed. Pneu-
monia, in 1923, when there were no antibiotics, was fairly
dangerous and required good nursing. I got no nursing; even the
so-called 'crisis' on the tenth day had to be fought alone. My only
grateful memory of a bad time is of the first, pre-dawn call to
prayer, ringing like a silver bell from the minaret, which told me
that another nightmare of darkness was over.

The call to prayer was a familiar Jedda sound, but the best
Izan I ever heard was chanted for me by the *Muezzin* of the Great

Mosque of Medina. He asked for a visa for Egypt, and I told him that His Majesty's Government would get their two shillings from me, if he would oblige me. He hauled his immense bulk up to my desk and held both hands to his face before letting loose a voice of bronze. When he fell silent, the street below my window was black with people.

Marshall left us and Reader Bullard replaced him. What manner of man he was, and is, can be gathered from his autobiography, *The Camels Must Go*, but his book does not tell of the admiration and respect in which his Levant Service colleagues always held him. He was not, I confess, easy to live with; sharing a flat was like living with one's conscience. For *l'homme moyen sensuel*, the austerity of his taste held too much of unspoken reproach, and the extreme disciplines of conscience, willingly accepted by himself, were sometimes unshared. He was an exemplar of study and he never ceased from its pursuit. I enquired, when he arrived, at what time he wished to be called next morning. He wished to be awakened at five o'clock, because he proposed to resume the study of Russian, before breakfast. He was reading the Russian novelists before I left, a year later, and he then passed on to renew acquaintance with the Classics. Bullard had an unfailing nose for the second-rate. He enjoyed Bach and Beethoven and classical jazz; but anything likely to find favour in a tea-shop made him sick, and many of our favourite records sang for us no more. His taste in books was no less eclectic.

During his régime, Rushdy Bey, the Commandant of Troops, ceased to visit the British Agency. This little villain had begun life as a P.T. instructor in the Turkish Navy, and the walls of his room were monotonous with portraits of muscular nudes. He liked a game of poker and used to present himself, uninvited, carrying a large bag of sovereigns, which was, in fact, the garrison's pay for the week. Otherwise, we saw but little of the Hejazi notables outside their offices. Sulaiman Qabil, the Mayor of Jedda, my favourite, had been to Cairo and had seen the tango danced in the Continental Hotel; this confirmed his conviction that Christianity had no future. Our wall-eyed office-messenger, Hassan Malik, had also visited Cairo, in Colonel Vickery's company. He had admired a lady ('. . . doubtless the daughter of an Emir . . .') who stood behind glass in Morum's Oriental Stores. Venturing inside to examine a surprising immobility, he stepped on the foot of a little boy in a sailor-suit, who uttered no cry. It was all very strange.

*　　*　　*

Our relations with King Hussein became strained as he became more and more embittered, more and more conscious of the Wahhabi threat. We could get no sense out of him on slavery, on treaties, on general-average (to which a shipwrecked consignment of gold for Rabegh was liable). The daily scandals of Dr. Nu'man Thabet's quarantine service remained unpunished. He by-passed us when he allowed Habib Lotfallah, a Lebanese millionaire from Cairo, to pose as his representative in London. Habib designed himself a uniform and entertained royally, but the Foreign Office was unresponsive to his importunities. He once reported to his royal master the words of the head of the Eastern Department: 'For God's sake, Habib, why don't you bring a bed and sleep here, while you're about it?' 'This will prove to your Majesty,' he wrote, 'how truly popular I have become with the senior officials of the Foreign Office!'

In the Spring of 1924, I became involved in a complicated commercial arbitration case between two groups of Patni merchants, whose flat pancake head-dress rivalled the gilt truncated helmet of their friends and enemies, the Bohra merchants, in picturesque improbability. The Marwaris in India are alleged to keep three account-books: one for their partnership, one for themselves, and one for the Inland Revenue officials: these Patni book-entries were labyrinthine. For the first and last time in my life, I was offered a bribe. A chinking bag of gold sovereigns was discreetly left on my desk, and returned without thanks. I have no idea how the case ended, for I was instructed, in May, to take the home-leave due to me and then proceed to Constantinople. This was where I most wanted to go.

I shipped to the Tetton Kennels the beautiful Saluqi bitch given to Marshall by the Emir Ali, and by Marshall to me, and began packing. When I called on King Hussein to take leave of him, he offered me the order of *Al-Nahda*, which he had recently invented; but Foreign Office practice dictated a refusal of this decoration. I explained our rules, with polite regret. He patted my hand. 'Dear Mr. Grift,' he said, falsely but charmingly, '*Anta wisámuna*—"you are our decoration!"' In place of the ribbon, he gave me an embroidered panel from the Holy Carpet (*al-Kiswa*) which had hung for a year on the Kaaba in Mecca. This silk draping was woven every year in Cairo and sent down to Jedda in great ceremony with the *Mahmal*. My panel bore a short passage from the Koran in gold thread and was for years a treasured possession.

Major Marshall left us for Netley and was appointed thence to head the bacteriological department of the Wellcome laboratories in Khartoum. This had been his heart's desire, but he was dead in six months. Lambie became a golf-pro in Canada. Pinder died tragically in Abadan. King Hussein lies buried in the great Mosque of Omar in Jerusalem.

He was an arrogant and difficult man, but one may feel compassion for frustrated human hopes. He had read into the McMahon letters a personal hope matching his high personal ambitions. These were unfulfilled, but he put on their phantom uniform and styled himself Overlord of Arabia and Caliph of Islam. He died in exiled poverty, knowing that his claim to these proud titles was a jest and an offence to other men of his faith.

As for Jedda, which I was to see again in a later incarnation, it is today enclosed in a brash sprawling suburbia of air-conditioned villas, macadam roads and swimming-pools. Only the secret streets of the old city and the annual press and bustle of the pilgrimage link it with the prison-town I was at last to leave, with fourteen sovereigns in my pocket and Bullard's copy of *Tom Jones* to read on board. The Jedda of King Hussein lay halfway down the Red Sea, on the left, just off the map; but now only memory can find it.

Chapter Four

Muslin Tapestry

It was an unusual house. It stood in the stony desert half a mile from the city, on a rise sloping steeply up from the southern road. It was four-square, with battlements and a machicolated roof, and a high wall surrounded it. This *Beau Geste*-type fortress-quality was deliberate; the house was planned for defence against hostile attack. Because it failed in this purpose when the moment came, my successor, Monck-Mason, was butchered by the mob; and I was very lucky not to be there in his place.

One of the more impressive rooms in the house was the downstairs lavatory, which had the furnishings and almost the proportions of a throne-room. Elsewhere an inevitable skimping of funds had betrayed the original dream. The windows posed as steel-strong, but their tin borders blew out at the drop of a hat. One sandstorm shattered twenty-eight windows in a night which we had to spend in a sheltered corner of the drawing-room floor, with wet sponges over our mouths. There were six alternative lavatories to the throne-room, but in all seven of them an unfortunate defect in the plumbing—which the original owner had personally installed, before enclosing it in masonry—produced a crossing of lines and an occasional effluence of hot water where this was markedly inappropriate. Our guests' anxious faces as they issued from an experience suggestive of most feverish body-temperatures were an embarrassment to their host and hostess.

There were three widely separate levels of flat roof, which enabled seclusion and sleep in hot weather in the 'meat-safes' which housed beds and lamps, for ourselves, our children and our visitors. The topmost roof-space was reached by a very narrow, very steep spiral staircase, and its low surrounding wall was, for some reason, capped along two sides with a horizontal shelving of corrugated iron, stretching six foot over the roof-space at a height of thirty inches from the ground. This may well have been the last redoubt of the fortress, for anyone lying up in the darkness of that shelving, with his gun-sights on the narrow staircase door, could wreak havoc on any invasion-force. My successor did not, perhaps, remember this unusual facility.

Halfway up the staircase leading from the ground-floor to the living quarters stood a large built-in stone-marten cage, complete with tree-trunk and branches for the animals to play on.

One wall of the office on the ground-floor was covered with bookshelves, one of which carried a number of unconvincing metal books. I found that by manipulating one of these bogus volumes I opened a door, leading to the *sardab* at cellar-level below. Here electricity and fans and an absence of any windows ensured coolness and comfort in the hot siesta hours. From the *sardab* another secret passage led into a dry well, outside the walls. Any tenant of the house menaced by marauding Kurds might plead, not unreasonably, for five minutes' privacy and prayer in an apparently sealed room, and then use this route to escape.

From three sides of the house one saw little but desert or the hazy distant silhouette of minarets that was the city. But from the main bedroom the view was different. I looked out of that window on my first morning and saw, in the middle distance, a great water-snake sliding under the sky. I have a minor passion for world-rivers. Nile, Tigris, Euphrates, Ganges, Brahmaputra and Indus are names carrying bourdon-echoes to my memory's ear. This was Tigris, the second of my monsters. On the farther bank a dishevelled white mosque stood on a hill, flanked by high green mounds and deep green hollows. The mosque was sacred to Nebi Yunus, whom we call Jonah; and the hill buries the palace of Esarhaddon, son of Assurbanipal, King of Assyria. The mound and hollows I was looking at were Nineveh.

*   *   *

The 1914 war brought Mesopotamia under British control—a major British objective. The campaign against the Turks which yielded this prize was mounted by the Government of India, and the Indian political service was strongly represented in the uneasy years of direct British administration which were followed in 1920 by the régime of the Mandate. This provided a deceptive formula, enabling a League of Nations cover for imperialist performances in Palestine, Iraq and the Levant States. The Arab nationalists were, however, not deceived, and a bloody rebellion in late 1920 shook London to a change of mood. The Emir Faisal, son of King Hussein of the Hejaz, was crowned King of Iraq—the Arabic name for Mesopotamia—in August 1921, and the blessings of an organic law, a constitution and treaty-relations blossomed. The perfectionist logic of a quintessential administrator, Colonel A. T. Wilson, was thus abandoned for a system which retained the fact of British authority while giving to the face of administration an Arab semblance, and the great Sir Percy Cox was able to steer a course towards self-government acceptable to many Iraqis. The British mandate was surrendered in 1932, when Iraq became a sovereign independent state in military alliance with Great Britain. Sir Francis Humphrys, the last of the High Commissioners, remained as Ambassador, to be succeeded by Sir Archibald Clark-Kerr, a Foreign Office man, in 1935.

I knew only three things about Mosul and its surroundings when I was sent there in September 1935. One was that this was the town where a butcher had prospered by the sale of human meat, horrid evidence of which was available on a picture-postcard circulating between the wars. Another was that the tangled affairs of the B.O.C., an oil company with British and international interests functioning at Qaiyyara, would be a major burden. The third was that the word 'muslin' derives from Mosul, its original place of manufacture. Some experience of the town and district, where violence is an accepted way of life, convinces me that the butcher might appropriately figure in any municipal coat-of-arms; but I have preferred a gentler association for my title.

Before leaving Alexandria I had consulted a grizzled veteran of Mesopotamian adventure called Colonel Bovill, but he did not help me greatly. He claimed to have held Bagdad in the hollow of his hand when General Maude occupied the place, by commandeering all stocks of rubber-goods and releasing these only in return for political advantage. This was a hazard of history unlikely to repeat itself for my benefit. The only serious advice he gave me, crystallising long years of experience, was, if ever using a Kurdish woman, to have a Flit-gun by my side.

My new duties, mainly of political observation, were not onerous: luckily so, because I had no vice-consul to assist me. My staff consisted of a portly Assyrian pro-consul called Efraim, and two Assyrian *cavasses*, acting as door-keepers and messengers. On the domestic side, I had two Assyrian house-boys, a Mohammedan gardener and an Assyrian sweeper; the cook was a Jacobite Christian. Any mental picture of heavily bearded Sennacherib-figures typing despatches or waiting at table would be a mere illusion of semantics. The Assyrians, whose problems were to be mine, will be separately and later discussed.

Their presence in the area does, however, explain the architecture of my consulate. In 1935 our landlord was one of Mosul's M.P.'s, but the house had been built by an eccentric cleric, a Mr. Panfil. By birth a Polish Jew and by ordination a Roman Catholic priest, he parted company with the Vatican and became a missionary in the service of an American organisation working for the conversion of the Assyrians to Presbyterianism. He seems to have allowed other considerations to outweigh his sense of mission, for he used the mission funds to erect this modern fortress, hoping that the Assyrian Patriarch, the Mar Shimoun, would purchase it for patriarchical residence. The price was probably too high.

My consular district was one of the most varied and picturesque in our Service. On one side of the Tigris lay the great Syrian desert, stretching to Damascus, and the black tents of the Shammar confederation were pitched in a world of immense empty spaces, postmarked with only the rarest wells. On the other bank of the Tigris lay Kurdistan, with its mountain villages, forests, gorges and waterfalls, and its fierce handsome men and women, all in a smothering of swaddled linens and coloured boleros, baggy trousers and bandoliers. Arbil (once Erbela), the capital of that province and one of the oldest continuously-inhabited cities of the world, stood perched on a high hill composed of its own past existences, some way short of the Kurdish foothills. If a well were sunk in that town, it would pass through six millennia or more of domestic history before reaching water.

Kirkuk, in the southern corner of this part of my responsibilities, had the moneyed importance of oil-wells, and flaming gushers turned a night-ride there into a Doré illustration of the Book of Daniel.

There was a British vice-consulate for Kurdistan under my supervision, stationed in a small village called Diana, at the far end of the Rowanduz Gorge. This was a relic from British mandate days, when it had been hoped to attract some trade-traffic from Persia by way of Rayat through the Rowanduz Gorge into Iraq. Our vice-consul had no duties in this respect. In the tragic week when Assyrian minorities were being murdered up and down Kurdistan, Edwin Chapman-Andrews made a series of sorties from Diana to save whole villages from extinction, but later the post hardly did more than provide me with an excuse for unforgettable excursions.

This was not the fault of the incumbent, an old friend from Cairo days. His observation of the Kurdish scene was penetrating, and his reports on blood-feuds and tribal politics were comprehensive, which is saying a lot. Mr. Finch's equipment for reporting on anything was, indeed, impressive, for he was all but omniscient. After serving in the first World War (characteristically as a gunner specialising in the obscurer problems of ballistics), he took a First in history at Oxford and, perhaps misguidedly, chose the Levant Service as a career. I could never understand why so much erudition failed to waft its bearer to the dizziest heights. After retirement and until he died, he was writing military text-books for the army.

The Kurds deserve a book to themselves, but not from me. They have produced many great men. Saláheddín el-Ayyoubi, our Saladin, was a Kurd, born in Tekrit. In modern times, Nuri Sa'id Pasha, for many years Prime Minister of Iraq, and his brother-in-law Jaafar Pasha, were Kurds. The race has great vitality and potential. But they have lived so long in remote eyries, separated from each other by barely passable mountains, that they are incorrigible individualists; when the challenge comes, they are apt, like the French or the Irish, to put century-old animosities before national unity. Their nation itself is scattered between Iraq, Turkey and Perisa, and some idealists hold that only imperialist tyrannies keep it fragmented and separate. I can imagine no cataclysm of history that would not leave any surviving Kurds with better reasons for internecine quarrels than for uniting.

Their hospitality is heartwarming. On the hot dusty drive to Rowanduz the bowl of *mast* or curdled milk, and the refreshment of *mastao*, a drink made of curdled milk and ice-cold water, welcomed us to the hills. I saw a good deal of this magnificent country, in visits to the poplars of Shaqlawa, to Aqra, to Zakho, or to the high plateau town of Amadia. But I can make no claim to close acquaintance with it. Everywhere it was a pleasure to see the women, unveiled and singing, as they worked in the fields. The men were more likely to be swaggering about on horseback, looking for a blood-feud.

If my district was picturesque, the people living in the Mosul 'Liwa', or administrative district, with their multitudinous faiths and creeds, were as colourful as the geography they inhabited. The Kurds and the desert Arabs were, of course, Moslems, but the Kurds are of Aryan stock, and different languages and racial origins made for different attitudes within Islam. Less familiar were some of the Christian minorities, the so-called Chaldeans and Assyrians. Unique were the Yezidis and the Sabaeans. Remains of ancient Syriac and other churches and monasteries littered the countryside. Some, among them Mar Behnam, standing in wholly Moslem villages, remain places of Christian pilgrimage. Others have become mosques. The great Mosque of Mosul, Jami'-al-Arbain, commemorates in its name the Forty Martyrs who suffered ordeal by cold water, and to whom, with St. Paul, it was once dedicated. The language spoken by some of these minorities is the Aramaic spoken by Our Lord: 'Why did you leave me?', spoken by a young Assyrian, would echo words that darkened the sky.

Away from the desert, the Moslem population of northern Iraq is not conspicuously Arab. Arabs there are, and plenty; but many have strains of Turkish, Turcoman or Persian blood, and the Kurds are a race apart. I found adjustment to the Iraqi man in the street difficult. Egyptians, who have very little Arab blood, have a keen sense of humour and have (or used to have) enough of an inferiority complex to sharpen their humour on jokes against themselves. The Beduin of Arabia have a sense of humour, also, and no complexes at all. The Iraqis, like the Palestinians, have next to no sense of humour, but their superiority complex is Manchu in its sweep. I could appreciate their virtues but could not find them *simpáticos*. They speak a clipped, thick-set Arabic, half-way between the classical simplicity of the Hejaz and the cockney liberties of Egypt, and their speech is spattered with Turkish and Persian words much as Pakistani Urdu is spattered with English. The *Mutassarif*, or governor, and I used to hold our conversations in classical Arabic, much to our mutual admiration.

When the Lord God planted a garden to the eastward in Eden, Tigris and Euphrates were two of the four heads of the river which 'went out of Eden to water the Garden'. Iraq thus meets us in the second chapter of Genesis, and it was to Iraq that Abraham sent his servant to find a wife for Isaac. In the context of the New Testament, also, the land came very early into Christian history; the Christians of the Mosul district have a long religious ancestry. The rock-monastery of Rabban Hormiz was a monastery in A.D. 300, and there was a Christian church in Mesopotamia long before that.

This church gained separate individuality, a new impulse of missionary zeal and a remarkable reputation when it broke with the Imperial Orthodox Church of Byzantium in A.D. 480, choosing to adopt the view of Nestorius that it was possible to distinguish the two persons as well as the two natures in Christ. The Nestorian Church, as it was then called, was followed in this schism by Christians in Persia and by elements of the Church in Syria also. Its activity became legendary. It established communities on the Malabar Coast of India, in the Yemen, in Bokhara and Tartary, and in China. The Tartar King who wrote to Alexius Comnenus, the Byzantine Emperor, signing himself Prester John, was a Nestorian convert. In a church at Jelu, in Kurdistan, Sir Henry

Layard found in 1850 'numerous China bowls and jars of elegant form and richly coloured, but black with the dust of ages', which had been 'brought from the distant Empire of Cathay by those early missionaries of the Chaldean Church . . .'. It is even possible that one of these missionaries of the late sixth or early seventh centuries may have had some influence on the eager mind of Mohammed himself, for there is a tradition of his acquaintance with a Nestorian monk. Certainly the Nestorians claimed privileges and protection guaranteed by a 'treaty' with the Prophet; Layard thinks there may have been some traditionary compact.

Known as the Nestorian Church for its doctrinal peculiarities, and as the Chaldean Church from its racial connexion with Mesopotamia, this ancient institution split, in 1552, into two conflicting halves. The breach, in fact, reflected geographical and perhaps racial, as well as religious, factors of dispute. The Assyrians, a subject-race since the fall of Nineveh, had from the first been the keenest supporters of the Nestorian Church. Over the centuries, they moved from the Mosul plain to the highlands of Kurdistan, leaving only a remnant settled at river-level. The inevitable tensions and growing difference of outlook between plainsmen and mountaineers led to a jealous rivalry for the Patriarchate, and one unsuccessful lowland abbot appealed to the Pope, who created him 'Patriarch of the East'. A Church of the Plains then feuded for two centuries with a Church of the Mountains. Later, when the Dominican Fathers settled in Mosul, the Church of the Plains became subservient to Rome and became known as the Chaldean Uniate Church, 'uniate' meaning a church adhering to its own rituals and appointing its own hierarchy, whilst at the same time acknowledging the sovereignty of Rome. According to Mr. Gransden, who is my authority for these events*, there were about 60,000 'Chaldeans' in my consular district when I was there; and these were loosely considered as Roman Catholics. The 'Assyrians', who had retained their Nestorian faith, had had, at that time, a recent past of turbulent adventure, pride and final tragedy.

For hundreds of years they had lived in pockets of the Hakkiari

* A. H. Gransden *Chaldean Communities in Kurdistan.*

mountains and other remote corners of Turkish Kurdistan, tough and fanatically devoted to what had become a rather misty doctrine; always exposed to attack or persecution from their Kurdish neighbours or the Turkish officials of the region. As a Christian minority, they were fair game; as fighters, they were respected. In 1914, on the outbreak of war with Turkey, the Assyrian tribes of Tiari, Tkhuma, Jelu and Baz, who lived in the Julamerk Vilayet of Turkey, broke out from their fastness and marched, women and children and all, across the mountains to join up with the Russians on Lake Urmia in Persia, believing that their faith and future were thereby secured. They were welcomed by the Russians as fellow-Christians, and—if I know them—soon began taking it out of the local Moslems. This paradise did not last long. The Russian Revolution punctured all Russian military balloons, and the hasty withdrawal of their new protectors left the Assyrians at the mercy of their newly-made enemies. During a nightmare exodus from Rezaieh into Iraq, when thousands of Assyrians died by the roadside, some British political officer or subaltern is alleged by the Assyrians to have guaranteed them British official protection.

Such a mass-immigration was embarrassing to the British mandatory authorities, but the menfolk were soon welcomed as recruits into the Iraq Levies, a British-officered force with mainly R.A.F. security duties. Their families found homes in villages in North Iraq already long settled by their co-religionists. During the period of the British mandate, the Assyrians served with ardour and, indeed, with religious zeal, for Moslems were the natural objects of their hostility. The fatal British officer-habit of assuring troops that they are ten times better than anyone else in sight, gave these Levies an overweening pride which the Arabs of Iraq found exasperating and provocative.

The end of the mandate, and its replacement by an unfettered Iraqi Moslem government, brought ruin to this small and arrogant minority. General Bekir Sidqi cordoned off their villages and gave his troops licence to avenge the stigma of inferiority which had marked them. Hundreds of Assyrians were butchered; the name of Simel village stank in civilised nostrils; and it became obvious that there was no future for an Assyrian in independent Iraq. Unfortunately, nobody else wanted them.

The League of Nations in Geneva sponsored appeals to all and sundry to find room anywhere for from twenty to twenty-five thousand unhappy refugees for whose welfare the British government felt painfully responsible. Their industry and craftsmanship, their Christian religion and high moral standards, their valuable military qualities, might have been expected to justify Australian or Brazilian hospitality; but no home could be found for them. It would be interesting to know what effect their settlement in Cyprus would have had on events there.

Finally, after years of argument and frustration in Geneva, the French government came up with a proposal that the Assyrians should be settled in Syria, under what was known as the 'Ghab Scheme'—a project for the redemption and *bonificazione* of an area, notoriously malarial, for the joint benefit of the French mandatory government and of a consortium of Paris banks. The Assyrians were to provide the labour on development and, later, the population cultivating the new crops. The League of Nations was to contribute heavily, as were the French and British governments, to the initiation of the scheme. Gratefully our negotiators commended this solution to their government, and an organised exodus of Assyrians from Iraq to Syria was started with League of Nations blessing, under the local control of Colonel Wilson, a former civil administrator of Mosul, and a Swiss engineer, Henri Cuénod.

By the time I reached Mosul, a number of caravans had already taken Assyrians to the Hassetché and Kemashlié areas of Syria, near to the Iraqi border, where they remained in a staging-camp, awaiting the next move west to the Ghab area. M. Cuénod was already a hostile critic of the whole venture. He went often to Beirut and Damascus, and he had become convinced by all he saw and heard on the spot that the scheme was a racket, designed to secure limitless finance from, among others, British government sources, for an uneconomic investment-project dreamed up by Big Finance in Paris. Moreover, the rigours of life in a malarial swamp could not, he thought, but decimate mountaineers unhappy in any plain. I made other enquiries, which seemed to confirm this pessimistic view. I began to fear not only that we were condemning our protégés to disease and death, but also that the unspecified extent of H.M.G.'s future financial responsibilities might well involve us in great expense and embarrassment. I reported these conclusions to the embassy in Bagdad, and they were forwarded, with no expression of disagreement, to London.

The able young man who handled this question on behalf of the Eastern department of the Foreign Office was, naturally, horrified by any prospect of having to resume his place in the Geneva orchestra and play, *da capo*, the monotonous discords of debate. I was told so, sharply, and was instructed to shut up and mind my own business.

This was a rebuff which I had no reason for resenting. But it still appeared to me that objections had been based on expediency rather than justice; and I was unhappy about this. I improperly discussed the issue frankly with my old friend Mr. Lumby, of *The Times*, when he passed through Mosul shortly afterwards. He was interested, and a short piece about the Ghab Scheme, under a Beirut dateline, soon appeared in his newspaper. This had the immediate effect of causing the French to throw up the sponge, and the Ghab Scheme was, for the then foreseeable future, stone-dead. The Assyrians from Iraq are now settled on the river Khabour in the Hassetché-Kemashlié sector of Syria, and they no longer cost the British government a penny. I find it difficult properly to regret this, the most unforgivable behaviour of my official life.

The Yezidis live mainly in the Jebel Sinjar, in the desert west of Mosul, but also around Ain Sifni, in the neighbourhood of their shrine, Sheikh Adi. They are commonly assumed to worship the Devil, and this reputation assumes a ritual of orgiastic horrors, entirely imaginary. As Sir Henry Layard discovered, when invited by the *Mir* of his day to be sponsor to his first-born son, it also involves equivocal responsibilities. Yezidis do not tell others much about their religion, and seem to accept some Supreme Being as ultimately in control. They do, however, put reverence for Satan before all else in their lives and ritual, believing that he will in due course be released from punishment and restored to his rank as an archangel; now he can do evil to the human race, but then he will have power to reward those who have sought throughout history to conciliate him. His name is never mentioned, and words beginning with the same syllable or even letter, or in any other way suggesting the sound of *Shaitan*, are taboo. Other taboos are lettuce, the colour blue, and buttons on shirt-collars. One very sacred object is an image of a bird, *Malik Ta'us* or the Lord Peacock, which is in the *Mir*'s keeping. His instructions to his flock are orally conveyed by messengers—there is a long tradition of imposed illiteracy—and these men carry small replicas of the peacock to prove their *bona fides*. Some ranks of their priesthood are hereditary and may even be filled by women. Their morals are exceptionally pure; their physical beauty is no less exceptional.

During my stay in Mosul, a running war was going on in the Jebel Sinjar between Iraqi forces, determined to impose conscription on this small and recalcitrant minority, and the Yezidis who fought from their bases in the mountain caves. The mere fact of having to wear button-up army-issue shirts was reason enough for Yezidi resistance. The fighting was never less than savage, and there was much killing and raping. Layard claims to have returned a Yezidi woman, who had been made a slave, to her grateful tribe. I was assured that no Yezidi woman who had been úsed by an Iraqi soldier would even consider a return to the tribe—defilement made her automatically outcast.

The Sabaeans of the Mosul region were not, I think, native there. They are more numerously found in other centres. They, too, have strange tenets of religion and a confused cosmogony. Popularly, they are assumed to venerate John the Baptist above all others. Wilfred Thesiger found them making boats for the Marsh Arabs in the Marshes between Kut and the Shatt-el-Arab. This would be a congenial occupation, for another of their articles of faith imposes residence near running water. They seemed to be gentle, dignified people, best known, perhaps, for their speciality of *niello*, familiar as 'Kut-el-Amara work'. Those napkin-rings and spoons with river-scenes annealed are made by the 'Subbis'.

Mosul also had, of course, its ancient colony of Jews. They

lived, and no doubt had lived since Old Testament days, in their own village, outside the city wall, direct descendants of those of the Captivity who sat down and wept by the waters of Babylon. Their Chief Rabbi and I were on calling terms, but they were not a comfortable group to frequent: their orthodoxy was extreme, and their total abstinence from any action definable as work for twenty-four hours each week made them all but unemployable, except by co-religionists.

There is a danger, when recording the origins and faiths of exotic communities like these, that perspective may be distorted; as if an impression were created that London is inhabited by its Italian, West Indian or Jewish elements alone. Minorities are interesting and they often affect history. Armenians are massacred; Sudeten Germans are Fifth Columnists; Syrian Christians invoke French interest and protection; Copts represent what is unalterable in Egyptian characteristics; Pakistan is born because Mr. Jinnah considers 80 million Moslems 'too many to be a minority in an independent India'. But it would be a false picture of the Mosul consular district that showed only the picturesque remains of communities retaining shreds of faiths dating from before the imperial spread of Islam, or claiming descent from Chaldean astronomers and Assyrian tyrants. There were also great numbers of more orthodox Christians of indigenous race, themselves a comprehensive 'minority', with the fears and suspicions natural to their status. The majority of my neighbours were, of course, Moslems; and in Mosul town Islam was a way of life practised with particular fanaticism.

*　　*　　*

Mosul was officially labelled 'unhealthy' for purposes both of leave and of pension; but I found it a much healthier place than Cairo, where millennia of dust blow about unwashed by any rain, with damaging effect on eyes and throat. Our Mosul sand-storms were, at least, made up of honest sand. The climate was stimulating: in summer, 120 degrees in the shade; in winter 20 degrees below freezing. This was good for our metabolism, which was kept in a state of constant adjustment. The summer heat made long-distance motoring uncomfortable. I sent my small family and the nurse up to Rayat on the Persian frontier for six weeks respite, which they spent under canvas, and the little caravan was most unhappy. More than once, driving back from Rowanduz with towels over our faces to retain some moisture in our breath, we would strip and lie, holding on to the wheels of the car, in the snow-cold water of the Lesser Zab. Crossing these flooded rivers was a special skill, and one had to remember to unship the fan, with water above wheel-level. In a winter world that became unrecognisable, my elder son made a family of snow-men, all wearing a white fez.

We had little social contact with our Iraqi neighbours. At official parties I might meet the Chaldean Patriarch, a figure of great age, great girth and great dignity, or the Dominican Superior, or senior Iraqi officials; but, except for the *Mutassarif*, Mustafa el-Umari, there were no exchanges of hospitality on that level. With only one local family were we on visiting terms: in the Rassam drawing-room I was interested to see souvenirs of the vice-consul who had aided Layard in his journeys and excavations, and whose adventures in Ethiopia before and during Napier's expedition are part of history.

One reason for an uncharacteristic abstinence from local colour was, of course, a keen anxiety not to compromise local friends. In those early days of Iraq's independence, every British official was by hypothesis suspect to Iraqi authority as a plotter, interested only in inciting various minorities to rebellion and revolt; anxious only to revive an imperialist past. A display of friendship might only damage its object.

The European civilian community was not large. The former civil administrator found it hard to stomach consular pretensions to precedence. The British commandant of police suffered the discomforts of reconciling a professional conscience with the new compromises expected of him. We had a formidably Irish judge and a scatter of businessmen and bankers. It was to No. 30 Squadron, R.A.F. that we owed most of the excitements and pleasures of life in Mosul society.

This squadron had been commanded by a redoubtable man,

'Tanks' Chamberlayne, whose overriding purpose had been to fit his men for war. Low-flying was encouraged, and every hazard accepted, if not imposed. Many of his officers had made the nightmare flight through the Rowanduz Gorge and back again, and one initiation-rite was the descent, first made by the Officer Commanding, into a nauseous pit in the desert where a myriad pigeons nested in a mass of guano centuries high. The squadron's bombing was the best in Iraq, and its *esprit de corps* was exceptional. But rules are rules; all that low-flying was officially condemned. Arthur Fiddament was sent to replace Chamberlayne, with instructions to restore discipline. His role made him unpopular, and in the field of personal relations No. 30 Squadron was not a band of brothers.

These young men, denied any family life by service regulations, were something of a social problem. One expects a buzzing of bees round any available honey-pot, but this was a hive of hornets. They worked hard to make life in Mosul enjoyable. They organised dances in the quarters where General Bekir Sidqi was later assassinated. They organised picnics to the streams behind Nineveh, or to the remarkable Parthian ruins of Hatra. To drive to Hatra in the spring, when winter's mud and summer's dust lay hidden by a multi-coloured carpet of wild flowers, was a delight and a pain, for our cars trampled like juggernauts through the anemones and lilies. Once there, apart from the tall buildings that remain, there was not much to see; but one pilot told me that mounds and hollows, hardly noticeable when one approaches the place on foot, become walls and fortifications when seen from a height of 5,000 ft.; and that, from twice that height, a further network of streets and separate houses becomes visible. This familiar phenomenon is splendidly manifest when one flies above Samarra, on the way to Bagdad. Nothing of interest can be seen at ground-level, but from the aeroplane one looks down on a great chariot-course in figure-of-eight loops, worthy of Ben Hur. Long-smothered irrigation canals become new again to airmen on this route, and the Caliph's boast that a bird could hop from bough to bough all the way from Mosul to Bagdad becomes suddenly and fantastically acceptable.

Mosul town was a rabbit-warren of stinking lanes, criss-crossing and confusing; but one long main street ran for the full length and crossed another, running the full breadth of this warren. The famous Colonel Leachman, the Government of India's answer to the Cairo Arab Bureau's Lawrence, had cut these swathes through slumdom, to enable at least a minimum of police-patrolling and control. His approach was delicate and diplomatic, for he called for a revaluation of all house-property in the town and received, predictably enough, some divertingly exaggerated minimisations of value, since some increase in municipal taxation was generally assumed. Armed with each landlord's sworn mendacities, he then requisitioned the property at the declared value, knocked it down, and built his two major arteries.

I never met Leachman living, but I had a shadowy association with Leachman dead. When, already a legend, he was murdered by a hostile Arab who escaped arrest, a reward was offered for the criminal's capture. Years later, a humble Armenian cobbler in Damascus spotted the man, and spent over a year cruising Damascus in a taxi-cab, with his brother beside him in the front seat, before he was lucky enough to pick up his quarry as a fare. The two brothers managed to drive with their prisoner across the desert to Bagdad and there to deliver him. But by that time interest in the matter had waned with a change of régime, and only a small sum was paid to set the Armenian up in business as a cobbler in Cairo, where he had taken refuge from Arab revenge. I was his paymaster there.

In one of the main streets of Mosul a ramshackle cinema showed elderly Westerns twice a week to an Arab audience rarely reaching double figures. Visits to this hovel were another form of team-expedition. We would arrive after dinner in the evening, equipped with ice-boxes in summer and with paraffin stoves in winter, and the manager always began the programme all over again for our benefit. Other clients must have thought the western way of life a strangely recurrent phenomenon. Every now and then a crackle of rifle-fire from the stalls meant that some unsophisticated member of the audience, eager that virtue should triumph, had pooped off, either to lame the horse or to shoot the silver screen through a villain's heart.

*　　*　　*

In the event, the various conflicting international interests involved in the British Oil Development Company found a formula for agreement, and their problems gave me no trouble. Later, in 1942, the concession was transferred to the Mosul Petroleum Company: I have not heard that any marketable oil has been produced. Qaiyyara, the company's headquarters some seventy miles down the Baghdad road, is not a place I wanted to visit twice. Great quantities of bitumen have been discovered there, and one smells the stuff long before the township comes into sight. The stench in Qaiyyara itself is all-pervading. I was told that one kind of gas, fatal in a 1 % mixture, poured out of the Qaiyyara field at 35 % strength. The staff bungalows, most hospitable to a visitor, were heated by throwing lumps of bitumen into a fireplace deepened to catch the burning liquid; there was a smear of black moisture everywhere. The phrase 'the Mosul oilfields' appeared often in political pamphlets of that time; but this was not a flattering reference to Qaiyyara; the oil in question was that of the great Kirkuk field of the Iraq Petroleum Company, 125 miles S.E. of Mosul, but still in the Mosul administrative district.

We drove past Qaiyyara without stopping, one winter's day, on a visit to the embassy in Bagdad. For over a hundred miles to the south of Mosul the ground was deep under snow; it was impossible to guess where the road ran. The camels we met or overtook were hopelessly at sea: their padded feet gave them no grip, and they slithered about like children on a slide. When the snow disappeared, the road was still invisible for miles on end. We drove across a wide desert plain with a choice of up to seven different tracks fanning out to the horizon. After Baiji, where the railway began again on this western route, we continued a long journey through Tekrit and through Samarra and Kazimain, both glorious with their golden domes. When dusk fell, there was a close expectation of bandits and this did nothing to make time

194

fly. On our return journey, we stopped to visit Ashour, the ruins of the first capital of the Assyrian empire. Its roofless dwellings lie, below ground-level, open to the sky. Many ancient sites leave this impression of smallness of houses and narrowness of streets, and in Ashour no grandeur of palace and temple and forum finds reflexion in a cramped and crowded slum of antiquity.

One very happy memory is of a drive that took us to Ain Sifni and on to the Yezidi country. We left the car some way from the shrine of Sheikh Adi, and went on foot to the point where tall trees stand like exclamations of surprise in the tawny desert scene. We found ourselves in a large grove of oak trees, unique in that part of Iraq, where ferns grew in the undergrowth and birdsong whistled from the entangled branches overhead. Within this grove, all life is sacred, and the birds knew it. Beyond, we came to the simple white-spired shrine where the saint is buried. Even though expected, that black snake, carved on the white-washed lintel of the doorway, shocks like a woman's blasphemy.

It was a Yezidi feast-day. We made no attempt to approach the shrine or the pilgrims, but sat watching them, entranced. There was continuous singing and dancing; gay and mischievous, or ritual and solemn. The young men and women were in festival dress; the men gorgeous in brocades, the girls with gold coins in their hair and a great billowing of coloured scarves. Only a few of the younger women were in simple white. I do not remember ever seeing more beautiful people. They paid no attention to us as they danced, or played complicated games in rings, or challenged each other to rivalry in some special skill. All was done with a gaiety and delight and transparent innocence primitive in its unconscious loveliness. When our driver whispered something about our return, I found we had been sitting there for over five hours. We turned again into the dark wood that separated the dust and glare of Baadri from the bright dancers, whose sunshine seemed to have dawned in another world than ours.

When Archie Clark-Kerr rang up from Bagdad to say that he and Tita were planning a visit to Mosul, it was to Sheikh Adi that I first thought of taking them. But there are not Yezidi festivals on every day of the year; and I suggested, after taking the necessary desert soundings, that we might visit the Shammar tribe, in the western desert beyond Jebel Sinjar. The Sheikh of this great confederation was Ajil al Yawer, a towering, handsome man, 6 feet 7 inches tall, and he was delighted to entertain His Majesty's ambassador and party. The Clark-Kerrs drove from Bagdad, with Vyvyan Holt, the Oriental Secretary, and a pallid, intelligent young man, some sort of honorary attaché, who for reasons not easily explained was known as the 'Dead Boy'.

The drive out to the Shammar encampment was dusty and uneventful; our reception there was enthusiastic. Holt and I were familiar with Arab hospitality, but the ambassador was not, and we were kept busy ensuring conformity with conventions. By that time the ambassador had developed his Scottish complex—his mother was a Kerr—and every detail of Bedu life was painstakingly compared and likened to the habits of North Britain: I got tired of the word *Iskotlanda*. My happiest memory of our days in the Shammar tents is of Tita Clark-Kerr, the original Pocket Venus, pacing the sands by the side of a gigantic Sheikh Ajil. Her questions about his sons revealed in the father a basic ignorance of their names. But he did know when each had been born. 'This,' he would say, introducing some pretty child, 'is 1930. That one over there is 1928. Next to him is 1931.' It was like being taken round a Cambridge College cellar. Sheikh Ajil's hospitality was not wholly disinterested, for there was talk of an extension of the railway from Tel Kotchek through Mosul to Baiji, and he wanted to obtain the contract for labour on the northern track.

During our last night in the desert the heavens opened and torrential rains brought joy to the tribe. Not to us. The road back to Mosul was a Cresta Run of bottomless mud, and our cars teetotummed about like tops, and slithered cannoning from bank to bank. Our cars had chains, and could be kept fairly steady; but the ambassadorial transport made only drunken progress. We all got out, bare-legged with trousers to the knee, and pushed or pulled, or tore brushwood and grass to lay beneath the whirring wheels. Archie showed the quality that was later to endear him to all in bombed Chungking by leading these endeavours, wearing, and that under duress, trousers only. His honorary attaché refused to take part. He read poetry. I saw him at one moment peer from the window of a spinning car at his unwearied master. 'How odd!' said the Dead Boy, and resumed his reading. We took nine hours for a three-hour drive home.

Not long after this excursion, Archie Clark-Kerr suggested that I should transfer to the consulate in Bagdad, hoping that I might do there the sort of work I had enjoyed in the Oriental secretariat in Cairo. His own Oriental Secretary, Vyvyan Holt, later to suffer as our ambassador in Seoul, was by formation a Yogi-soldier, and by experience an old Bagdad hand who detested all forms of social activity and confined his contacts with Iraqis to the office and the polo-ground. I had to explain that, as British consul, my duties would lie with the British community, who would certainly resent, as 'playing about with Iraqis', any efforts of mine to cultivate and to entertain the people of the country. I was, however, very willing to exchange Mosul, the place where my marriage had finally broken down, for Bagdad. After a brief leave, I found my immediate successor, Maurice Eyres, already installed in Mr. Panfil's castle and handed over to him. His father, Sir Harry Eyres, had been a great figure in our service, and Maurice himself was one of its adornments. He had a philosophy which eschewed any excess, not least of zeal, and admirable taste in food and wine. He only remained a few months in Mosul.

The ambassador's invitation to Bagdad may well have saved my life, for it was less than two years after my departure that a group of young hotheads in Mosul were planning a demonstration outside the house of my elderly and world-weary French colleague to mark their displeasure at the French government's refusal to ratify a draft treaty with Syria. While they were assembling, rumours from Bagdad, made circumstantial by German drafting, told them not only that the young king had met a tragic end (which was true: in a car-accident), but also that the British had planned and effected his murder. The young politicians decided to transfer their hostile interest to the British consulate. This was in early April 1939, when Monck-Mason was already installed as consul.

o

He had sent one *cavass* to take a flowery message of condolence to the mutassarif, and the other *cavass* was busy in a garage of the town. The consulate was therefore unguarded. The demonstrators were joined, when near the building, by a gang of navvies working on the site of the projected railway-station, and these men did not leave the tools of their trade behind them. Crowbars and pick-axes soon opened all doors to the mob, which began by setting the ground-floor ablaze.

Monck-Mason spent precious moments on the upper floor in choosing a hiding-place for the wireless-set which I had sent up to him the week before. When the demonstrators crowded up the staircase, he did what I should probably have done: he started to make a speech in Arabic. This was soon cut short by a pickaxe through his brain. Fat Efraim hid on the top roof; the cook, screaming, flung himself over the banisters and escaped through the flames. After an hour or more, troops, alerted by our Irish neighbour, arrived and stopped the trouble.

This episode is, I fear, typical of the place of its occurrence. You will find the same dark stain of blood in any tapestry of Mosul weaving.

Chapter Five

Non-Belligerenza

Mr. Nevile Chamberlain's declaration of war with Germany found me on a Yorkshire beach, convalescing from a split-cartilage operation which I should have had, but could not afford, any time in the preceding thirty-three years. Remembering those Russians who hastened to our succour in 1914 with snow on their boots, I was interested by a suddenly universal rumour about our new death-ray, which was guaranteed to stop any invading tank in its tracks. The cars of farmer A, near Staithes, young B, up Whitby way, and a fleet of other vehicles had, circumstantially, found themselves mysteriously unable to proceed. I suppose this synthetic encouragement was dosed out by higher authority.

I informed the Foreign Office that I was making immediate arrangements for return to my post in Baghdad, where I had served for two years after leaving Mosul. I was instructed to stay where I was: other plans had been made for me. It was two months before I could learn what these plans were, and only when ignorance of my own future had become a bad joke was it confided to me that I was to go to Albania, as Consul-General.

Some element of furtive purpose in this appointment is under-standable. The Italian invasion of Albania on Good Friday, 1939, had been followed by the withdrawal of our legation, with one vice-consul left to attend to current affairs, and by firm non-recognition of Albania's new status. It was presumably assumed later that British recognition might count for merit in our effort to keep Italy out of the war; but the great British public would certainly have protested had this recognition been advertised at a moment when we were already busily fighting Italy's Axis partner. My appointment as Consul-General in Albania, which required King Victor Emmanuel's signature on my *exequatur*, discreetly and implicitly recognised his imperial authority over my new consular district.

I enquired about my goods and chattels left in Bagdad, and was assured that these might safely be transferred to Albania, because there was every hope that Italy would not enter the war. This official optimism was to cost me dear.

I crossed the Channel on a cold, blustering day, and the voyage from Dover to Boulogne took over four hours, because of mine-fields. This seemed a very long time to a nauseated passenger half-choked by the obligatory Mae West lifebelt round his neck. I had a diplomatic passport and was second off the boat at Boulogne. Ahead of me, already warming himself at the station restaurant fire, I found Sir Seymour Hicks, who invited me to join his party for luncheon—it was then 3.30 p.m. With Claire Booth, the actress, and Tom Webster, the cartoonist, he was on his way to entertain the troops; and he reacted thunderously when a gangling young officer came up and asked whether he formed part of Miss Gracie Field's troupe. We had a very long, very good and very well lubricated meal, and I was laughing most of the time.

After London's black-out, Paris seemed strangely pallid and twilit, and the thrill of finding illuminated fountains and a blaze of street-lamps in Rome was tonic. I stayed some days with the Scriveners, in search of an embassy briefing on Albania which I never found. Rome was blatantly non-belligerent, advertising everywhere Fascist contempt for the decadent West, while reserving hostilities for a later date. George Labouchere, then a Second Secretary, was in trouble for tearing down one insulting poster. My visit included a luncheon in an Orsini villa whose lovely rooms were hung about with Cardinals' hats, and a first meeting with Alan Moorehead. The desert war then lay ahead of us, and I suspect that Alan was still primarily and resentfully thought of in the Beaverbrook enterprise as Lucy Milner's husband.

I shared a carriage from Rome to Bari with a tough young Fascist bound for Tirana, and crossed with him to Durazzo, where Herbert Gamble, the vice-consul, and Frank Borman, the archivist, welcomed me to Albania. The three of us made up one-half of the total British community in the country.

Before the Italian invasion of that spring, there had been a small but select British colony. Frank Stafford and General Percy had run a local gendarmerie, British-officered, but they had gone. With them, Mrs. Pennington of the Aubrey Herbert Institute and Mrs. Hasluck, whose *Albanian Grammar* I studied, had followed our Minister Sir Andrew and Lady Ryan to England. I was left with one Maltese born in Corfu, living in Porto Edda, one U.K.-born Albanian in Tirana, and a derelict British mechanic who had for years lived with and on an Albanian washerwoman.

The diplomatic corps of Ryan's day had also melted away. The German Minister stayed on as consul-general; and Greece, Yugoslavia, Turkey and Rumania had made consuls-general of their former counsellors or secretaries of Legation. But France, the United States, the Scandinavian countries, and all others previously represented, still refused to recognise the Italian rape of Albania: my consular colleagues were exclusively Balkan. The German and I bowed stiffly to each other at official receptions, and I found him sympathetic, when deviously approached, to my efforts to succour the small group of German and Austrian Jews who had fled to King Zog's shelter from persecution, and were now in jeopardy again. We could do little to help them, and only extracted one (Christian) Jewish girl, who was able to find a home in Edinburgh. Many obtained visas for the United States, only to find that the Italians prevented their necessary journey from Albania to Naples to catch their steamer. The German consul-general in Tirana was liberal-minded about this; but Mussolini was by then more Hitlerian than Hitler's own representative, and those pathetic passports, officially stamped with the Star of David and with the compulsory first-names of 'Abraham' and 'Sara', were a total obstacle to travel.

Giacomoni, the former Italian Minister, had remained in Tirana as 'Lieutenant-General'; he was nervously pompous in the role of Head of Government. Madame Giacomoni was as popular as he was not, and was indefatigable in good works. The real power lay with the Secretary-General, Piero Parini, a handsome fanatic whom I had known in Egypt when he was Head of the Organisation of Fascists Overseas, a key-post in Fascist machinery. Indeed, the Cairo Residency had vetoed his appointment as Minister to Egypt; and his awareness of this fact, and of my own connexion with Cairo, did not sweeten our relations. Unlike conditions in Ethiopia, another victim of Fascist expansion, there had been no pre-invasion European and anti-Fascist Italian residents in Albania. Our wartime society was almost exclusively composed of post-invasion Italian service elements and post-invasion Fascist officials and propagandists, all missionary-minded and actively eager for their country's entry into the war against Western decadence. The hostility shown by Britain to Mussolini's invasion of Ethiopia, and the economic sanctions then unsuccessfully imposed, had excited passions barely concealed in all professional Fascists. Their conversation was continuously provocative, and inflammatory anti-British posters proclaimed Italy's arrogant contempt for British policies and British statesmen.

Apart from a few members of the Albanian Quisling régime under Verlaçi, we met few Albanians at Italian parties, and could not prudently entertain them ourselves. One pretty contact used to whisper treason while we were dancing, but I never tried to encourage confidences which might be suicidal. To salute all but a few Albanians in the street was to condemn them to sharp discomfort in the Questura. We were always followed by the secret police when in Durazzo or Tirana, and our telephone was always tapped.

The mass of Albanians were still numbed by the sudden shock and complete success of the April invasion. They were cowed: an uncharacteristic Albanian attitude. It might have been otherwise, had King Zog decided to withdraw north from Tirana, to destroy the mountain roads at strategic points and to lead his tribesmen in resistance. Instead, he chose to accompany his queen and their two-day-old son to sanctuary in Greece, and this his people did not forgive. Later in the war, I strongly advised against a plan for parachuting Zog into his native mountains: I felt sure that no one would follow him.

One can appreciate the feelings of a husband and father, but these sentiments, if they clash with patriotic purpose, are less acceptable in Albania than elsewhere. The country has a long history of implacable resistance to foreign authority, and the most ancient race in south-eastern Europe, descending, I believe, from the earliest Aryan immigrants, has retained its individuality for millennia in wild and inaccessible mountain strongholds. Gibbon is often quoted as describing Albania as a country, within sight of Italy, which was less known than the interior of America of his day. Even the Turks, in their four hundred years of domination, had to grant the Albanians exemption from taxation and from conscription, and had to leave to them their own laws and customs. North of the Via Ignatia, running roughly from Durazzo to Salonika, are the Ghegs—Spanish in morose and haughty pride; south are the Tosks, more affably Italian in character. The tribes of the north are mostly Moslem, but the Mirdite confederation there is Roman Catholic: religion is less important than tribal ties. The sister of a Moslem friend, formerly ambassador in London and Minister for Foreign Affairs, was called Afrodita. All have, or had, a savage attachment to the vendetta as a way of life, ordained by their 'Law of Lek Dukajin', and in some tribes only one quarter of the men died a natural death. These blood-feuds excluded women from their operation. There are girls in those high mountains who bring to marriage the purest European strain of beauty.

I never managed to learn Albanian, partly because I should have found no one to speak it with. It is a most venerable language. I cannot believe that it really gave to the Greeks the names of their divinities—indeed I am incompetent to discuss it—but it has an interesting quality, a sort of shorthand of familiar words: the Albanian for 'friend' is 'mik'; for 'dog', 'kien'; for 'Alexander', 'Lek'. It is tempting to think of these curtailments as originals, but they may only be adoptions.

★　　★　　★

The British Legation in Durazzo had been the only one standing outside the capital, and a new Legation-building was already under construction in Tirana when Italy's occupation shifted all local diplomatic representation to Rome. This promised me a

fine residence for the distant future, but there was then a wide
enough difference between diplomatic and consular salaries and
allowances, particularly in matters of furnishings and accoutre-
ments, to darken the prospect of a move from Durazzo. I was in
no hurry to furnish the large new building at my own expense
and to live palatially beyond my means. Life in Albania was
aggressively expensive. In King Zog's time, the 'gold franc'
was soundly based on a large gold reserve, and Sir Andrew Ryan
got value for his money. The Italians shipped all the gold to
Rome and imposed an artificial rate for the Italian *lira*, so that
prices rocketed and we suffered a grave financial haemorrhage in
loss on exchange. Fuel for our fires or the kitchen-stove, or for
heating the two bath-geysers, was a local thorn-bush, and a small
bundle cost eight shillings. Heating cost us many pounds a day.
Other daily expenses were comparably shocking. My appeals for
reconsideration of my allowances to compensate for this prejudice
were only answered two days before I left the post.

Our house in Durazzo, where Vice-Consul Gamble and I lived
and had our office, was picturesque and charming, (Borman
lodged elsewhere). It had foaming wisteria over the gate, an old
well-head in the courtyard, and one wall of the house dated from
the Venetian occupation of the fourteenth century. As an ex-
Legation, it had been officially furnished and equipped. We had a
Moslem cook, a Moslem house-boy and a Roman Catholic
chauffeur and handyman, Kol (Albanian shorthand for Nicholas).
The Albanian secretary, Mr. Triphoni Toni, had been there for
many years. Our *cavass* was a large Russian, Porphyry Gladky,
imported by Sir Ralph Hodgson when he was promoted to
Albania from the consulate in Moscow. Kol's pretty blond wife
and her sister laundered for us and did some housework.

For some months, I enjoyed life; the strains of work in an
all-but-enemy country were cumulative. We exchanged entertainment with our Balkan colleagues, and I learned unwillingly
to live with the convention of tipping after private parties, and
watching my own domestic staff line up after luncheon with
hands outstretched.

When the Giacomonis gave a party in Tirana, I used to spend

the night with the Yugoslav Miltitch and his wife, who were most hospitable. His vice-consul, Crititch, interested me, for he was marked by the experience of drowning in Lake Okhrida the year before. He had been rescued long after life seemed extinct, and he remembered much of what he had seen and felt before he was, most unwillingly, resuscitated.

On Sundays, we went for picnics along the coast, which was less attractive than I had hoped. Those lovely rocky cliffs rising from the blue Adriatic in Yugoslav tourist-posters give way, further south, to cliffs with feet of clay, and the sea was turbid and muddy for a long way out from the wash and erosion of their soil. Our tramps over those hills showed us monstrous lizards and strange plants, all catalogued for us by the omniscient Borman. Asphodel was a disappointment.

Our only excursion was to Kruja, north of Tirana, the home-town of the legendary Skanderbeg, whose ruined citadel we explored. Under his leadership, for the first and last time, all the tribes of Albania had united against the Turkish invaders. But of Albania I really know less than of the Southern Sudan. We never went south to Vallona or Argyrocastro, or north to Scutari, or east to Lake Okhrida and Koritsa, or even to Elbassan and Berat in the centre of the country. Tourism would not have been an acceptable excuse, and we had no other. Before long, we dared not stray far from our office.

In those early days we went for wide-ranging country walks, over smooth hills capped with little farms and across stile after stile (they have a very special stile), field after field, and olive-grove after olive-grove, trying to lose ourselves before unwinding the thread of our wandering. These walks, also, had to be abandoned, as the growing animosity of official and unofficial Italy inflamed to threaten our peace of mind.

The day came when a clamour of shouts and curses took me to a window, and I saw a large crowd, exclusively Italian, demonstrating noisily against us. The various *bonificazione* projects provided huskies for such occasions. My vice-consul had gone to Tirana on official business, and the archivist and I had to watch while the mob surged towards the house. But their attention soon focused on a young man who clambered nimbly from outhouse-roof to balcony, and from one roof-level to another, until he reached our flagpole, tore the flag down and threw it to his friends below, amid loud cheering and applause. This was a horrid thing to see. We had no fire-arm in the house, and I do not think it would have been advisable to use it, had we had one. With hindsight, I realise that I should have turned the fire-extinguishers upon the young acrobat, but that thought came too late. I felt ill with frustration and shame, and I later heard that several Albanians were seen weeping in the streets.

I reported the event to Tirana at once, asking for the punishment of all concerned and reserving my Government's right to demand any satisfaction they thought appropriate. I also demanded an immediate apology, and this was forthcoming. My report to London produced a reply from Lord Halifax, deploring the outrage; but he asked me to accept the apology as satisfaction enough, because His Majesty's Government did not wish for any exacerbation of relations with Italy at that moment. The pulling down of a country's flag had, in the past, been a *casus belli*.

We had been under much strain for months past. Gamble, on his return from the capital, was shocked to hear what had happened. Our chauffeur, Kol, was even more shaken, for news of the outrage removed his reason. The cook and houseboy brought him into my bedroom at 3 a.m. next morning, haggard and raving, and he was taken to hospital. Gamble was shaving when I went in to his room before breakfast. 'Kol went mad in the night!' I said. He stared at me, turned up his eyes, and fell flat on his back in a faint. While I was doing the obvious things to restore him (he was never made aware of this faint) I found myself hoping that Borman, at least, would report for duty as usual that day.

After that, we were too apprehensive of some organised irruption by Fascist extremists, in which our office safe and its ciphers and confidential archives might be a target, to risk leaving the house unoccupied. We had not had much straight consular work to do beyond occasionally quoting to Messrs. Dunhill the price of briar-roots. Our main activity was to identify and indicate to the Rome embassy any *mostre*, or military insignia, we observed; and the military attaché in Rome was thus able to inform London of the arrival, location and/or possible departure of this or that Italian Division. As we had valuable local assistance in the collection of this information, our archives on the subject were dynamite. By the spring of 1940, the possibility of danger to our ciphers and files became an obsession, and we yearned to be rid of them. Any officer allowing a Foreign Office cipher to be compromised is Public Enemy No. 1 in Whitehall. And we held our informants' lives in those thin manila files.

Meanwhile, in Rome, our ambassador's efforts to keep Italy out of the war unwearyingly continued. Sir Percy Loraine had an uncanny gift of influence over the foreign statesmen he had to deal with, notably manifest in Ankara. Count Ciano, Mussolini's son-in-law and Foreign Minister, was responsive to this influence; he played much golf with the ambassador and they talked about a possible Anglo-Italian treaty. Italy desperately needed coal. Britain offered all the coal she needed, and offered a practical interest in a long and comprehensive shopping-list of Italian goods: aeroplanes, materials for uniforms, anything the Italians wanted to sell. Such an agreement, commercial in appearance, could not but engage on our side the interest of all Italian industry, gilding Italian neutrality and riveting the Italian businessman tightly to a hope of British military success. But Mussolini, whom Loraine was able to meet only twice during his tour in Rome, refused to go back on the word he had pledged to Hitler. Italy's entry into the war became only a matter of time.

When war breaks out between two countries, various courtesies are still observed: arrangements are made for a third party to take charge of the interests of each of the combatants—the Swiss are in great demand in this role—and all officially representative persons are given safe-conduct out of the enemy country to which they are accredited. One of the last things done is to burn ciphers, codes and confidential archives; but do this too soon, and you cut yourself off from home. Correspondence about the various procedures that are indicated when the risk of war is (a) possible, or (b) certain, kept us busy; long cipher-telegrams on which we all worked, seemed always to arrive in the early hours or late at night. We discreetly packed up our possessions, most of which we should have to leave behind us. We hoped to be able to drive Gamble's Chevrolet and the official Armstrong-Siddeley, laden with our personal effects, by way of Koritsa into neutral Greece. I had no United States colleague to whom to hand over British interests, and I received no alternative instructions about that. I made sure that our three rather dim compatriots had warning to get out of Albania while the going was good.

The one exception to Italian bloody-mindedness in uniform was Admiral da Zara, commanding the naval base at Durazzo. He was unfailingly friendly, and always caustic about the régime. He came from a Venetian family hitherto historically cavalry, and the horse figured largely in his thinking. Over the tea-cups, he would ask me which was the top-weight for the big race at Ponte-fract on Wednesday, or what I fancied for the 3.30 at Salisbury tomorrow. When we were counting the days for war to start, he offered to keep in safe custody any treasures of silver, pictures or books I might care to leave with him. I was touched by this almost improper suggestion, but felt it impossible to take advantage of it. I did, however, ask him to accept and drink to my health in some.cases of whisky, which I saw no reason to present to the security police. I next heard of him when he formally handed over the Italian Grand Fleet after the Italian armistice. I have no doubt he at once asked the nearest British admiral for all the latest news of the turf.

We did not listen regularly to the Italian broadcasts, finding their propaganda-content too nauseating. But by God's good grace we did hear Mussolini, in the early evening of June 9, announce for the following morning the outbreak of hostilities. All our fires were hurriedly lit; and for ninety minutes we stoked them with apparently uninflammable ciphers and codes, and with shoals of despatches and flimsies. All was ash at last: our relief was orgasmic. As we straightened up in a stench of burning, two Italian functionaries from Tirana belatedly arrived—thank Heaven for that terrible road!—to discuss our immediate future. One was Rainaldi, late Italian Consul-General in San Francisco, who had recently been appointed *Chef de Protocole* in Tirana. We were told that we were to accompany our visitors to Tirana at once, and sleep there, before leaving by air next morning for Brindisi and by train from there to Ancona. A couple of suit-cases each was the limit of our luggage. I asked whether our colleagues in the embassy in Rome had been similarly restricted on luggage, and insisted on permission for us to send one cabin-trunk each by sea from Durazzo to Greece, for collection as and when possible. As Signor Rainaldi was professionally embarrassed by my inability to hand over the charge of British interests to anyone in Tirana, I wrote, explaining the situation, to the United States ambassador in Rome, giving Rainaldi a copy. Foreign Office authority to burn my ciphers reached me as I entered the 'plane next day.

On our journey to Ancona we were accompanied by Rainaldi, and by an officer and a non-commissioned officer of police. Rainaldi was courteous and friendly throughout, and the others were strictly correct. These stirrup-cup courtesies were my first and last experience of official Italian politeness.

In an Ancona hotel, we were detained for two days, as hostages for the departure from Malta of the Italian consular staff there, delayed by their own side's bombing operations until June 13. I made every excuse for contacts with Italians while so detained and was granted permission for a hair-cut and a manicure, which made possible some discreet enquiries. All my visitors professed to deplore Italy's entry into the war.

At last, on June 13, we were put on board the *Conte Rosso*, just home from a Far Eastern cruise, spotless white and luxurious. When our consul from Rhodes had arrived, the British embassy and consular staff were ready to sail, and were due to do so at 8 p.m. But during the morning, Scrivener took me aside and told me that the Italian Consul-General in Canada, Count Manassei de Collestatte (who had married Lord Perth's daughter) had been unable yet to leave Canada with his staff, and the Italian government required hostages from the *Conte Rosso*, which would sail without them, for his unimpeded departure from Canada. Specifically, they asked for one consul-general, two consuls, three vice-consuls and, I think, a press-attaché; and I was chosen to lead these hostages. I protested that I had already done time in Ancona, but selections had been made by pricking lists at random with a pin, and I could not dispute my destiny. I was also asked, very properly, to keep my immediate future to myself, so as to avoid discomfort to others on board. There was no obvious way of sending the little group to which I was to belong back to England, and I was annoyed by the prospect of a long sojourn in wartime Italy.

News of this predicament somehow leaked. Herbert Gamble came up to my deck-chair in the afternoon and asked if what he had heard was true. When I said that it unfortunately was, he replied: 'I should like to stay behind with you.' This, from a friend who had shared every turn of the screw in our garrison-life in Durazzo, was almost too much for my emotions, and I shall never forget it. In the event, the United States ambassador in Rome was able to ensure an Italian exodus from Canada, and at 8 p.m. we all sailed together for Lisbon, where we were to change ships with the Italian embassy officials from London. The *Conte Rosso*, floodlit at night and with the word DIPLOMAT in huge letters on her sides, had been cleared with all submarines and warships in the Mediterranean before we set out to sea.

*　　*　　*

We were an unlikely boatload, for some of the wives of the subordinate staff of the embassy were Italians, who had never left Italy before; and there was at least one unhappy German wife. Many of the men were unsure of another job in wartime; none of us knew where we should go next. The Italian sailors were frankly contemptuous of so civilian a party, and two British Council officers, who used to knit all day long while chattering together, convinced them of Anglo-Saxon decadence. Sir Percy Loraine kept himself to himself as far as the crowd could see, playing bridge all but uninterruptedly, in three long morning, afternoon and evening sessions, to distract his mind from the reception that awaited him. Sir Noel Charles was more or less O.C. passengers. I found great satisfaction in the feminine company that had been lacking in Durazzo. The naval attaché and his assistant Taffy Rodd came close to heart-failure when they saw through a port-hole the Italian Grand Fleet swanning about in the Mediterranean, and had no means of reporting what they had seen. We were under strict wireless silence, and we had no news of the fall of France.

Before we reached the Mediterranean, I had written a sonnet which may convey some impression of the strange ambience of that voyage.

REFUGEE CRUISE

Day after day, on every cabin-wall,
Luminous pennies from the mint of June;
Night after night, an Adriatic moon
Lays on the sea's blue breast, a silver shawl.
Life uncontinuous; strange, synthetic noon
In which no past or future shadows fall;
Life in a vacuum, isolate and small;
A bar of silence in a broken tune.
The world they loved, or prayed for in their soul,
Barred at both gates, to memory and to dreams,
By War's immense and alien sentinel.
Only their eyes betray, when each one seems
To hear the chime, the tocsin or the toll
Of Destiny's irrevocable bell.

At Lisbon, we left the comfort of the Lloyd Triestino for the rigours of the *Monarch of Bermuda*, which had made three trips to Narvik during the evacuation, and was literally lousy. We were reminded, if necessary, by the skeleton staff of stewards, that there was a war on.

★　　★　　★

Our unusual voyage ended in Glasgow, on a Sunday morning, and we travelled to London that night. I sat up for more than half of it in Sir Percy Loraine's compartment, drinking very brown whiskies out of sleeping-car tooth-glasses. I never saw him again.

Italy's entry into the war may have angered Mr. Churchill, and Sir Percy may have become something of a scapegoat. He was—I fear, contemptuously—offered the supervision of Germans interned on the Isle of Man. When the Windsor constituency fell vacant, I heard that he had been a candidate for Conservative nomination; wealthy privy councillors with a lifetime's experience of public affairs are not negligible candidates. But a young man who had been his honorary attaché in Rome was selected. If this was a disappointment, it was forgotten when stewardship of the Jockey Club and the prowess of the good horse Darius combined to bring congenial interests and satisfaction to the evening of a distinguished life.

If I never saw my much-loved Persian rugs—and much else—again, this was not the fault of the Italian authorities in Albania. In the matter of official and personal property belonging to the diplomatic and consular services, Italy had far more at stake in the British empire, with its then massive openings for foreign representation in the Dominions, than the British had to leave in Italian hands when war severed relations. It was much to Italian interest to safeguard our possessions carefully. Our own effects were taken from Durazzo to Tirana and there held under seal in the cellar of the skeleton British Legation building. I have no doubt that at the time of the Italian armistice all was still in good order. After that, unfortunately, His Majesty's Government seemed to lose interest in Albania; certainly no intervention such as prevented a communist take-over in Greece was approved. Hopes that the partisans might prove friendly; that their brand of communism would be benign; that the Albanian coast and what lies behind it might be saved for democracy, have shipwrecked on hard facts already obtrusive when these hopes blossomed.

Scraps of news came out from time to time. Albania's communist leader, Anwar Hoxha, formerly a clerk in the Albanian consulate in Brussels and later a schoolmaster in Korçe, seems to have been of less real importance than his head of police, Koço Xoxe, once an apprentice tinsmith of Korçe. This man was responsible for boiling the feet of the wealthy nephew of Lef

Nosi of Elbasan, until he betrayed his uncle's hiding place; for beating Shevqet Verlaçi—the Quisling's wife—until she died; for shooting the two brothers of twenty-two year old Mohsine Kokalari and leaving her unable to walk, because of a broken back. The treatment of 'enemies of the régime' in Albania matched any competitive revolutionary horrors.

After the German evacuation of Albania, while the situation there was still malleable, a small British military mission went in, and discovered what remained of my possessions. In the cockpit of fighting between the Germans and the Albanian (communist) partisans, Tirana had been a battlefield. The mission found, in our Legation cellar, a scattering of papers and some battered silver-ware; two dead Germans; a lot of books trampled over the floor; an all but complete set of the *London Mercury*, and three dead partisans.

Chapter Six

Persuading the Sphinx

1

In July, 1940, when Mussolini's navy was lording it in the *Mare Nostrum* of Fascist mythology, civilians travelling from England to Egypt were sent either by troopship round the Cape or by overnight flight, over enemy territory, from Lyneham to Cairo. The air route was reserved for Very Important Persons and their staffs, and had its own discomforts. Mr. Churchill, cabinet ministers, ministers of state and other notables had to don rubberised clothing and travel, in an unheated and unpressurised York aircraft, well above the weather, with one stop at Malta. The altitude imposed an oxygen-mask, and it was the task of one crew member to ensure that no one fell asleep. A visit to the lavatory meant unplugging one's mask, running for it, and plugging in again when there. The Cairo Embassy always had a doctor at the airport, in case of need.

Less exalted travellers, myself among them, circumnavigated Africa to reach Suez from Liverpool. On arrival in September, 1940, I was informed that our ambassador had decided to make use of me in the Publicity Section of the Embassy. There were friends, both British and Egyptian, who lamented this appointment, insisting that I might have enjoyed more interesting and rewarding employment if Sir Miles Lampson had named me to be Assistant Sanitary Man in the local asylum, or Deputy Corpse-Washer at the local lazaret. All that mattered to me was that I was back again in Egypt, for Egypt is one of the loves of my life.

The publicity section was housed in No. 8 rue Ahmad Pasha, where Vivien and Jessica Cornelius had so long kept open house, in Garden City. It was directed by a Sudan civil servant, Reginald Davies, whom I remembered from earlier days, and he was assisted by another Sudan hand, Frank Cottrell; by a sparkling Canadian couple who had come from Estonia, the Arnold Smiths; by a bevy of army wives controlled by the experienced Mrs. Lawlie Tomlyn, and by Fuad al-Mughabghab and his corps of translators. Arnold Smith now heads the Commonwealth secretariat.

The section had no responsibility for direct relations with the Egyptian press, which were handled by Williamson-Napier in Chancery. It did the obvious wartime things, devising ways of projecting in Egypt the mass of material received from London. As I soon discovered, it enjoyed the poorest reputation in Cairo, where its staff were written off as bungling amateurs in a not very creditable line of business. Indeed, malice and all uncharitableness seethed in the local propagandist world, which had far too many mansions. The uniformed specialists in Greek, Italian or Free French affairs despised our civilian status. A swarm of heterogeneous organisations labouring in the same field as ourselves took pleasure in torpedoing our better efforts. One young orientalist, who played it as a Mohammedan, was special poison. Local war correspondents thought us a poor joke. I was not, therefore, attracted to my new job, but I determined to make something personal and effective of it. I put up a large notice in English and Arabic on the wall behind my chair: NO RECOMMENDATIONS ACCEPTED OR GIVEN! and prepared to propagand.

This notice frustrated the secret purposes of many of my visitors. In Egypt as elsewhere in the East, the recommendation or 'chit'—in Arabic *tawsiyya*—is the bane of authority. Newly arrived managers or officials are the worst offenders, for they see no harm in scribbling a line to a friend asking him to do what he can for so-and-so or for so-and-so's graduate son. The friend, unless he can pass the buck, has the ungrateful task of saying 'No!' Except in the rarest possible cases, I refused to play this innocent and deadly game. When people called whom I had never heard of before and claimed that my personal acquaintance with the General Manager of Shell morally obliged me to invoke his interest in some relative, I was rude, and made an enemy for life. I had, some years before, asked Spinks Pasha, the Inspector-General

of the Egyptian army, to ensure that the deserving son of a most
deserving father received no less consideration than others in his
candidature for the officer's school; I was told that there were
fourteen vacancies in the school; that Sidqi Pasha, then Egyptian
Prime Minister, had written sixteen letters recommending different candidates, and that my letter must follow his into the waste-
paper basket.

Edwin Chapman-Andrews of our service, then serving in the
embassy, had been allowed to take a commission in his father's
old regiment and go to Khartoum, in order to join the Emperor
Haile Selassie on his militant return to Ethiopia. He kindly offered
me the use of his pleasant flat, overlooking the Nile on Gezira. I
settled in and acquired a car and a driver.

There can have been few periods in British history less favourable to impressive projection in Cairo. Egyptians, by and large,
find moral arguments relatively unconvincing. Lip-service is
paid to principles, but personal advantage is what counts. In a
war which had already given Hitler Norway and Denmark, Bel-
gium, Holland and France, as well as Poland and Czechoslovakia,
the betting in the Mousky was not on Churchill; and during my
two years at No. 8 the sweeping successes of the Japanese in the
Far East in conquering Malaya and Singapore and sinking British
battleships right and left—not to mention Pearl Harbour—
weighed the scales even more notably against us. It was a surprise
to me to find so many Egyptians who, despite these omens, still
expected a victory for democracy. They were a minority.

I consulted one or two good Egyptian friends; one in particular,
who may wish to remain nameless, was unfailingly resourceful
in ideas and methods of approach. The starting-point of my own
thinking was the sceptical attitude of all Egyptians to anything
smelling of propaganda, and on that base I built my own propagandist efforts.

I was convinced that all the pro-British articles which
Williamson-Napier inspired in the Arabic press were discounted
from A to Z by Egyptian readers as being something Mahmoud
Abu'l Fath or Karim Thabet, or some other journalist, had been
well paid to produce. If an Egyptian were to read in a wartime

newspaper that the British Fleet had sunk a German trawler, he would not believe it. But the same man would give instant credence to some item of news whispered to him behind closed doors under an oath of secrecy: indeed, if he was informed of the event in confidence, he would believe that a British trawler had sunk the German Fleet. I decided to eschew the written word and to rely solely on word of mouth. London readily agreed to proposals, put up by me and commended by the Ambassador, that I should form and exploit an organisation specialising in 'Arabic Whispering'. Within very few weeks, we were in business. I hoped to use what I knew of Egyptian mentality to get our message across. This promised more interest than putting little figurines of a trouserless Mussolini in Xmas crackers, or using Charlie Chaplin's Jewish tailor in *The Great Dictator* as an argument for Egyptian sympathy.

In the recruitment of agents, I was largely guided by the advice of my Egyptian friends, and I have no doubt that an element of racket could, here and there, have been discovered; but this I wrote off as an ingredient in the omelette. I had, when the whole machine was working, some 350 agents in all strata of local life, and I could, at the drop of a hat, get any story I liked into Abdin Palace or a native brothel. Where possible, I tried to recruit from the men who had had the spirit to volunteer for civil defence duties, which involved real hazards during the air-raids soon to begin.

One early professional deformation I suffered from was a contagion of Egyptian habits of thought. I have referred, when discussing elsewhere the initial hesitation of the proletariat in 1918 to accept the 'Wafd' as genuine nationalists, to a distortion of reasoning which makes the obvious solution of any problem unacceptable to an Egyptian, who prefers more tortuous explanations. This trait had to be constantly remembered in 'psychological warfare'. As an example: if, uninvited, you tell a fellah that your name is Smith, he is likely to ask himself why you said this; to deduce that you have some ulterior reason for doing so, and to assume that your real name is Jones. When Mahmoud was asked why he called Abbas a liar, he explained that Abbas had told him

he was going to Tantah, and that he had, in fact, gone there!
The Italian air-raids on Alexandria, which destroyed a mosque
and killed hundreds, looked like jam for an anti-Italian propagandist, but in Egypt the truth always boomerangs. 'I know why you
tell us about this,' I was informed; 'you want us to be angry with
the Italians; but we know that it is the R.A.F. who are bombing
Alexandria, just so that you can speak as you do!'

The Germans had two simple lines of propaganda in Egypt
during the war: that Hitler was a Moslem, born in Egypt (I
was shown his mother's house in Tantah), and that, when he won
the war, the poor man would get the rich man's land. These were
most effective talking-points; the victory of 'Mohammed Haidar',
as he was locally known, was prayed for in every village. But in
the Arabian Nights atmosphere of Egypt, even the most attractive
slogans backfire. A police officer in Shebin-el-Kom told me that
two bleeding and battered fellahin had been brought in, charged
with mayhem. It transpired that they had been sitting amicably
side by side, thinking of Mohammed Haidar and dividing the
Pasha's many acres between them, field by field, until the last field
divided them, and they fought to the death for its ownership.

When Wavell's later victory in the desert brought the first
German prisoners of war to Egypt for internment, I asked him to
allow one batch to be marched from the Bab-el-Hadid terminus to
the Bab-el-Louq station, rather than transit Cairo in closed lorries.
It seemed important to me that Cairo should see these exhausted
youths in defeat, and abandon its belief in a race of supermen.
Wavell agreed, and the march took place. One of my agents came
to me the same evening and begged me never to allow such a
thing again. He had been having his weekly shave, at the hands of
an eighty-year-old barber on a mat on the pavement, and the old
man had asked him in a whisper if he knew that Mohammed
Haidar was now in Egypt. Yes, he had continued, it was blessedly
true; he had been among the Germans who crossed the city that
morning! My agent protested that this was impossible, and asked:
'What about those British soldiers with rifles, who marched by the
side of the Germans?' 'They were showing him the way!' said
the old man, finger on nose; and that was that.

Our procedure was to equip our agents with talking-points, which I drew up every day in the light of the day's news, the local preoccupation of the moment, or just fancy, and leave it to them to get these points across in their own circle. Sometimes two agents would stage an argument, leading to a scuffle, in a coffee-shop, one of them shouting the anti-British case until over-whelmed by the others' reasoning. A popular local charlatan, who claimed to read without seeing, and to answer, any question written down and held in the questioner's hand, was paid a small monthly retainer to ensure that at the parties he was often en-gaged to amuse he always answered the one about who was going to win the war in a satisfactorily pro-Allied way.

The holy men who squat here and there outside Egyptian villages, and pronounce on Fate and miracles, were one target of mine, for they had much influence. An agent would travel from village to village, unobtrusively leaving a gift of food and sweetmeats by the dervish's side, but delaying long enough for a greeting. He always explained that he had had no alternative to a respectful visit, because of his dream; and relation of this dream showed the dervish of the moment standing in Paradise, with the Holy Prophet's arm around his neck and the Holy Prophet's foot on Mohammed Haidar's neck. That was all the agent said, but it was enough.

I learned much of value about current Egyptian thinking from the myriad enquiries made by my agents, who daily asked what replies should be given to this or that anti-British argument encountered. I doubt if even the Embassy Oriental secretariat were better informed on popular attitudes and popular grievances, especially grievances. Many of these, unfortunately, arose from the impact of our local war-effort on Egyptian life.

Analogous grievances had blazed up during the 1914–18 War. This time, they took new shape. From my professional point of view everything possible had to be done to associate the mass of Egyptians with ourselves in a common interest in British victory; but the professional thinking of the military authorities ignored the mass of Egyptians altogether.

When Egyptian staff was needed for the first civil administration to be set up in Cyrenaica, Sir Philip Mitchell, all glorious as a Major-General, left all recruitment to Fuad el-Mughabghab, a Syrian Catholic on our office staff; as a predictable result, only Syrian Catholics got jobs. The engagement of Egyptian Moslem clerks and accountants would have brought us good dividends in the family sympathies of hundreds in a country where jobs are always scarce. I commented on this in a minute to the Ambassador which he read aloud at the high-level weekly meeting. Sir Philip promptly asked Wavell to expel me from Egypt for criticising the army; but Wavell saw no need to do so.

We were buying vast quantities of foodstuffs, eggs and vegetables, and firewood, for the needs of an expanding desert force, and their purchase might most usefully have been organised by a joint Anglo-Egyptian purchasing board, financing its own supply and transport. The producers, all native Egyptians, would then have received good prices—for everything was paid for—and would perhaps have felt some gratitude. But the army was in too much of a hurry for such arrangements to be acceptable. 'There's a war on.' They argued that Mr. Cohen and Mr. Ovadia and the other big contractors, all of some minority religion and quite unrepresentative of the population, were able not only to offer, but to transport to Mersa Matruh, or wherever, the massive supplies required. The fellahin received 1939 prices. The contractors made very high profits. Nothing made us more unpopular.

Alarmingly frequent were stories of bribery at G.H.Q. in the allocation of various contractual services. I had never conceived it possible that this charge could be brought, but my agents' reports were circumstantial. I reported, after long hesitation, to the Ambassador, who passed the message on. Next day I was summoned by General Haining, Churchill's 'Intendant-General', a sort of Super-Q, and called on him, expecting instant execution. He thanked me for my report and asked me 'how high' I had got. I said I had a full colonel. He said he had a brigadier, thus scoring one point. He also said that definitive proof in such cases was the hardest thing in the world to obtain.

I am not suggesting anything characteristic, and this last grievance should not be taken too seriously. In a conscript army, there will always be roughly the same percentage of black sheep as in civilian life: no more, no less.

During 1941 and early 1942, as our desert strength built up by hundreds of thousands, the number of base-troops in and around Cairo also increased to some sixty or seventy thousand men. These troops may or may not have had something of an inferiority complex; what is certain is that they soon exhausted the attractions provided by devoted workers—among them Lady Russell's Club and, with Helen Besly, her 'Music for All'—which, to troops on leave from the desert, offered blessed recreation and relief. The base-troops were also peculiarly a target for the minor extortions of Cairo shopkeepers, beggars and pimps and they developed no friendly feelings for those around them. The problem of the built-in percentage of delinquents in a conscript army soon began to affect the lives of all in the town, for a small minority of hooligans in uniform seemed to take over the streets of Cairo.

The young women in our Office were charming, but in no way provocative; every one of them had one or more unpleasant experience in the street or on her own front doorstep. So did most other young women, by my reports. Private houses were invaded, and the Mohammed Ali Club was a popular port of call for drunken and violent soldiery. The persuasion of Egyptians to the British way of thinking was not helped by the handful of untamed toughs who strode about, looking straight in front of them, striking out lethally at anything wearing a *tarboush* without even glancing at its face. The evening cinema became a hazardous pastime, for after it one might find two husky privates in one's car, who preferred to fight rather than go away. General Haining explained that military police are born and not made, and cannot be improvised; he had far too few of them.

Local taxi-drivers went on strike one day for the right to have a friend sitting beside them in the front seat. One of them had taken two Canadians back to their camp at Maadi by night, and on arrival they had crowned him with a beer-bottle and cut his throat with the shard. I should have liked to see a public execution in this case, to prove our goodwill to the Egyptians and *encourager les autres*; but, of course, the culprits were never identified by any of those who knew their identity. Loyalty to one's men is a fine thing, up to a point.

I found few Egyptians unwilling to make allowances for the behaviour of men on leave from the desert, while wishing that someone else might be the target for their holiday mood. The scenes in Alexandria after the evacuation of Crete, which led one pasha to ask who would defend the town that night if the Germans attacked, were accepted and allowed for: those men had been in Hell and had come out the other side. I proposed, in vain, a desert Yoshiwara, between Cairo and Alexandria, where all the bright lights and women and carousal of which men had dreamed in the desert might be theirs, without this constant pressure on innocent Egyptians. I lived in fear of a day when some poor castrated and crucified British sergeant might be found in a lonely street, for that would have started big trouble. That day, mercifully, never came. But Egyptian memories and resentment of those months of daily humiliation surely inflamed emotions later, on 'Black Saturday' and during the confrontations of Anglo-Egyptian tension.

★　　　★　　　★

I had thought that my ideas about the importance of purely oral propaganda were original; but dear, admirable Freya Stark, who came from work in Aden to Egypt, had reached the same conclusions, and she went on from there to practise a philosophy of persuasion which made other organisations, based on the money-motive, look old-fashioned, crude and rather dirty.

Her results were extraordinary, and nobody was ever paid a penny. The creation and activity of her 'Brotherhood of Freedom', as she has explained in her autobiography, found inspiration in the originating and spreading of *ideas*. The direction of effort was towards the encouragement of our friends, not the convincing of our enemies. The key-thought was Freedom. The three basic rules were (i) to believe in one's own sermon; (ii) to see that it must be advantageous, not only to one's own side but also to that of the listeners; and (iii) to influence indirectly, making one's friends among the people of the country distribute and interpret one's words.

Miss Stark was attached to our office without in any way belonging to it; and I used to supply talking-points for her to use or ignore. She was ably seconded by Mrs. Hore-Ruthven and Lulie Abu'l Huda, and later by other enthusiastic disciples. The 'Brethren' were organised into small cells, all actively co-operative, and the organisation snowballed to tens of thousands. Its success, which was invaluable, owed everything to the simplicity and sincerity of Freya herself, and was a remarkable instance of the persuasive power of positive good.

She had a little flat on the *Bahr-el-A'ama*, the gut of Nile on the far side of Gezira. There, once a week, she kept open house for students and staff officers, officials and farmers, merchants and journalists. It was a privilege to join these gatherings; they had the simple unity of purpose and the shared happiness of other meetings, long ago, in the Catacombs of Rome.

2

In World War II, Egypt was never a belligerent. Bombs were dropped on Egyptian towns, but the targets were British. There were no attacks on specifically Egyptian objectives, such as the Aswan Dam. But Egypt was well in, if not 'of', the war. Cairo had its open-air restaurants and its cabarets on hotel roofs, the blatancy of bright lights and unrationed luxuries and gross material prosperity; but the young men who drank and danced there were only briefly absent from the desert fighting. War rumbled beneath the dance-floor, and we were asked to pay for our drinks at the time of service, 'because of the risk of air-raids'. These became frequent enough to be a nuisance.

The mass of Egyptians went fatalistically about their business, profiting from new opportunities to turn an honest or dishonest piastre, convinced of their own traditional ability to conform to any conceivable future situation. But for others there was a constant excitement in the air and a quicker pulse. The local intelligentsia devoured their daily ration of eight newspapers greedily.

Britain benefited from the instinct which prefers the devil it knows. But Hitler's anti-Jewish measures had, because of the Balfour Declaration, found many sympathisers in Egypt; and large sums of money had been laid out, during the nine months before Italy joined the war, to secure the interest of leading local politicians. As was only human, also, an urge to reinsure against all risks persuaded many to hedge their bets. Tewfik Doss Pasha, a leading Copt and politician, used to fall on my neck at every news of a British advance in the desert, and cut me dead in the Club at the first signs of any retreat.

One result of the persecution of the Jews in Europe was a change of attitude by the Sephardim Jews of Egypt, most of whom had opposed the concept of a National Home for Jewry in Palestine, fearing, like Edwin Montagu in England, its easy argument against their own established position elsewhere. These anti-Zionists became fervent supporters of Zionist policy. Nowadays, I suppose, outside the inflamed territories of Arab and Moslem sentiment, whatever the built-in injustice of the Balfour Declaration, the hellish spectacle of Belsen and Auschwitz has placed the Jewish Home in Palestine firmly if fortuitously beyond discussion, and a revival of past history and origins is dismissed as being no longer relevant.

I soon found it more easy to uncover anti-Italian prejudice than anti-German, for an Italian occupation of Egypt threatened new and powerful local competition at low levels. There had never been a stonemason or house-painter, navvy or grocer, of United Kingdom origin in Egypt: apart from anything else, Lord Cromer did not encourage such immigration. But as Libya and Abyssinia had shown, Italy had no lack of potential settlers, eager to emigrate and to compete with any local talent as labourers and artisans.

Those Egyptian political parties professing democratic ideals— the Liberals and the Wafd—were inclined to favour our cause. The Ittehadists and others dependent on the Palace for their political livelihood wanted Italy to win. King Fuad had displayed a lifelong predilection for things Italian; this led him to invest much of his large fortune there, which may have helped to explain his son's strong personal bias. Seventeen Italians were retained in

King Farouq's service during the war. Most of these were employed on the lower levels, as valets and kennel-men; but the King's assistant private secretary, Puli, was an Italian. Kennelmen can be trained to manipulate wireless transmitters, and valets can become their master's counsellors.

From time to time the real black hatred for Egypt's British association, which time had mellowed elsewhere to a cynical acceptance, could be glimpsed, as a heritage of earlier grievance. When Rashid Ali al-Gailani and his masters, the 'Golden Square' of army officers, swung Iraq into pro-Axis attitudes in 1941, one legendary figure, Aziz al-Masry, whom Britain had rescued from a Turkish revolution before the First War, decided to desert the high post of Chief of Staff which Farouq had given him in the Egyptian army, and fly to Bagdad, to join up with Rashid Ali, the Germans and the ex-Mufti of Jerusalem in their exploitation of anti-British opportunity. His pilot was a young Egyptian air-Force officer, Yusuf Zulfiqar Sabry—later my colleague on an International Commission in Khartoum—whose brother, Ali Sabry, was for many years Nasser's Prime Minister. The aircraft crashed with no loss of life, in the Delta, and with it many secret hopes.

The moods of the European community were calculable by reference to recent history. The French colony was split down the middle. The (Vichy) French Minister, a gentlemanly Corsican who did not go out of his way to be obstreperous, was expelled with his Legation staff in early 1942; this led Farouq to dismiss the Prime Minister responsible, with consequences of crisis. The French diehards on the Canal were, as always, strongly anglophobe, and many French bankers and businessmen in Cairo shared with them and with relatives in France a prejudice in favour of Maréchal Pétain and against an upstart who did not have tradition's consecration. Baron de Benoît, the Canal Company's representative in Cairo, was firmly Gaullist; Madame was for the Marshal. Many wavering French sympathies were lost to us on the day France had to ask for an armistice, because nobody responsible for the weekly dinner-dance at the Gezira Sporting Club thought it appropriate to cancel that gay little function.

Levantine Egypt was surprisingly friendly, except for those most marked by a French educational formation. The large Jewish community had its own reasons for being pro-Ally; the others might well have sat on an ideological fence. Quite a few young men went into uniform, and their wives and sisters were decorative in canteens and soldiers' clubs and hospitals. These ladies were probably looking forward anxiously to some post-war collection presented by Molyneux or Jacques Fath, and they much disliked a war that came so near home. '*Tu sais, Grafftey*,' one lady said to me, '*cette guerre n'est pas aussi sympathique que l'autre!*' Whether, as I rather smugly assumed, it was an old British association, or some other more cogent reason, that put them squarely behind us, they were certainly well-disposed.

A new glitter came to Cairo drawing-rooms, when King George of Greece and Prince Paul settled down in Cairo. Aly Khan was seen here, there and everywhere; General de Gaulle came out to stake his claim to Syria, and left behind him Madame Catroux and the admirable General, in that apparent order of importance, to represent Free France and to feed the fiery journalist Canéri with material for his Gaullist news-sheet.

Our Ambassador's niece reappeared in Cairo in a Molyneux-designed uniform, with about thirty other lovelies who combined beauty and efficiency in exceptional degree. They formed a unit commanded by Mrs. Mary Newall—herself no slouch—and drove military motor-cars here and there to the distraction of pedestrian males. Their commandant, esoterically known as 'Pistol Mary', appeared to reserve to herself the liberty of decorative scarves and nail-varnish, and this provoked some mutinous mutterings.

These were also the days of the desert war correspondents who made history. Alan Moorehead of the *Daily Express* and Alex Clifford of the *Daily Mail*, who were daily cheered on in noisy competition by their newspapers, amicably shared a flat in Cairo, where Lucy Moorehead coped with a new baby of marked personality. Richard Dimbleby completed the trio. Older hands like Arthur Merton, and the batch of Americans, achieved less instant fame.

One of my most valued journalist friends, Stanley Parker of the

Egyptian Gazette, threw down his pen and disappeared into uniform when his owner, our local British millionaire, moved from Egypt to the Cape. This act of emigration by the unofficial head of Alexandria's British community was too much for his servant Parker, who wrote some fairly scorching stuff on the subject before abandoning local journalism for a second distinguished military incarnation.

The ebb and flow of desert war was an alternation of climax and anti-climax, emotionally exhausting. Triumphal progress, stimulant of a hundred talking-points, would suddenly become retreat, with an ominous crescendo of German gunfire.

After the disaster of Crete, Randolph Churchill came to Cairo to act as spokesman at G.H.Q., and he attended our daily publicity committee-meetings in the Embassy. We were left by Randolph in no doubt that the next time would be the last and that our troops might henceforward, if they wished, keep one hand behind their backs. I was happy to hear this, for my brother Tony was now commanding the 3rd County of London Yeomanry (Sharpshooters) in the desert, where, I am told, they put up a magnificent show. After the disappointment of the 'November Handicap', reaction from early optimism was painful. It would be unfair to blame Randolph for speaking to his brief. His tempestuously controversial utterances were, however, sometimes an embarrassment; not that this would bother him. I was informed that he once proclaimed to the population of the Mohammed Ali Club bar that his father had been a lifelong Zionist, and that he was a Zionist himself. In so Moslem a setting, this may have been a courageous statement of conviction; from the publicity angle the setting was badly chosen. His circulars to officers had a mixed reception.

*   *   *

The appointment of Minister of State in the Middle East which Lord Lloyd had been promised went to Oliver Lyttelton, whose secretariat included Arthur Rucker, Bill Iliffe, Henry Hopkinson and other heavyweights. Henry's first question to me was to ask why we had not already bought up every politician in Egypt:

the difficulty lay in finding an acceptable channel of payment. The presence in Cairo of a full cabinet minister, with blanket responsibility for the whole Middle East, was valuable. Beirut no longer needed to refer to the Foreign Office, or Berbera to the Colonial Office, for rulings on one similar problem, because Mr. Lyttelton represented both departments up to a certain level of decision. His office co-ordinated the supply and shipping of many increasingly scarce materials to all points in his diocese, and the rational distribution, between parish and parish, of locally produced foodstuffs and other needs. In practice, the local Arab monopolist handling those precious heavy-duty tyres, or petrol, or foodstuffs, made a killing, in spite of the critical supervision of the Middle East supply centre's branch offices; but the basic idea was right. Later, the Americans claimed their share of these responsibilities, and wide areas of ground were then made fertile for their own massive trade-invasion of the Middle East at the war's end.

One small corner of the British wartime community deserves an admiring glance, for this was a nest of singing-birds. On the staff of the British Council, or in academic groves, was a group which included Robin Fedden and Lawrence Durrell, and many talents seemed to be whetted by the ambience of those war days. They were impelled to pronounce essentials in a world of flux and menace, and they did so, eloquently. The quality of their fantasy valuably restored the sense of proportion of others who lacked their special vision.

I used to lunch off sandwiches and beer by the Lido swimming-pool at Gezira, where one of my more stimulating cronies was Major Wintle, then doing some small administrative job, which he hated, at G.H.Q. He was lucky to be there at all. Having lectured at the French Ecole de Guerre before the war, after collecting a D.S.O. in the earlier struggle, he knew personally many influential French officers; and, when French collapse was imminent, he had the brainwave of flying across and making a personal appeal to one friend who might well be able to bring the whole French Air Force to us across the Channel. He was working in June, 1940, in a department with R.A.F. connexions, and was able, illicitly and urgently, to order an aircraft to be prepared for his trip to France. His urgency was all too contagious, for the plane was ready ten minutes before time and its readiness was reported to the wrong person. His plan misfired. Bureaucracy was outraged. Hot words were exchanged; insulting charges were made, and the alleged movement of a hand towards a revolver sent Wintle to the Tower. There his Grenadier warders became his slaves when he refused their usual services, proclaiming that no one in the Brigade of Guards knew how to polish a pair of boots. After his acquittal on all charges and twenty four hours after his release, the cell he had occupied was wiped out by a German bomb.

He was a stimulating lunch-time companion. He had decided that he would be best employed circulating from office to office in G.H.Q. every evening and asking each officer what he had done to win the war that day. Those many whom he would expect to reply in self-congratulation at having put the War Office right about a misprint, or at having dished some rival intelligence organisation, would be transferred forthwith to Tobruk.

The wise innovations of technique in officer-selection adopted during the war seemed, indeed, not to apply to the staffing of Headquarters posts. Christopher Summerhayes, a 1914 veteran and an experienced Arabist and administrator from our Levant Consular Service, was posted to supervise a native labour contingent in Port Sudan. I found Laurence Lockhart, who had a First in Oriental languages and was for years the Anglo-Persian Oil Company's liaison-man with Persian officialdom, issuing pencils and stationery in a G.H.Q. basement.

Major Wintle's last wartime exploit was to smuggle himself on board a ship carrying Vichy French sympathisers on a voyage of repatriation from Beirut to Occupied France, in order to see for himself what was going on there. I do not know if he fulfilled his promise to me to travel as a pro-Pétainist piano-tuner. He managed to get ashore under false colours, but was soon spotted and imprisoned. He found his way home unscathed. That implacable eyeglass, that arrogant assumption of complete authority, somehow extracted him from Admiral Darlan's gaols and freed him for later British notoriety.

Our intervention against the French authorities in Syria, whose old-fashioned mandate-style rejection of Arab aspirations was a considerable political embarrassment in wartime, was never forgiven by General de Gaulle. Characteristically he interpreted our attitude as betraying an intention of British usurpation of French influence. Our Minister of State in Cairo had some uncomfortable interviews with him. This development brought me, also, much extra work. Walter Smart, Oriental Secretary in the Residency, was absent on leave at the time, and the Ambassador asked me to take on all his work as well as my own. I was handicapped by severe conjunctivitis, which kept one eye under a shade and therefore—for an astigmatic—allowed only the briefest concentration with the other before all became a blur. Those three weeks of massive paper-work were uncomfortable, and I welcomed Smart's return.

★   ★   ★

Soon after Farouq came of age, at 18, on July 29, 1937, he had appointed Ali Maher Pasha to be his *Chef de Cabinet*, a post of great influence because of its dual function of liaison between the King on the one hand and his ministers and the foreign representatives on the other. The Pasha's father had publicly insulted Lord Kitchener; one of his brothers, Ahmed Maher, though later a Prime Minister, had been tried for murder; from a narrowly British point of view, Ali Maher came of bad stock. He had taken the opposite side in politics to his brother and was leader of the King's Friends. His influence on young Farouq was wholly unfortunate.

I have never met a more compulsive ambition. When I was far down in Residency hierarchy Ali Maher invited me to dine alone with his wife and himself, and the evening was uncomfortable. Their longing for the accident of politics which might pave the way to his premiership was nakedly advertised: I was assumed to be able to pull the essential string.

Both brothers were short and stocky. Ahmed was fleshy and had fat chops; Ali Pasha paid annual visits to Tring where he lived on orange-juice, and returned fever-eyed and wrinkled; a small ravenous wolf driven by furnace-heats of ambition. I can hardly believe that his normal temperature was normal.

Before King Fuad's death, which had come in May, 1936, nine months after I left Egypt for Iraq, the heir apparent had been but rarely seen, for Fuad had a deep contempt for Egyptians and discouraged contacts between his son and the public. I was told that Farouq first saw the Pyramids when he was twelve. A succession of English nurses and governesses brought him up, and his only venture out-of-doors was to drive his little car around the Palace gardens. In July every year, I had had to select and order the book which the High Commissioner was to give him on his birthday. His schoolroom coffee-table was assumed, rather implausibly, to groan under the weight of an accumulation of such titles as *The Uniforms of the British Army* and *The Castles of Britain*, all most expensively bound, bearing the royal monogram in gold. I saw him first at a ceremony organised by Imperial Airways when he was standing in for his father, a pretty boy with charming manners. The King had bought for him 6,000 acres of the best sugar-cane land in Keneh and had given him the title of *Amir-al-Sa'id*, or Prince of Upper Egypt.

Lord Lloyd had wanted Farouq to go straight from Abdin Palace to Eton. His Oriental secretariat was unenthusiastic. Without the experience of an English prep-school, where children are conditioned to schoolboy English conventions, the treatment of a new boy at an English public school, whatever his origins, seemed unlikely to induce feelings of affection for the British way of life; indeed, royalty in embryo is likely to have its bottom kicked more than most, if only in the interests of other boys' later memoirs. We favoured a good tutor, and an English university later, where the wide pleasures which rank and wealth provide might be agreeably associated with thoughts of England. I personally hoped to see some hard-bitten young cavalry major as the Prince's tutor; someone able to help him to excel on a horse, with a gun, in a boat, and, by his own prowess and tact, to impress on the future King of Egypt standards and a code of behaviour not otherwise easily picked up. Neville Ford, who had once bowled for

Harrow, was selected; it would be unfair to assess his tuition by its end-product.

When it was suggested to King Fuad that Farouq might advantageously blossom as a cadet at Woolwich, the King showed unexpected enthusiasm for the idea. Some element in this seemed to derive from his own pleased surprise, on arrival at the military academy in Turin, to be expected by his fellow students to 'make himself naked', for this was the circumstance he recalled when expressing his parental approval. Farouq was sent to a Richmond villa, for preliminary acclimatisation and further study, under the care and tutelage of the admirable Ahmed Mohammed Hassanein Bey. This choice of bear-leader was a good one: Hassanein had already made a reputation as an Olympic fencer, a pioneer aviator and an explorer of the remoter Western Desert. The same qualities of initiative and courage were not so noticeable in his father, the last Egyptian admiral before the British occupation. He, being instructed to take the Fleet to Malta, replied after an undue delay: *Malta mafish!* ('Malta isn't there!'). He had been unable to find the place.

One cannot guess what good Farouq might have found in the companionship and example of a remarkable man or, later, in the disciplines and opportunities of Woolwich, which he never reached. King Fuad's death in May, 1936, compelled his son's return, still immature and malleable, to Cairo and its pressures of overwhelming ambition.

He may well have needed no encouragement in anti-British attitudes, but he was credibly reported to receive constant guidance from Ali Maher Pasha, not only towards an autocratic conception of his relationship to his people but also towards a mistrust of all and every advice coming from the British Embassy. His heredity made the first lesson congenial; the second, gradually inflamed by our Ambassador's manifest dislike of the young King, soon became obsessive. Actions and reactions on both sides exacerbated a mutual animosity; and Maher Pasha was always at hand to place the worst interpretation on any British gesture or remark. Had Sir Miles Lampson been replaced in Egypt when the 1936 Treaty brought its radical change to Anglo-Egyptian relations, the path of goodwill might have been smoother. But the same six-foot-five of British officialdom who had given Farouq those boring books and, perhaps, patronised him as a child; the High Commissioner whose authority had been an offence to all from King Fuad downwards, still represented Britain, though now in a role allegedly entirely different. No sensitive young man cares to be reminded, even by his own memory, of the day a visitor knows that he has wet his trousers; but this was the sort of emotion Maher Pasha was able to evoke in his venomous persuasions.

In the month before the outbreak of war, Ali Maher Pasha was appointed Prime Minister. He included no Liberals in a cabinet of Independents and Saadists (a new grouping of dissident and anti-Nahas Wafdists). The assistance prescribed in the treaty was duly offered to Egypt's ally, and the period of the 'phoney war' was spent in argument about Nahas Pasha's demand that Egypt's association with Britain in the war should be bartered for further political concessions. In parliament, Abdurrahman Azzam Pasha (of all people) proposed that Egypt should inform the Axis powers of her willingness to give their troops free passage across Egypt from the Western Desert to Palestine. German elements in Egypt were firmly interned.

Markedly less firmness was shown to the large Italian colony in June 1940, and the first Italian bombs had fallen before the Italian Minister left Cairo. Ali Maher Pasha's attitude became equivocal and embarrassing, and it was only after his dismissal at the Ambassador's insistence that the Italian Legation packed up on June 22. Hassan Sabri Pasha, an honest and able man, succeeded him, but he died while reading the speech from the throne in November. From then until January 1942, Hussein Sirry Pasha was Prime Minister, ably seconded by a brilliant wife. When King Farouq's annoyance at the expulsion of the Vichy French Legation from Egypt led to Sirry's resignation, it became clear that the King planned to re-appoint Ali Maher Pasha, who now urged immediate Egyptian reinsurance against an Axis victory, in Sirry's place. The students and rabble in the streets screamed: '*Ala'l imám, ya Rommel!*'—'Forwards, Rommel!', with no flicker of objection from the authorities. Sir Miles Lampson pressed for a Prime Minister who commanded a majority in the country, enabling control of the internal situation, and only Nahas Pasha filled the bill. Lampson's request was refused. A situation of real danger threatened.

All indications at the time suggested that the Bari and Berlin wireless-stations were getting their Egyptian news items from reports transmitted from one of the King's estates. By an unusual decision of wartime security, the diplomatic missions in Cairo no longer had the use of ciphers; and no other source for the daily Axis pinpricks could be easily conceived. The new hazard of an actively hostile Egyptian administration seemed intolerable, and His Majesty's government were therefore asked to approve the forced abdication of Farouq and his replacement by the elderly Prince Mohammed Ali, younger brother of the ex-Khedive. London agreed.

Organisational arrangements for this *coup* were not easy. Sir Miles Lampson had booked an audience with Farouq at 9 p.m. on February 4, 1942, and this he proposed to attend accompanied by the G.O.C. British Troops in Egypt (General Stone) and by a heavyweight personal bodyguard of half-a-dozen officers, all over six foot tall. British tanks were to roll into Abdin Palace court-yard, and a staff car was to fetch Prince Mohammed Ali at the appropriate time and bring him to his new throne. Decoy-cars would lead any pursuit astray while King Farouq was being taken to a battleship. A brainwave about sounding all air-raid sirens well in advance of the time of the audience, to allow the tanks to roll in along streets empty of the public, had to be abandoned at the last moment; someone remembered that any air-raid alarm automatically brought out large forces of Egyptian troops in support of the palace guard.

Sir Walter Monckton drafted the instrument of abdication for Farouq's signature. His expert assistance was possible because of his recent appointment to Cairo to control all British publicity activities in the Middle East. But King Farouq could not be expected to abdicate on British embassy foolscap, and nothing appropriately impressive and anonymous could be found in war-time Cairo. The document, I am told, had a dingy look.

We went to bed that night expecting to wake to a new king. One can be sure of nothing, but I suspect that Egypt's shock of sentiment at a brutal action and at its resultant change might soon have passed. Any regrets for Farouq might fade to hopes of Mohammed Ali, a new fount of honour and influence. Speculation is futile, for there was no abdication. We earned, and duly collected, the resentment and obloquy of a nation deeply humili- ated and insulted in the person of its King merely, or so it appeared, in order to impose one Prime Minister rather than another. Farouq was left with no diminution of his power to tease. Last- minute thoughts over dinner had persuaded the Ambassador and the Minister of State to decide that the young King should be given another chance, and it was Farouq and not Prince Moham- med Ali who was to be asked to say: 'I will be good!'

Farouq put on a brave show. Offered the choice of 'either . . . or . . .', he chose the abdication formula. Ahmed Hassanein Pasha, now his Grand Chamberlain, twice pulled Farouq's hand from the paper, pleading with him to stay; and then he threw down the pen. What would have been his last words as king were: 'You might have given me a decent piece of paper!' This echoes another, perhaps apocryphal, abdication remark: 'Of course, there would be no ink in the bloody inkpot!'

His Majesty's government entirely approved the decision taken by their representatives. We in the Embassy were, not surprisingly, boycotted by all our Egyptian friends after this 'humiliation-by- tank' of their King. Nahas Pasha was condemned even by his own supporters for accepting the premiership in an atmosphere of armed blackmail. The younger Egyptian army officers were out- raged.

*　　*　　*

When Farouq had a serious motor accident later, on the Suez road, he was more deeply scarred by this than was expected at the time. From then seemed to date the grossness of person and the accompanying self-hatred, with the coarseness of speech and behaviour which marked him in any social circle. He may perhaps have blamed the British doctors who attended him in the emergency for this development of a Hyde personality. The descendants of Mohammed Ali the Great had bequeathed to him a dark heredity, which found obscene flowering not only in his *Musée Noir* but also in horrid reflections in his own character.

One story, told me by Ahmed Seddik Pasha, may be enough. Farouq was interested in any odds and ends the Italians might have left behind in Cairo and he desired news of every inventory made by the Egyptian sequestrators of Italian banks or businesses. The bank of which Ahmed Seddik was sequestrator had a safe which the King coveted, and orders were given for this safe to be delivered at Koubbeh Palace. This was done, not without much sweat and labour, by half a dozen herculean porters, who installed it in a basement and were there congratulated personally by their King. He threw gold pieces into a bucket and invited them to compete and to reward themselves for their exertions by fishing as many out as they could. When they stood up screaming—for the liquid in the bucket was not water but vitriol—the king laughed. Ahmed Seddik had seen the men, and the state of their hands, within an hour of this bestiality.

3

To our Ambassador the war had brought unusual problems. The position of the head of a diplomatic mission in a country intimately involved in hostilities must be powerfully affected by the presence elsewhere in the capital of a General Officer Commanding-in-Chief whose demands are paramount and whose own attitude may be one of impatience with strictly political considerations. Too complete a genuflexion to General Headquarters is only less dangerous than too haughty an interpretation of Foreign Office instructions.

The qualities required in this situation are not always gracefully displayed. An old friend of mine called Goldie was, in days of pre-history, manager of the leading bank in Ethiopia, and he cabled his head office in Cairo for a ruling on the handling of a young Ras, importunate for an extended overdraft. He was instructed to be 'tactful but firm'. As he told me later: 'I said to the fellow: *"Majesté"*—that was the tact—*"n'oubliez pas que vous êtes nègre!"*—that was firm, I thought.' Sir Miles Lampson, in his day-to-day relations with Service chiefs and at the weekly top-level meeting, met all his problems with firm and tactful diplomacy. In addition to uniformed pressures, he had further scope for skill in adjusting himself to the appointment of a senior cabinet minister as minister of state in a diocese which included Lampson's own parish. His conduct during the war years certainly dazzled Mr. Churchill, and he was rewarded with a peerage while still a serving ambassador: a very rare honour.

His staff, and the British colony in Egypt, had mixed views about the Ambassador and his lady. She was his second wife, the daughter of a famous Italian specialist in tropical diseases, Sir Aldo Castellani, who had received high honours from Mussolini for services during the Abyssinian war. Lampson's efforts to secure the expulsion of the Italian elements on King Farouq's personal staff were met by a coarse retort that he should first get rid of his own Italian in the embassy.

Lady Lampson was active in good works during the war, and ambulances bearing her name were a feature of Cairo's wartime traffic. Unfortunately, relations between her organisation and the official British Red Cross became embittered. There was an age-gap between them of over thirty years, but this did not prevent the happiest of unions, for His and Her Excellency shared the blessing of ebullient vitality. They both had a deep thirst for life in any of its physical manifestations, and both were apparently indefatigable. After a succession of late nights, there followed a succession of early mornings when they were ready and eager for whatever exercise an excursion to the Fayoum, or a duck-shoot, might dictate. This shared delight in living seemed to be a close bond between them.

Sir Miles Lampson himself was always a little larger than life. When he decided to learn to fly, under instruction from the R.A.F. at Aboukir, he took his test on the day he was due to leave for a holiday in England, and ended up, cheerful but in some disarray, upside-down, with petrol pouring over him. The Foreign

Office, valuing his services, forbade further experimentation in the upper atmosphere. He had a rather lordly way of taking other people's services for granted, and his treatment of his staff was rather selective. I was one of the lucky ones, but I was shocked, when acting briefly as Oriental Secretary, to read some of those red-ink minutes he had addressed to Walter Smart, a precision-instrument of great worth and sensitivity: the Ambassador might have been admonishing an under-gardener.

Despite its provocation, embarrassment was caused by the frequent public expression of Sir Miles Lampson's bitter antipathy to King Farouq. Even those Egyptians who were ill-disposed towards the King resented his public disparagement by our Ambassador. As we had learned when King Ghazi of Iraq died in a car-accident in Bagdad, the sentiments of a nation for its ruler reflect more than moral criteria. Lampson's favourite story, which may well have been true in every particular, concerned the shooting by King Farouq of all the lions in captivity in the Cairo zoo. This was recorded as being part of an urge to exorcise an evil omen, for the king had been disturbed by a dream of lions, and Ali Maher Pasha had reminded him in whose coat of arms the lion is prominent. Much offence was given by the frequent broadcasting of this anecdote.

Looking back at the thirteen years of his mission in Egypt, I think it was marred by very few mistakes. The last High Commissioner and first British Ambassador had, indeed, the fairy-gift of luck. He should never have been left in Cairo, once the 1936 Treaty was signed; but that was not his mistake. I personally regret that the plan for Farouq's removal on February 4, 1942, was not firmly carried through, but then I do not know what considerations led Lampson and Lyttelton to draw back at the last moment. Most regrettable was the Ambassador's unwillingness, once the tide of war had receded from Egypt, to use his great authority to enforce immediate implementation of the treaty he had signed, by the withdrawal from Egypt of massive British forces; by the evacuation and cession of barracks and installations; by the winkling out from the polo-fields and the flesh-pots of Cairo of hundreds of officers, and by the limitation of British troops in Egypt to the 12,000 in the Canal area promised and provided for in the 1936 Treaty. The effect of such strictly correct action would have been electric, and a long and gratuitous provocation of Egyptian national sentiment would have been prevented—who knows with what results?

★   ★   ★

In my own small field of endeavour, things went rather better than I had dared expect. It is not easy to gauge audience-reaction to propaganda with precision, but I was able to deduce from my agents' reports a gradual acceptance of optimism. For this, world events and not mere 'Arabic Whispering' were responsible: we witnessed superhuman Russian resistance to German invasion; we guessed the immense potential of the American contribution; we glimpsed the prospect of a Second Front. I was personally lucky enough to pinpoint Stalingrad as the precise map-reference at which the Russian tide would turn. I take no credit for this. Simply, in my instructions to my agents, I decided to wager on one point on the Russian map, and I pronounced for Stalingrad before its selection was more than fortuitous. The little stir created by this pot-shot of prophecy set up a fair wind for our other lines of whispering.

Nearer home, a cloud of war was blowing up which threatened to extinguish the British position in Egypt. As Rommel and his Afrika Corps pressed on towards Alamein—where they were to be held, had we known it—nerves, mine among them, became frayed. I can remember few more distasteful evenings than one spent in the Ambassador's box at a charity preview of Charlie Chaplin's film *The Great Dictator*. The German wireless had that day blared out threats against Badi'a Massabni, Karim Thabet and others who had committed themselves to activity on our behalf, promising them death by slow hanging in Ezbekia Square within the week. To watch, and to be expected to find amusement in Chaplin's funny business with the dictators, while the tramp of German soldiery was shaking the sands, was almost impossible for me. I had nothing to fear in the matter of personal safety from an invasion of Egypt, for my survival was more or less assured by diplomatic convention, or so I believed. But the film did not make me laugh.

Already the reputation of General Rommel among our troops was alarmingly high. I once stood near a group of soldiers watching a rugger match at Gezira Sporting Club, between South Africans and Maoris. When my neighbours wished to encourage particular violence, they shouted: 'Rommel 'im! Rommel 'im!' I found the new verb humiliatingly significant.

I may, perhaps, record two men's personal reaction to those days, when the menace of a German irruption loomed most darkly. When the British fleet, which had attracted many a bomb on Alexandria, sailed away to Haifa; when the sky above General Headquarters in Garden City was murky with the smoke of burning records; when hitherto respectable British citizens rushed to their banks, to remit to the safety of London the totality of their accounts, Sir Alexander Keown-Boyd, temporarily in Addis Ababa on business, cabled his Cairo Bank with instructions to purchase a large slab of Egyptian government stock. And Sir Miles Lampson ordered the re-decoration of the outside of the Embassy building, with painting of the street-railings as a first priority. At that moment in time, the fresh green paint on the railings of what had been written off as a doomed property was more effective for good than any whisper of propaganda that his publicity section could have thought up in a month of Sundays.

*   *   *

On March 21, 1942, Walter Monckton promoted me to be Director of the Office in the rue Ahmed Pasha, much to my pleasure. Not much later I was even more pleased to be summoned by Nahas Pasha, the Egyptian Prime Minister, who was an old friend and enemy and warmly congratulated on our work. He told me that he had been watching us carefully and was satisfied that what we were doing was in the best interests of Egypt and in the interest also of the democratic way of life which he personally favoured. Few, if any, people could have given me more welcome congratulation.

Nahas Pasha offered me, in exchange for a not unreasonable *quid pro quo*, the use of the whole Egyptian government machine in the cause of our propaganda. When London accepted his terms, he appointed a committee of three consisting of Amin Osman Pasha (later murdered), Georges Dumani Bey (a Syrian journalist and Wafdist polemist) and myself, to concert detailed procedures. We met once; and various measures of valuable co-operation were agreed.

To me, this was a dream come true. Here was an opportunity of influencing Egyptian opinion on many levels, through a mechanism which controlled not only governors and mudirs but also inspectorates and officialdom from the top to the bottom of the administration. The ubiquitous secret police were as much part of this machine as the *shaikhs* who preached their sermons in every mosque, every Friday. But our committee's first meeting was also its last. On May 16, 1942, the Ambassador received a cable instructing him to arrange for my urgent transfer to an Indian Ocean post. I squealed. Sir Miles kindly echoed my squeal. No argument availed. Anthony Eden's telegram had ended with the potent words: 'Prime Minister agrees.'

My own post as head of the publicity section was put into commission. When the wise, Sudan-trained Arabist, who was to continue the specialised work I had initiated, called on Nahas Pasha, to take up the threads of collaboration, he was informed that the Prime Minister's offer had been strictly personal to myself and was not hereditary.

★　　★　　★

My regret at leaving Egypt was not solely due to the enforced abandonment of an interesting job. I was obliged to assume, and rightly, that this separation would be final, for the Cairo embassy, held today by a Levant colleague, was not even a remote possibility for me in the circumstances of the time. Of the twenty-six years of overseas service preceding this transfer I had spent sixteen years in Egypt: time enough to learn to love the country and its people and to make some claim to understand them. I cannot accept anyone's claim to an understanding of the thinking and behaviour of another race if affection is not its basis. Being personally unable to develop any special feelings of affection for Brahmins or Sikhs, I naturally find their motives and reactions incomprehensible.

A claim to particular awareness of what makes Egyptians tick is, indeed, presumptuous. Sometimes it has meant no more than that the speaker has found in the Mohammed Ali Club congenial friends of his own social class. Often the claim reflects a closer experience, but one coloured by some prejudice in the matter of behaviour. British administrators in Egypt as in the Sudan were inclined to prefer the solid worth of *shaikhs* and village-headmen who might be illiterate but were also honest and respectable, pillars of the system of established order, to the brash young *effendis*, mouthing political slogans, preaching change, menacing a paternalistic establishment. It was the *effendis* who won later elections and brought their adolescent humiliations to inflame a new political relationship.

It is fashionable nowadays for historians to lay much blame on British functionaries in Egypt and the Arab countries for their neglect of the *effendi* class: students, junior officials and others easily written-off as 'half-baked'. It would be fairer to limit this blame to a later period of history than we have reached in these memoirs, for it was all but impossible, before the end of the second World War, for a member of the Cairo Residency or Embassy staff to meet and cultivate that age-group. Those elements of the Establishment now discredited—the Turco-Egyptian élite, the traditionalist landlords and their like—were still in effective control of affairs; they could not be ignored. The young men who found those pot-bellied and diabetic generals and time-serving politicians unacceptable were, no less ardently, hostile to any British presence in Egypt; they certainly made no move towards friendship with us. The Egyptian press, often a source of useful contacts, was still largely dominated by Syrian and Lebanese journalists who did not share the enthusiasms of the young

Egyptian hothead. I had working with me in Cairo during the last war many different types of *effendi*: Miss Freya Stark similarly made wide friendships in that field. Until then, a Residency contact would have been thought of by the *effendis* themselves as more compromising than desirable.

As for the Egyptian army, which was to be the fulcrum of nationalist upheaval, that world was always barred to Oriental secretariat interest. There was a British Inspector-General, or a later British military mission, and none of us had the right to poach on these preserves. None of us was likely to meet socially at a friend's house those younger officers—often of relatively humble origins, ignorant of any foreign language and hostile to all more privileged by birth or education—whose personal sense of privation bred and nourished their socialist and revolutionary thinking.

The assumption that long experience of a country can, overnight, become valueless was interestingly displayed by one post-Farouq ambassador in Cairo who refrained from discussing Egyptian affairs with the many senior British ex-officials resident in Egypt, or, indeed, with members of his own staff whose experience dated from some way back; believing that Nasser's radical changes of method and philosophy invalidated any counsel they might offer. He had, of course, a point: many personal and individual channels of approach to local thinking have been cataclysmically affected by Nasser's punitive measures against wealth and influence. But is this more than a superficial objection? Does the national character change with a change of régime? I personally believe that national characteristics are a proper subject of study in any Chancery.

Few people have been more completely revolutionised in recent history than the Russians. No régime has more dramatically swept away the conventions of its country's past. But some constants remain. What, in present Russian systems of censorship, of secret police and delation, of prison camps, of official infallibility, is different from the system of the Autocrat of All the Russias?

After such obtrusive suggestions of a claim to some experience of Egyptian attitudes, I should, perhaps, go on record in assessment of Egyptian behaviour during the years of Nasser's régime.

Unfortunately, in all that concerns the sweeping changes made in the economic and social structure of Egypt, commonsense rather than pusillanimity dictates a prudent hesitation. These are fields in which the reaction of the man in the street or in the fields is subjectively decided by personal interest. It is fourteen years since I was able to ask questions in Egypt, and the essentially individual arguments for or against this or that measure cannot be a matter for generalisation. The régime has scythed down all the tall flowers in the Egyptian garden: there is nothing much above sweet alyssum height in sight. They have reduced the areas of wealth and influence to an authorised acreage per plutocrat of one hundred acres or less. They have distributed the land of the pashas to the fellahin who were their tenants. These are all textbook procedures of revolution. Nasser did not invent them.

If more good than harm has resulted from extensive victimisations, confiscations, sequestrations and distributions, it would not be proper to condemn them. Sentiment may suggest that some geese who laid the golden eggs were slaughtered in the application of a theory to economic facts. Without the advantage of a personal inspection no judgment can be valid.

One thing is certain: appearances in Egypt are always deceptive. Demonstrations of conformity are part of the Egyptian's natural armoury.

I hope that the distribution of land to the peasantry may prove to be a blessing. In 1956, when I was last there, I heard many grumbles that the fellahin had been better off in the bad old days. An old-fashioned landlord was always ready to remit the rent in a bad year. He could be relied upon to find the money for the precious seed, from which he and his tenant would benefit in harvest. There was a relationship of shared interest, lacking today, when the owner of some fractional acreage has to deal with cold-blooded government officials and tax-collectors. I can only hope that adjustments may have been made to ensure mutual satisfaction. Meanwhile, let nobody take any public demonstration at face-value. People who flatter themselves that they know what

Sir Miles Lampson
(later Lord Killearn)

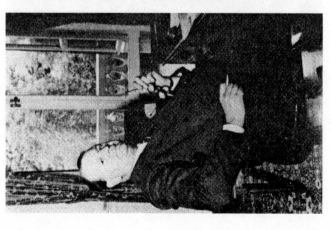

Sir Percy Loraine

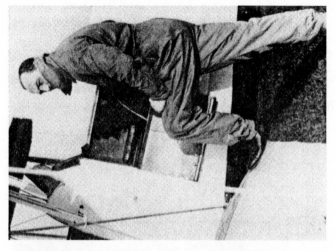

Lord Lloyd

Rowanduz Gorge, Kurdistan

Kruja, Albania

their cats are thinking are rarely right; and *Bast* and *Sekhmet* were Egyptian deities.

Egyptians, as a race, are not easily moved to demonstrations of resentment against their rulers. They bow to the wind, and survive. They are buoyed up by the conviction that, sooner or later, even the heaviest jackboot will step on that banana-skin. This trust in Allah to produce for every autocrat the desired *khazouq* is something that no Mr. Big in Cairo can prudently ignore. The clamour of adulation that greeted the well-beloved General Neguib now swells from the throats of a notably conformist populace—in which a favoured class of syndicalists sets the note—for his usurper. It will greet Gamal Abdel Nasser's successor with undiminished applause.

In the field of Egypt's foreign policy, I am more ready to express an opinion. Here it means little to say that Egyptians have behaved exactly as I expected. What is significant is that they do not seem to have behaved as Nasser himself expected.

In any analysis of the various ingredients bubbling in the witch's cauldron of the Middle East, a major factor of aggravation is the involvement of Egypt, under her President's pressures, in a role of alleged Arab hegemony and adventure, for which nothing in Egyptian history or the Egyptian temperament fits her. Egypt is not an Arab State in any racial sense. While sharing the general Mohammedan and the particular Arab resentment at Britain's implantation of a Zionist Israel in Palestine, Egyptians were rather contemptuous of Arabs, until higher authority made that mood unfashionable. They were, for millennia, content to be Egyptians; content to attend to their own affairs; content to eschew the imperialist and military adventures of their hitherto alien rulers. They are dwellers in a Nile valley; their strength is to survive. What has been manifested recently in the distant Yemen, and, on two tragic occasions, in the Sinai desert, was foreseeable and inevitable, given the traditions and character of this ebullient, humorously self-sufficient and closely self-regarding people, who have endured worse hardships than a modern police State in silent and indomitable patience.

Any friend of the Egyptians must hope that their historic

and innate distaste for the part Nasser has forced them to play has now been clearly enough displayed, and that they may now be allowed to concentrate on their own considerable domestic problems, leaving dreams of Empire and the clash of arms to others who enjoy such things.

Chapter Seven

Sovereign at Sunset

1

It sometimes happens in Foreign Office service that one is posted as vicar in a parish where one formerly laboured as junior curate. If little that is substantial has altered, previous experience then becomes valuable. If, as when I left the Hejaz as Vice-Consul and returned twenty-one years later as Minister, the harvest of the earlier incarnation is, except for its instruction of what is immutable in the local character, old rope, much needs to be forgotten and much needs to be revised. The theatre is the same, but the scenery and the performing cast have changed beyond recognition. The play may be about Roundheads and no longer about Cavaliers. Such a comprehensive change imposes, in the present case, a rather ponderous programme note.

Orthodox Moslems—the Sunni as opposed to the Shiah—follow one or other of four different rites, and it must be remembered that Islam is a code of law as well as of ritual. The Wahhabis of Saudi Arabia follow a code differing far more widely from the other three than those three differ from each other. This is why I found so much changed in a post previously familiar.

The four systems were variously codified by scholars seeking an orthodox interpretation of the Prophet Mohammed's 'Revelation' of the Qur'an and an orthodox reflection in canon law of the *Sunnah*, or religious practice, manifested in the Prophet's own behaviour and speech. There was a mass of available tradition and commentary on his attitudes and utterances, not all of which carried unchallenged authenticity, and this corpus of tradition, known as the *Hadith*, probably confused the scholars more than it assisted them.

The *Encyclopaedia Britannica* is a more suitable place than these memoirs for an analysis of the testing and transmission of tradition and of the application of a kernel of truth to differing speculative principles, which stamped each accepted code with its author's own philosophic prejudice. It is enough here to record the name and rough territorial acceptance of the three principal codes. That of Abu Hanifa, is followed by the Turks and by Moslems in Central Asia and West Pakistan. The Malikite school is popular in Upper Egypt; and the code of Ash-Shafei obtains in Syria and in Malaya. Egyptian loyalties are divided, for the Delta is apt to favour Ash-Shafei. This classification does not attempt to cover the whole Moslem world, much of which is not orthodox at all; and some principles of one rite have been accepted by adherents of another.

There is a fourth rite, and that is why the matter has been raised: the Hanbalite school. A puritanical minority within orthodox Islam eschew all sources but the literal Qur'an and the best authenticated *Hadith*. They prefer literal interpretations to any speculation. This fanatical fundamentalism makes them as unpopular with other Moslems as Plymouth Brethren would have been with the Inquisition. Much in the religious practice of the other rites is to them error, grafted on by Egyptian or Persian superstition, and as such abhorrent to a Hanbali Moslem. He sees in the otherwise universal reverence for Moslem saints and their tombs a heretical attempt to promote some other person or thing to a share in the attributes of divinity. He allows no shadow of doubt that there is no god but God.

This creed, condemning all that is not visible in the literal interpretation of the Qur'an or in those traditions of the Prophet's life that are conclusively authentic, was given new strength and a new purpose in the mid-eighteenth century by the preaching of a Nejdi divine, Mohammed Abdul Wahhab, and the interest of an 'Anaza Emir, Mohammed ibn Saud, who pledged his family and his sword to support the newly redefined faith. The families of Saud and of Abdul Wahhab remain in close alliance two hundred years later, and all Arabia knows it.

The present domination of the Arabian peninsula by the House of Saud is not the first of its adventures in aggrandisement. Mohammed and his son Abdul Aziz won Nejd and al-Hasa; the grandson, Saud ibn Abdul Aziz, went further afield and raided Kerbela, sacking the shrine of the prophet's own grandson. After ten years of desert raids and counter-raids, he occupied the Hejaz and the Holy Cities of Mecca and Medina. These twistings of the Caliph's tail brought armies from Egypt, but it was another sixteen years before the Wahhabis were beaten back to their home-base of Dera'iyah in Nejd, the town razed to the ground, and one lonely Saudi princeling left surviving to escape the massacre. This was Turki, the great-grandfather of the Ibn Saud to whom I was to be accredited as His Majesty's Minister.

Two sons of Mohammed Ali Pasha, then scheming for a throne in Egypt, led the Egyptian expeditions in Arabia. One, Emir Toussoun, owed his life to a certain Ibrahim Aga, who headed the storming-party in the siege of Medina and was the first to enter the precincts of the Prophet's Tomb. This man, a native of Edinburgh called Keith, had been captured when a gunsmith of the 78th, in Macleod's Square at El-Hamád in 1807, and had preferred Islam to release. The right-hand man of Mohammed Ali's other son, Ibrahim Pasha, was a certain Soliman Pasha (to whom an earlier reference has been made) formerly Colonel Joseph de Sève, who had fought against us at Trafalgar as a sailor and only did not fight against us as a soldier at Waterloo because he was then on Maréchal Grouchy's staff. He entered Mohammed Ali's service in 1819 and his blood ran in Farouq's veins.

During the nineteenth century, the House of Saud had its ups and downs. Faisal ibn Turki and his son Abdullah clawed back parts of their lost Nejdi lands, and the alternation of strife and alliance with the powerful Rashids of the Jebel Shammar was as chaotic as the Wars of the Roses. Low-water mark came when Faisal's son, Abdurrahman, with his boy Abdul Aziz, had to seek the sanctuary of exile with the Shaikh of Kuwait.

The legend of Abdul Aziz began when he and a handful of companions captured from the Rashids his family capital of Riyadh. The legend grew from year to year with his success in inter-tribal fighting, in judicious peacemaking and in numerous, no less judicious, marriage alliances. When the 1914–18 War broke out, he was already courted by Residents in the Persian Gulf and by the Government of India, whose unconcealed antipathy for the Sherif Hussein of Mecca reflected a prejudice in favour of his Wahhabi rival. Abdul Aziz was content to allow the British to exercise some control over his foreign policy, so long as they acknowledged the territorial integrity and independence of Nejd and paid him a considerable subsidy. The pro-Turkish manifestations of his neighbours in the Jebel Shammar and in the Yemen during the war added lustre to a commonsense attitude. In December, 1915, he signed a treaty with the British government which formalised these relations.

Tension with Hussein of the Hejaz was made inevitable by the arrogant tone and imperialistic claims made in Mecca, and was envenomed by a dispute over two small desert townships, Khurma and Taraba, both in remote Hejaz territory but both inhabited by Wahhabi sympathisers. In an earlier chapter I have mentioned my own vain efforts to persuade King Hussein to join Abdul Aziz Ibn Saud in acceptance of British arbitration offered in this matter, and the failure of this initiative combined with H.M.G.'s withdrawal of the subsidies paid to both men to encourage Ibn Saud to take the law into his own hands. In August 1924, his fanatical 'Brethren' seized the town of Taif, a summer resort for the Meccans, with some bloodshed. This circumstance persuaded Abdul Aziz to use methods of siege and blockade rather than of a bloody onslaught whose success, though certain, might bring him obloquy in the Moslem world. Slow but relentless pressures led to the abdication of King Hussein, who left for Akaba and, later, Cyprus: also to the liquidation of all Hashemite authority in the Hejaz, when Hussein's eldest son, the Emir Ali, after a few months of gently futile monarchy, sailed away to join his brother, King Faisal, in Baghdad. Abdul Aziz Ibn Saud was then able to declare himself 'King of the Hejaz and Nejd and its Dependencies', and by 1937 he was in treaty relations with Transjordan, Iraq, the Yemen and Egypt. An unwieldy title was abandoned when he chose to put his thumb-print on the map

of a peninsula so large a part of which is now known as Saudi
Arabia.

I looked forward to meeting him.

★   ★   ★

When I arrived in Cairo *en route* for Jedda, I learned that His
Majesty King Abdul Aziz ibn Abdurrahman al-Faisal Äl Saud,
more concisely known as Ibn Saud, had left Arabia for the first
time in his life on February 12, 1945, and was aboard an American
destroyer bound for Suez. President Franklin Roosevelt, on his
way home from the Yalta Conference, had invited the King to
meet him on board the U.S.S. cruiser *Quincy* in the Bitter Lakes,
hoping to be able to persuade Ibn Saud to a less intransigent
attitude towards Zionist Palestine. The story of this episode as
told by Colonel Eddy, then American Minister in Jedda, portrays
Mr. Churchill as jealously incensed by this impending confrontation and the king as hesitant to accept Mr. Churchill's own
request for a meeting until Mr. Roosevelt's approval and consent
had been obtained. The British version claims that the King
informed our Jedda Legation that he would only travel to Egypt
if he could meet the British Prime Minister as well as the American
President, and that this was gladly arranged. Arab good manners
would dictate a diffident reference to a Churchill meeting in conversation with the President, but this would not be more than a
convention of formal politeness, not literally intended.

The Roosevelt–Ibn Saud conversations might well have had
an influence on later relations, for they were cordial and friendly
and led to assurances by Mr. Roosevelt that he, as President,
would never do anything which might prove hostile to the Arabs;
and that the United States government would make no change in
its basic policy in Palestine without full prior consultation with
both Jews and Arabs. But his four separate attempts to win the
King's sympathy for the rescue and rehabilitation in Palestine of
the suffering Jews of Europe all shipwrecked on Ibn Saud's
insistence that Germany and the Germans should provide all
necessary compensation, and that Palestine, one of the poorest

and smallest countries in the allied camp, should be spared any further quota of European refugees.

Colonel Eddy's brochure, *F.D.R. meets Ibn Saud*, which is the *locus classicus* for this moment of history, from which these details have been recorded, ends his story with President Truman's remarks eight months later, when four American envoys from the Arab countries were told, in reply to their representations on the deterioration of American political interests in the Near East: 'I am sorry, gentlemen, but I have to answer to hundreds of thousands who are anxious for the success of Zionism; I do not have hundreds of thousands of Arabs among my constituents.' The envoys had already been kept waiting idly for four weeks in Washington, because President Truman was advised that it would be impolitic to receive his ministers from Arab countries, no matter how briefly, before the November Congressional elections.

Mr. Churchill had flown from the Crimea to Greece, and after the onward flight to Egypt his ears had not popped as they should; Lord Moran ordered rest in bed. There I found him, in a villa near Mena House, when I called with Stanley Jordan whom I was replacing in Jedda, to finalise arrangements for the large luncheon which the Prime Minister was to offer to Ibn Saud and his suite. Mr. Churchill, many-splendoured in a Chinese-dragon dressing-gown, welcomed us from behind an immense cigar and asked how things were going. The luncheon-party was to be given in the 'Hotel du Lac' on Lake Fayoum, a favourite shelter for illicit honeymoon couples, and security precautions imposed the arbitrary expulsion of all those then resident there, to minimise the hazards of assassination. I was less worried by security considerations than by religious scruples on the royal guest's behalf. Tobacco and alcohol are alike anathema to Wahhabi believers, and His Majesty, who, like his ancestors, was Imam of the sect, claiming the authority of a leader in prayer and ruler of a theocratic state, had never seen or smelled the unclean things. I feared that for Mr. Churchill to offend in these particulars might exceed hospitable propriety and diminish his guest in the eyes of his own people.

'What about that cigar?' I asked, and explained our problem. There was a longish pause.

'No!' declared Mr. Churchill. 'No! I won't pull down the flag! I feel as strongly about smoking as His Majesty feels about not smoking.'

There was obviously no argument, but I asked him to refrain, if possible, from smoking before going out on to the hotel verandah balcony; and this he was good enough to do. I do not know what persuasions I should have used if the Prime Minister had ever visited King Ibn Saud in Riyadh, for the act of smoking there would have been a real offence.

'And what about alcohol?', I continued.

Mr. Churchill looked alarmed. 'What about it?' he asked. I explained some more. The answer was immediate! 'We will have opaque glasses.'

And these we had at the luncheon, which was a great success. The Prime Minister sat between the King and the Emir Abdullah, a younger brother of Ibn Saud. Mr. Eden, opposite him, sat between the Emir Mohammed and the Emir Mansour, sons Nos. 3 and 8. I sat on the other side of the Emir Mohammed and did some of the interpreting on both sides of the table. The opaque glasses with which the infidels were equipped contained very brown liquor, but a small crisis threatened when the King, turning to Mr. Churchill, insisted that he sample the famous water of the Jar'ana Well, near Mecca, which had accompanied him from the Hejaz. On page 398 of *Triumph and Tragedy*, Mr. Churchill records that this was the most delicious water that he had ever tasted. I can only insist that, as observed from across the table, he excused himself, on doctor's orders, from acceptance of the proffered cup and called out: 'Anthony!' to attract Mr. Eden's attention, before pressing him to drink from the famous desert spring. As a good subordinate, the Foreign Secretary complied with good grace. Possibly Mr. Churchill's memory made Mr. Eden's reactions his own.

The Prime Minister made no effort to convert Ibn Saud to indulgence towards Zionism, preferring to leave that to the President, and I was relieved to hear from him, at that bedside audience, that this was his intention. My relief was the greater because of the argument which he then said he would have used, had the matter been discussed. This was to the effect that Great Britain 'had done a lot for Faisal, by making him King of Iraq, and for Abdullah, by accepting him as King of Jordan, and that it was for the Arabs now to do something for us'. This is an example of what the French call '*le vide des grands hommes*': British favours to Ibn Saud's most embittered dynastic enemies were hardly an ingratiating argument.

Arabs are not unique in saying to each hearer what he wishes to hear, careless of later confrontations of statement. This may explain the many divergences between Colonel Eddy's version of the King's attitudes on this Egyptian trip and that of British officialdom. He tells us that the King compared his return voyage to Jedda in a British cruiser most unfavourably with life in the U.S.S. destroyer *Murphy*. We had the same story in reverse, with deep gratitude for the large compass set up on the cruiser's deck to enable instant identification, at any hour of the day or night, of the correct path of prayer to the *Qibla* of Mecca.

While in Egypt, His Majesty saw and essayed for the first time a railway train, and there is a legend that he rode part of the way to Alexandria on the footplate. One of his first acts on his return home was to order the Arabian-American Oil Company to instal a railway-line between Riyadh and the Persian Gulf. With small justification other than the royal whim, this railway now slithers round and over the most inhospitable dunes of the Nefud desert.

*　　*　　*

The Jedda I lived in from 1920 to 1924 still slept in the pilgrimage-dust of centuries and we were a strictly enclosed community. Only a white barracks on a hill and a distant palace stood outside those walls. Its streets were a path for lurching camels and the home of tribes of pariah-dogs. No electricity gave us fans or flameless light; our water came to us from 700 miles away by sea; survival was an ordeal.

In February 1945, the plane bringing the outgoing and incoming British Ministers to Saudi Arabia landed at a modern airport, and we drove through a small suburb of villas and embryonic gardens to the familiar Medina Gate in the city wall. Lorries and a scuffle of little cars impeded our progress to what had been the house and offices of the Dutchman Van de Poll and was now the residence of His Majesty's Minister. From its windows, the view of Jedda seemed little changed. But within was an air-conditioned study and an air-conditioned bedroom, pleasant living-rooms with good English furniture, and running taps in the bathrooms and water-borne sanitation as a last surprise. The broken-down condenser of an earlier day had given place to an impressive apparatus adequate for all the needs of the town; skinny Arabs still ran up the back-stairs with *tanakas* of water on their shoulder-yokes, shouting: '*Ya satir!*' to warn any womenfolk of the household of their male approach; but they brought enough and plenty for our occidental refinements. The Legation Chancery and offices were housed in the building I had known as my home for some long and uncomfortable years.

Jordan stayed on for a few days before leaving me, and I was distressed to find how poor an opinion he had formed of all around him, because such attitudes are always reciprocated. He spoke hopefully of an appointment as our Ambassador in Tehran, but his future lay in a Trade Commission office in Jerusalem. As is customary, I took whatever he wished to leave at his valuation, and found among other things in the store-cupboard three dozen tins of pig's trotters, which were at least secure from pilferage because no Moslem servant would cook, let alone eat them. I also found myself in possession of a dozen and a half large tins of a breakfast cereal new to my experience, and only on reading the small print later did I realise that Torbet Lactic Oats were medicinal and carminative. The flatulent sufferer is advised to take one dessertspoonful, to wait and see whether that is enough, and, if the necessity becomes manifest, to take another. This system of hit-or-miss suggested laboratory experiment rather than an established régime, but I was unfamiliar with a product rarely found in a diplomatic commissariat.

Our Legation staff was not large. Eldon Ellison was Head of

Chancery; Geoffrey Baker and Morgan Man were junior secretaries, Morgan being responsible for the Oriental Secretary side of the work. He had good Arabic but even better German, and could have passed as a young Hamburg man-about-town anywhere in the Reich. What had been our living-quarters on the top floor were given over to cipher mysteries involving a serious young poet called Michael Poole and a willowy beauty who should have been a girl. At the heart of the machine were two ex-N.C.O.'s who had chosen life in Jedda between the wars, Cyril Ousman and Willy Horne; and they, helped by Alan Roy, made the wheels of routine and clerical activity go round. Moira Man and Dorothy Ousman were the only wives, and Dorothy was a legend I had never met but knew of long before our meeting. For years she had established a position of social authority in a community and ambience unimaginable in her Staffordshire home, imposing standards of behaviour and adaptations of convention to which successive heads of mission, if not their wives, had dutifully bent the knee. Any bachelor minister was assured of experienced guidance in the arrangement of his furniture and the management of his household, and any wife was assured of a stimulating competition of wills if she differed, however firmly, from the rulings of a blue-eyed, golden-pompadoured arbitress of accepted tradition.

The Middle East supply centre in Cairo had for years organised the rationing to Saudi Arabia, as to other countries in the diocese of our Minister of State, of essential commodities in wartime short supply, and the co-ordination of local economic activity; and its Jedda office, like others, had amassed many files of valuable economic and commercial information. American association with the centre had been strongly built up in Cairo by Mr. James Landis, with the result that the Jedda office was predominantly American-staffed. When the centre began detaching itself from the outposts, this circumstance brought to my United States colleague a massive and precious supply of men and facts and figures, and I was only able to snatch from the dissolving structure one solitary British corporal; but he was worth his weight in gold.

John T. Davis (the initial stands for Tillett) was a grandson of the famous Trades Union leader Ben Tillett, and a man of parts. He had not taken up the history scholarship to Oxford which he was awarded, preferring to win First Class Honours in Economics at Birmingham University. Rotting in idleness in wartime Cairo, he had taught himself Egyptian hieroglyphics and was encyclopaedic about the Pharaohs. In such trade work as fell to us, he was invaluable. In fairness I should say that the M.E.S.C. archives in the U.S. Legation were ostensibly available for our consultation at any time, on official request.

Surprisingly, and regrettably, our relations with the American Legation were a little precarious. Colonel William Eddy, the Minister, was an admirable choice for the post. The son of Presbyterian missionaries who lived and died in Syria, he was born in Sidon and spoke fluent and good Arabic. He had been Professor of English at the American University in Cairo and at Dartmouth College; President of Hobart and William Smith Colleges; U.S. naval attaché in Cairo and Chief of the O.S.S. in North Africa at the time of the Allied landings. We were on most friendly terms. But in those closing months of the war America was becoming convincedly aware of her imperial destiny. Until then, non-involvement in Middle East affairs had well suited America's mood. Theodore Roosevelt might tell us, in Egypt, to govern or get out, but this was advice from the side-lines. No United States President would have touched an American mandate for Syria, in spite of the King–Crane Report, or the American mandate for Armenia mooted at the same time, with a bargepole. With a growing sense of power, this isolation from the Middle East came to be regarded as due to a colonial conspiracy, aimed at preserving for Britain and France their dominant position there; and a merely passive disapproval of our monopolistic attitudes yielded to an impatient urge to replace the old by the new. A conviction grew, in the State Department and outside, that the United States had only to succeed Britain and France in direct confrontation of the Arab world for friendship and sympathy with the West to blossom in the desert like a rose. With no sullied page of history to deny, with so much goodwill and hope to offer, old hostilities must surely fade for lack of cause. This might be called the Wallace Murray–Loy Henderson syndrome. It powerfully affected Washington policies and economics in the Middle East, and it inevitably involved some slight embarrassment of mind in those of our friends whose task it became to substitute American for British influence.

Except for its failure to assess the damaging effect of U.S. interest in Zionism, no one need criticise this theory or the policy which reflected it. The first lesson we had to learn after 1945 was that nobody owed us a living: the war-years before the Lend-Lease Bill and Pearl Harbor interested only ourselves. And as far as my parish of Saudi Arabia was concerned, I had every reason to welcome American involvement in Arab affairs and the creation of an oil-lobby in Washington potentially offsetting the hitherto unchallenged lobby influencing attitudes on Palestine. I was delighted to see some desert sand in American shoes. But although every goodwill was manifested by H.M. Minister, American susceptibilities were extreme. Years later, when I was on an international commission in Khartoum in 1954, my eleventh-generation American wife was informed by the U.S. representative of that time that I had a very good dossier in the State department; but, while in Jedda, I was more than once accused to London of being 'anti-American'. King Ibn Saud often complained to me that he hated having to choose between his friends in the matter of contracts: if we and the Americans would only agree between ourselves on 'who should get what', he would happily conform. He said the same thing to Senator Pepper, when he was in Arabia, chasing some aviation or telecommunications business. The Senator cabled to the President complaining that the British minister was, according to the King, the only obstacle in the way of American success; and this was passed on to Whitehall. I was exculpated, but my successor was compelled to superannuate himself at the age of fifty-four for no other, and for just as grotesque, reasons. However cordial our relations with Bill Eddy, Merritt Grant, Bill Sands and the rest of them, there was always this hazard of attack from some visiting politicians or businessmen, more aggressive and brash than our diplomatic friends.

The American Legation was an impressive building (now, I believe, abandoned for something better) standing some way outside the town on the edge of the sea. It had full air-conditioning and every modern comfort, and on its wide roof a weekly assembly watched a series of British or American films. The American unofficial community was numerous and expanding. Aramco, who handled the oil concession granted in 1934, which had begun pumping oil in 1939 from its field at Dhahran to the refinery and port of Ras Tannura on the Persian Gulf, had an office with mainly representational duties in Jedda and a houseful of friendly folk whose air-conditioning was always colder than anyone else's. Another American group ran the mining syndicate exploiting the *Mahd-al-Dhahab* or Cradle of Gold, between Mecca and Medina, a mine not worked since the days of Sheba. The pilots of Ibn Saud's Dakotas were also American. British civilians were now a minority. A joint committee selected the weekly films from an assortment containing much trash.

Any graphic representation of the human form is condemned by Moslem orthodoxy, and this Semitic abhorrence, deepened by the alien subject matter of idolatry, barred all natives of Arabia from the silver screen. During the war, propagandist zeal had supplied our Legation with films and a projector, and Willy Horne installed the works on our Legation roof and prepared to show the non-Moslem population of Jedda what they were missing at home. The first film shown had some wartime message, no doubt, but this was not exclusively plugged. Miss Brenda Marshall, when the plot required her to remove some lingerie, produced strong reactions in the crowd of Jeddawis who had been squinnying up four storeys to a distant flicker of picture, from their packed position on the city wall. There was a sudden and universal gasp as the garment fell, and with it the wall and its human burden fell also, in a confusion of collapse. After that we were instructed to place a screening of wood on the street side of our improvised cinema.

We only gave occasional shows, and to some of these the local Saudi officials insisted on invitation. *Brief Encounter* was movingly played, but our sound track went haywire that night. No voice was audible, and the incessant whine and screech of the sound suggested heavy traffic in the railway station.

My French colleague was a former Moroccan official called Max Rageot, a busy and friendly person, except when shadows fell over Anglo-French relations. We shared an interest in the fate of pilgrims from West Africa, for there were French as well as British *Takrunis,* and in collaboration we were able to obtain some advantage for them. But in June 1945, the Syrian and Lebanese Governments refused to buy a withdrawal of French troops, and a transfer of duties to local levies, by signing French-drafted treaties of alliance, giving France the privileged military, economic and cultural position demanded. The French bombarded Damascus, causing much loss of life. Britain intervened, taking over the military occupation of Syria and enforcing the withdrawal of French troops and French officials to Lebanon. This bruising blow to French pride brought my colleague round at white heat, and his enraged protest ended on a surprisingly high note: '*N'oubliez pas que nous avons le Moufti!*' It can hardly have been a coincidence that the notorious Amin el-Husseini, ex-Mufti of Jerusalem, who had been declared a war criminal for his association with Hitler and was in French custody, soon made his reappearance in the Middle East, as a focus of anti-British activity.

A second Arab war criminal, Rashid Ali al-Gailani of Iraq, who had also been in French custody, was conveniently able to make his escape to the Middle East at much the same time; but his potential for harm was blunted by Ibn Saud.

The admirable Daniel van der Meulen was Netherlands Minister. I had known him off and on for some years, and his noble chestnut beard had grizzled since our first meeting; but he was always active and imaginative in co-operation on pilgrimage affairs, and well-informed about our parish. His own experience went far beyond it, for he had travelled widely in the Hadhramaut and hinterland of the Gulf, and had lovely photographs, and not a few books, to show for it. The only bank in Jedda was Dutch, run by a friendly and disillusioned man who was seconded by Sayed el-Attas, a charming Hadhrami from Java. Van de Poll,

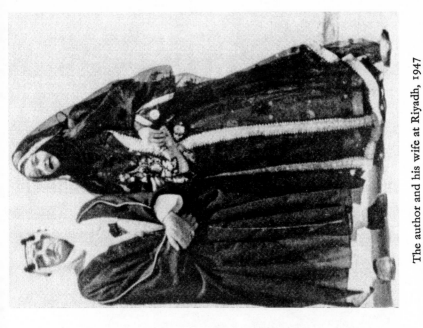

The author and his wife at Riyadh, 1947

Ceremony at Ta'if, 1945

H.M. King Ibn Saud

the prosperous merchant of 1924, was a shadow of his former self, now back where he started and financially embarrassed. He haunted the fringes of Jedda social life, and was more or less dropped when he married a very young Bedu shepherd-girl.

Saudi-Hashemite tensions prevented any Jordanian representation, and the Iraqi Minister's official life was not easy. I had known his brother in Bagdad, and this helped me to a welcome from him. The Egyptian Minister, el-Amroussi Bey, was rather overshadowed by Madame, whom everyone loved. She was a daughter of an old friend of mine, Hassan Shawarby Pasha, who was always to be found wearing white spats at one particular table in Groppi's, and she gave refreshingly unascetic parties in a country where most Moslem Legations were ostentatiously abstemious. She knew that party-success is assured by half a bottle of gin in the fruit-salad.

The British civilian element in Jedda far outnumbered the total European population of my earlier sojourn there. Messrs. Gellatly, Hankey still showed the flag, and the rival firm of Mitchell Cotts supplied another contingent. I was able to help combat one local mischief by persuading the King to engage a London oculist to organise a fight against trachoma, and young Dr. Longinotto from Moorfields did yeoman work. I trust he also benefited from royal generosity in the reward of services rendered to the Palace and its *harim*. My Cairo dentist, summoned to Riyadh to pull a few royal teeth, took three weeks off from his Egyptian labours and returned with a hatful of gold.

Some way away to the north of Jedda, a British locust mission had their camp and headquarters; and their work, too, was of great value. They criss-crossed Arabia in their search for hoppers, and became very knowledgeable about geography. Unfortunately, one swarm of locusts did great damage to the King's Riyadh gardens and he abandoned all faith in modern methods. He told me that the beating of tin cans and waving of garments in the air were tried and true forms of attack and that the locust mission's endeavours had no effect other than the poisoning of young locusts which the Beduin wanted to eat.

Facile princeps in the small British colony of departments was a man whom we saw but rarely in Jedda, the explorer H. St. John Philby, normally resident in the King's suite in Riyadh. He was more of a problem than all the other Britannics put together.

He is generally remembered as a man of action, but his academic equipment was remarkable. He had been a scholar and head-boy of Westminster, and a major scholar (Classics) of Trinity, Cambridge, where he won a First in the modern language tripos, before serving in the Indian civil service and acquiring Punjabi, Pushtu and other languages. Administrative service in Iraq led to his mission to Ibn Saud in 1917 and his crossing of Arabia from Uqair to Jedda. He came back to Ibn Saud from a not very happy appointment as chief political officer in Amman, and it is from about 1925 that his best-known incarnation—the desert explorer, the Muhammedan convert, the trusted adviser of King Ibn Saud—begins. This phase of his life is well and fully recorded in his own books.

I had known him for a long time (in the Oriental Secretariat in Cairo we saw a good deal of traffic to and from the world to our south), and always liked and admired him personally. When a London businessman asked me whether Philby would be a good choice for the post of resident director of a company called Sharqieh Ltd he was forming in the Hejaz, I commended his selection. This company, which gave Philby a living for many years, had some excellent agencies, including Marconi's and Ford's; but I have an idea that the London businessman who had thought it up ended by regretting his choice of agent.

He was congenitally 'agin the Government', and the difference of opinion which had separated him from Whitehall in 1924 grew to an obsessive antipathy for His Majesty's government and all their works. He had stood as a Peace Party candidate before the war, and retained this attitude after war broke out. My friend Stonehewer-Bird, our minister in wartime Jedda, was embarrassed when Philby stormed into his office, turned off the wireless and announced that all BBC news was a lie and that only Berlin and Bari told the truth. When Philby planned and set out on a visit to lecture in the United States, a tip-off from the most exalted source advised examination of his suitcases, and, when this was done at Karachi, he was detained under the notorious clause 18(B). His brother was commanding the Indian navy contingent in Karachi harbour at the same time as the distinguished explorer whom Sir Andrew Ryan referred to as 'Sinjallah Philby' lay in official custody. Sir Andrew, as a practising Roman Catholic, disapproved of conversion to Islam.

Having heard from Stonehewer-Bird of Philby's embarrassing behaviour, I was horrified to hear, just before leaving England, that he was at large again and was to return to Saudi Arabia. We were still at war, and I disliked the thought of vehemently anti-British utterances by so influential an old friend. But the pressures from his socialist friends of Peace Party days had been irresistible: I had to accept the fact of his return.

Messrs. Mitchell Cotts had taken over the running of Sharqieh Ltd., and Philby was more useful to them in Riyadh than in Jedda, which he only rarely visited. He made some effort to trail his coat provocatively, but I refused every invitation to quarrel and told him that I would not even argue with him. This brought peace. He knew that he was always welcome under my roof, even if he had to gate-crash parties to get there.

He was very proud of his son Kim. Did he suspect, or would he have cared, that his habit of automatic condemnation of every aspect of British Government policy might be a seed-bed of treason?

I had one opportunity of avenging his long denigration of British policies. Ibn Saud was discussing Philby with me after dinner, with unusual objectivity, ending his remarks with the loyal statement that Philby would always be for him the man who had chosen to throw away a brilliant career in British service rather than obey London's orders to work with the Emir Abdullah in Amman for Ibn Saud's discomfiture. This is so far from Philby's own published reasons for his resignation and abandonment of his Amman job, which in fact followed a difference of opinion about the level of grants-in-aid and his growing dislike of the intrusive expansion of Palestine Government influence, that I was sorely tempted to corrective protest.

I preferred to leave the legend undisturbed. After more than twenty years, what did it matter?

$$\star \qquad \star \qquad \star$$

The Holy City of Mecca can only be seen from close at hand, for it lies in a hollow of encircling hills. The four main routes of access are marked, well on the hither side, with white columns, marking the limit of infidel approach. I have been to three of these points, and at one of them, near the little village of Shumaisi, King Ibn Saud suggested a meeting to enable me to present to him formally my letters of credence. Disguised in white uniform, my staff and I drove up the Mecca road, where a fire which flared up in my large official Humber Pullman car involved us in energetic business with desert sand and brought us in some dishevelment to the King's camp. The car, which carried seven passengers in comfort, carried no extinguisher.

I thought it polite to make the usual speech, when presenting my Letters, in Arabic rather than English, and this irregularity of protocol was obviously welcome. After the official proceedings, we changed into Arab clothes and were entertained to a royal meal. All travellers in the interior of Saudi Arabia, which may be considered as beginning just outside the Jedda conurbation, were expected to wear Arab clothes, and the first gifts received by distinguished visitors on their arrival were camel's-hair cloaks and associated linen drawers and robes, with head-cloths and the gold-thread fillets to bind and secure them. The outfit was, to some, most becoming: a narrow bearded face gained great dignity from the *kuffiya* and the *igál*; but not mine. However, I soon forgot my unconvincing appearance and found the robes of obligatory travesty easy and comfortable to wear.

King Ibn Saud was now nearly seventy years of age, but still *muy hombre*, very much a man. Tall and very deep-chested, he looked impressively square-hewn, despite the slight stoop of age and the arthritis which imposed an outer ramp for his transport to the first-floor level of his Jedda palace. He had lost his left eye by neglect of an infection, and a recital of his battle-wounds and scars was an illustration of history; but he still had more than the mere remains of great physical strength, and the gentle hands and charming smile that made many love him. His life and miracles have been so exhaustively recorded by Armstrong and Philby and de Gaury, Benoist-Méchin and van der Meulen, and other predecessors of David Howarth, that it would be impertinent of me to recapitulate these Arabian events. Only where his past continued to affect my present will some reference be necessary to the days before arthritis and age diminished Arabia's most remarkable scion of our day.

I soon fell under his spell. His Arabic was not easy for me to understand, being a mixture of the classical (which I could follow) and tribal and beduin locutions (which I could not). His voice, too, had no timbre, and much was said in a hoarse whisper confusing to the ear. His preoccupations were both economic and political.

In 1945, the oil developments in Eastern Arabia had not yet produced the flood of royalties that came later, and revenues from Aramco were not yet large enough, by royal standards, for royal needs. The company was under constant pressure for advances, or for initiatives mortgaging royalties for years ahead, and this state of something short of complete affluence irritated and embittered the King. Finance was not made easier by desert practice. There was no government account into which oil royalties were to be paid; there was not even an account in the King's own name. Whatever Messrs. Aramco had to pay went into a New York bank account in the name of Shaikh Abdullah Suleiman, the Saudi minister of finance, in which his own personal fortune was also kept, and his signature alone was operative. Shaikh Abdullah Suleiman was the button the King pressed when needing cash.

He needed a great deal. He then had thirty-seven living sons, and they all, as they attained years of indiscretion, expected palaces and wives and Cadillacs which a doting father could not refuse them. But a far more severe haemorrhage of income flowed from Ibn Saud's treatment of the tribes.

The famous night when Riyadh was recaptured had been

followed by years of skirmish and campaign against desert princelings and tribes guilty of *shirk*, that infringement of divine attributes which is anathema to a Wahhabi; and as each tribe succumbed to conquest it was subjected to Wahhabi disciplines. Ibn Saud's next step was to create one fiery organisation in which all tribal loyalties melted, and this, the military brotherhood of the *Ikhwan*, became an invincible weapon of expansion. The *Ikhwan* forgot their parochial animosities in the new fervour of puritanical and iconclastic Wahhabi zeal, and their loyalty went, after God, to the Imam of their militant faith. With such swords in his service, Ibn Saud was able not only to extend the limits of expansion to include his dominions as we knew them; he could, and did, also threaten Iraq and Transjordan. I personally believe that the Brethren might have overwhelmed both these territories in their victorious advance had not Britain, as mandatory power, offered the genius of John Glubb and the protection of her diplomatic persuasion. The frontiers between the Hejaz and Transjordan, and between Nejd and Iraq, were drawn with due acceptance by Ibn Saud of the obligations of old friendship as well as of hard fact. Indeed, the high contracting parties agreed to differ on the definition of the Hejaz-Transjordan frontier, and Ibn Saud only agreed to the status quo existing under our Mandate 'until favourable circumstances permit a final settlement'.

The hardest part of his task in 'breaking the thorns of the Beduin' came with the dissolution of the *Ikhwan* and their urban settlement in over a hundred desert townships. His chief commander, Faisal al-Dawish, rebelled, claiming that the Holy War against the *mushrikin* must not be abandoned, but discipline prevailed. The raiding and the plundering and the internecine desert strife of long tradition were ended. These habits could hardly have survived long in an age of air-raids and tanks; their ablation from desert life was none the less surprising, and complete. But, as one result of the King's policy, great hordes of pauperised Beduin lived in idleness on his charity outside the town of Riyadh. The dole necessary to keep alive this ever-growing beggar population was the main item in the King's expenses for which Shaikh Abdullah Suleiman was called on to provide.

Apart from these financial worries and, of course, the constant preoccupation of Palestine, Ibn Saud's most nagging grievance in my day was the hard fact of his encirclement by hostile neighbours. He claimed to have desisted from invasion of British mandatory territory in Iraq and Transjordan out of loyal friendship for the mandatory power; but, to his annoyance, Britain later abandoned both mandates and sponsored Iraq and Jordan to independence, slipping out from under, as the King saw it, and leaving him to Hashemite enemy neighbours. He was by origins not a Bedu himself, being of the settled people of 'Anaza, and he had some contempt for his incalculable nomads; but he was Arab enough to share their dislike of frontier-lines drawn on a map with no reference to the essentials of pasturage and wells. In the old days an Arab could travel, with no passport or customs-trouble, anywhere in the Arab world, and tribes could move in winter or summer to feeding-grounds or watering-places now separated by Syrian or Iraqi or Jordanian cartography from Ibn Saud's authority. He found this intolerable, and often said so.

There was one happy day when he thought he had found a gap in the official Syrian frontier with his own and with Iraqi territory; the various official maps certainly seemed to say different things about one corner up at the top. This loophole he planned to exploit in the interests of customs- and document-free travel for man and beast; but I left the country before any experiment was tried.

The framework of his government and administration was resilient, primitive and ramshackle. The King's eldest son, the Emir Saud, was Viceroy of Nejd; his second son, the Emir Faisal, Viceroy of the Hejaz and Minister for Foreign Affairs. In this departmental duty he was assisted at various times by three persons, all of non-Saudi origins, and in other government departments a Syrian or Moslem Lebanese was often found in charge. The Finance Minister was, and had been for years, Shaikh Abdullah Suleiman, a Nejdi from Aneiza who had worked when young in a Bombay coffee-shop. He was nervous in attitude towards the King but always prepared to take excessive risks. He was the only Finance Minister I ever met who drank methylated spirit.

The only other Minister was the Emir Mansour, the King's eighth and very much loved son, who was Minister of War.

Office in the State brought great rewards in perquisites if not in salary. A series of peculating officials, led by Shaikh Nejib Salha, settled in Cairo after their exposure in Arabia and bought up the biggest and best of Cairo house-property.

. The King, whose authority was absolute, was concerned to enforce the Wahhabi way of life both as a rule of individual conduct and as a system of government, and to adapt to the solution of twentieth-century problems a seventh-century philosophy. He relied, just enough to avoid trouble, on the *Ulamá*, or religious divines, who administered the canon law and trained those officials, known as the *Mutawwa'in*, who executed the administrative functions called for under that law. The consent of the *Ulamá* was necessary for any administrative innovation, but here, as when he imposed wireless by broadcasting the Qur'an, the King was always master. The great provinces of the country were kept in loyal dependence by the great families of Sidairi, Jiluwi and others, all linked with one whose many marriages never excluded the politically expedient. Minor officials, alas, were generally related to their superiors: nepotism is not considered heinous in oriental assessment.

Ibn Saud did his thinking aloud about problems of the day when he summoned his *Diwan*, or privy council, to advise him. The same penury of local talent that brought Syrian adventurers into the administration filled the *Diwan* with an assortment of alien advisers. Partly, also, by design, this heterogenous group contained no ingredients for any 'ganging-up'. Shaikh Abdullah Suleiman there shared influence with Shaikh Yusuf Yassin, the King's secretary and head of his political department. This assiduously busy man was an Alawite from Latakieh, and he acted as the King's mouthpiece and as general obstructionist to the diplomatic missions. Fuad Hamza, a Druze, had preceded him on the foreign affairs side, and Shaikh Hafez Wahba, an old Cairo blacklist friend from 1917 and now a K.C.V.O., took some part in Council discussions when on leave from his London embassy. He was an Egyptian, and an Azhar graduate. There was a respectable Hejazi from Medina; a Cyrenaican, Khalid el-Qarqani; a Tripolitanian, Bashir Sa'adawi Bey, and, not to be overlooked, Philby.

I was once privileged to attend a privy council meeting, when in Riyadh. We went to a lower room after the evening meal, and sat round the wall. I sat next the King, who patted my hand reassuringly from time to time. After a kneeling scribe had read out his monitoring of the wireless-news, the King began commenting on it, calling on one or another for his views. No one seemed anxious to do more than echo his master's voice, but Philby, in his role of court jester, spoke up and rebuked the King for what he thought mistaken opinions with complete familiarity. These corrective interventions were valuable, and the King knew it. Now and then some detail of exotic wartime geography or obscure personality was referred to me for elucidation. It was an unusual evening.

In June 1945, hearing that Lord Wavell, now Viceroy, was flying back from England to New Delhi by way of Cairo and Bahrain, I asked him if he would consider a visit to King Ibn Saud *en route,* having obtained the King's warm approval of this suggestion beforehand. An R.A.F. Lodestar brought the Viceroy from Cairo to Jedda early on June 3 and he was welcomed there by the Emir Mansour. In the King's private apartments in the Khuzám Palace, a carnival atmosphere reigned while we assumed the ritual *sirwals* and *thobs,* draped *abayas* and adjusted *kuffiyas* and *iqáls.* Breakfast was more of a masquerade than a meal.

The R.A.F. machine took the Viceroy, Sir Evan Jenkins and an A.D.C., with the Emir Mansour, and I followed in Ibn Saud's private aeroplane. At Buwaib landing-ground, 50 kilometres from Riyadh, the Emir Khaled, fourth son of the King, awaited us with spare sets of Arab clothing. At four o'clock we reached the Badia Palace, our home in Riyadh, to be welcomed by the Emir Saud; and all hopes of a wash had to be abandoned. We waited on the King at 5 p.m. and dined with him after the sunset prayer on the roof of the *Qasr-el-Murabba'* Palace. The reed-like voices of five blind devotees, chanting the Qur'an, blended with the droning concert of distant water-wheels behind the bravery of brocades and gold of Ibn Saud's fantastic bodyguard. As usual, after dinner, rose-water and frankincense and perfumed oils were ceremoniously applied, but the King made an unusual gesture in conducting us to a point from which we could look down into his private wing of the Palace.

Lord Wavell persuaded the King to tell the story of his capture of Riyadh, forty-odd years before, and there was a moment when I expected to observe a detailed comparison of wounds. 'Soldiers always understand one another,' the King remarked, remembering that he had a field marshal as a guest. On our drive home, the Emir Nasser, the dark-skinned mayor of Riyadh, showed us the famous spear-point in the citadel-door and the bloodstains, still startling on the wall, which remain from the night when young Abdul Aziz won the first of many desert victories. I told the Viceroy of the King's statesmanlike clemency after victory; he always sought to spare the family of his enemies, but to keep them close enough for supervision. The sons of his arch-enemy, Ibn Rashid, were brought up with his own and lived in comfort in Riyadh. The infant son of the Governor of Riyadh, whose killing had been described to us, was now the most trusted among Ibn Saud's followers and guarded him during sleep.

This visit, with the banquet and the chanting, was typical of many: the routine rarely changed. I have been present at even more splendid feasts and looked down a diminishing perspective of roast camels. Other occasions were simpler. Ibn Saud was not a great eater, and preferred to our succession of viands a great bowl of warm camel's milk, slightly curdled, which I found delicious. I asked him, in all sincerity, that I might never be overlooked when it was served, and he always remembered this. He professed to be worried and distressed by my celibate state and applied the frankincense and oils with his own hand, spreading fragrance with a glass rod from a flagon of perfume over my hands and wrists. He swore that the aphrodisiac effect was proverbial. I did not wish to controvert the experience of one who had had one hundred and twenty-five wives, and who refused to abdicate alcove responsibilities while life lasted; but I felt that the King's assurance that no woman could resist me, once his perfumes were upon me, might, if realised, cause some raised eyebrows in our community, which contained no unmarried woman. I used to leave His Majesty smelling like all Soho at a christening.

The King's habit of giving presents to his guests was a constant problem. These ranged from one set of Arab clothing for the humblest, through the gold watch bearing the King's name and the gold *khanjar* dagger, to the gold sabre, mounted, in the most exalted cases, with brilliants. These were variously predictable. Surprises came when the greater included all the less, and when pearl necklaces, Persian rugs and diamond rings sweetened the farewells. Nothing was ever given in the King's presence. A chamberlain discreetly laid the surprise-packet in the visitor's room. Mr. Churchill, after the Cairo meeting, and the Viceroy, after his visit to Riyadh, were embarrassingly indemnified for their gestures of friendship.

Ideally, a guest should be able to return such generosity with presents no less generous, but this was impossible, and it was the selection of gifts for royal acceptance that made our problem. Perfume was the commonest currency of gratitude: the King seemed never to have too much of it. Mr. Churchill turned over all his treasure-chest to H.M. Treasury and they presented the King with a Rolls-Royce. Lord Wavell scored a bullseye with a charming illuminated Qur'an. When Sir Alan Brooke visited Jedda with Admiral Tennant and General Paget, I asked him what he had decided about this and learned that he had brought a walking-stick, to relieve the King's arthritis. It was the loveliest thing: a heavy malacca cane, all but transparent and tawny as treacle. But my face fell when I saw it, for it had a pigskin handle, and this is not a contact welcome to a strict Moslem. It was too late to improvise any alternative, and the beautiful thing was presented, rather in the hope that Ibn Saud, never having seen pig-skin, might not know it for what it was. He continued to use the trusty old wife-beater we all knew so well.

It may be shocking to look a gift-camel in the mouth, and a royal beast at that, but I sometimes wondered whether Ibn Saud really knew what was being given in his name. Some of his guests found themselves with impressive necklaces of artificial pearls, or Persian rugs deeply defaced by moth. The picture of some store-keeper or minor chamberlain cooking the Treasury inventory in his own financial interest was insistent.

The sequel to the Ibn Saud–Churchill exchange of gifts was unexpected. The King had been promised 'the finest motor-car in the world', but the British Ministry of Supply were lucky, in the circumstances of 1945, to find the one firm of coachbuilders who had had a new Rolls-Royce on their hands since 1939. This was to be the present of His Majesty's government, and we were asked to advise on structural refinements and coachwork. I con-sulted those best informed on His Majesty's tastes and prejudices and recommended a gun-rack, running-boards long enough and wide enough to accommodate three of the bodyguard on each side, with chromium hand-holds for their support, and a vast armchair for royal comfort behind the driver's seat. Cyril Ousman had had first-war experience in Rolls-Royce armoured cars, and I asked him to nurse the lovely silver-grey bird across the desert and deliver it, after ritual ablutions, to the King in the Palace courtyard. Ibn Saud exclaimed in admiration when he saw the car, but before Ousman left him he heard the King tell his brother, the Emir Abdullah, that he could have it. He had noticed that it had a right-hand drive. This was something we could not have changed and, indeed, had not thought of, since the rule of the road in Saudi Arabia is what the King cares to make it. But no one had told us that the King sometimes sat in front, on long drives across the desert, and he had instantly seen that he could not do so in the car given to him without sitting on his driver's left: an intolerable humiliation by oriental convention. The finest motor-car in the world was unusable.

In 1912, this convention of honour attaching to the right-hand position led the Khedive's aide-de-camp, Colonel von Turneisen, to call out a Greek friend in Alexandria and shoot him. The man had offered him a lift, after an official funeral where traffic-control went awry, and he had imprudently put the colonel on his left.

As in earlier days with King Hussein, I found most pleasure in listening to Ibn Saud on other subjects than those of our joint official interest. He made shrewd comments on his contemporaries, dividing them into three groups: '*Rájul wa nusf rájul wa la'sh rájul*', literally, 'the man, the half-man and the non-man', which in his interpretation meant the intelligent man who yet takes advice, the unintelligent man who takes advice, and the unintelligent man who refuses advice. One Egyptian national leader was '*Kathír al háraka, qalíl al báraka*', 'busily active, and ineffective'. The art of diplomacy he summed up as '*Kalám láyin yághlub haqq báyin*', 'smoothness of speech will get the best of right, however manifest'. His admiration for Churchill needed no Arabic saws for its expression.

He had no sense of figures; anything over one thousand defeated him, which must have complicated discussion of barrels and royalties. I once found him in tears, and he explained that he had just learned that there were as many as 5,000 Jews living in the city of New York. I did not correct him. Shortly before, an administrative act of British policy in Palestine had been held up for three weeks in deference to presidential anxieties about the mayoral election in New York.

It is in a context of arithmetic that I most happily remember him. Having received the present of a camel from a man in al-Hasa, he instructed the Amir of that province to pay him the conventional return-present of 300 rupees. In Arabic, a nought is represented by a single dot, like a full-stop, and His Majesty's reed-pen spluttered. The Governor wrote back, asking if the King had not meant to give the man the usual recompense of 300 rupees, instead of the 300,000 rupees apparently ordered in his letter. Ibn Saud's reply was immediate: 'Pay him,' he wrote, '300,000 rupees without delay. No one shall say that my hand is more generous than my heart!'

2

As the war drew to its close, British heads of mission in the Middle East were summoned to Egypt to hear from Sir Wilfred Eady of the Treasury the stark facts of Britain's economic plight. In the hospitable Fayoum Oasis hotel where Ibn Saud had been entertained, we were told that the essentially unthrifty house-keeping, which alone had enabled us to win through, now had its aftermath in accounts rendered by India, Egypt and other countries where our war-effort had run up immense bills. Most of us, I suspect, had not realised that so scrupulous a reckoning had been kept of expenses incurred in Egypt and elsewhere. The tally of sterling balances owing to these creditors made us fearful of impending bankruptcy.

I enjoyed the renewed contact with many old friends more than the cause of it, but I had to leave Egypt before the end of the conference: a cable from Jedda informed me that Ibn Saud required my immediate return and that he would await me in the desert, at Duwademi, to the west of his capital. I flew down to Jedda at once, and halted only long enough to assume Arab clothes before flying on to Duwademi in one of the King's Dakotas. As nobody had ever landed an aircraft there—and may well never have done so since—I was happy when the American pilot put us smoothly on the ground. I went to the King's camp, and every-one else left his tent as I came in. The King's news was indeed startling.

Ten days or so earlier, he had been asked by a Western frontier official whether permission should be given to three Syrian journalists to proceed to the royal audience they requested. It is alleged that Ibn Saud was always easily tempted by two prospects: that of a new and effective aphrodisiac, and that of hearing some dirt about King Abdullah of Transjordan. He may have expected the latter when he authorised the journalists' entry. On arrival at Riyadh, they were admitted to his presence, and two of them then retired, with salaams. The third, showing his face to the King, electrified him by announcing: 'I am Rashid Ali!'. The King cried out that there is no Strength and no Power except in God, and asked to be left alone.

The most notorious and most embittered Iraqi rebel against the Hashemite regime in Iraq had sought sanctuary with the Hashemites' chief dynastic enemy.

In 1941, when many doubted the chances of British victory, a revolt of four popular Iraqi generals, 'the Golden Square', had found an accomplice in Rashid Ali al-Gailani who formed a pro-Axis Government. The Regent, the Emir Abdulillah, Nuri Pasha and other leaders fled for their lives, Nuri being smuggled out to the R.A.F. station at Habbanya under a rug in the American Minister's car. Emir Abdulillah's sister, the Queen-Mother, and her little son King Faisal, were held in uneasy detention in Shaqlawa, in Kurdistan. The discomforts and apprehensions of the British community beleaguered in the embassy have been vividly described in Freya Stark's autobiography. Thanks largely to landing facilities provided by the Vichy French authorities in Syria, German aircraft ferried German specialists into Iraq, and the great oilfields of Kirkuk were occupied. Hitler was fortunately unable (because of Crete) to follow up this success, and the rebellion collapsed on the intervention of Glubb's famous Arab Legion and of a British Brigade group from Palestine.

Rashid Ali joined the ex-Mufti of Jerusalem in flight to Germany to seek Hitler's protection, and, like the Mufti, he had been declared a war criminal and handed over to the French for safe-keeping. Like the Mufti, he had somehow been enabled to find his way back to the Middle East, where he could do us the maximum of mischief.

The King asked me what he should do; he was unwilling to play the trump-card now in his hand. I could only suggest that he treat Rashid Ali hospitably for the period prescribed by Beduin tradition and then put him over some frontier. I did not consider suggesting extradition to Iraq, let alone surrender of his guest to British hands; but I hoped the King might be persuaded to wish him on to some other Arab territory, such as Kuwait, and that sooner or later we might thus catch him. I was, of course, unsuccessful in these recommendations. Whether or not Ibn Saud thought that it suited him very well to have Rashid Ali on a string, he professed complete inability to deny him the right of indefinite sanctuary. He said that if he became responsible for Rashid Ali's capture, at however many removes, his *harím* would spit in his face. And so it had to be left.

For a long time, Rashid Ali lived in virtual seclusion in Riyadh. Later he was seen here and there in the town, and finally he joined the privy councillors round the wall. I never heard that his presence in Ibn Saud's capital did us or the Iraqis any harm.

* * *

The visit to Jedda of Lord Alanbrooke and his party had been a considerable local event. But during their brief stay, another and for me more eventful visit brought new loveliness to a dinner-party which I had been promised to find memorable. The word was an understatement. Before the party ended, I knew that Jane was the woman I must marry. During the weeks that followed we saw much of each other and had much talk. When the decision was reached, she flew back in the early Spring of 1946 to the United States, for the necessary formalities.

I was summoned to London that summer for discussions on Britain's role in the Middle East in the changed circumstances of near-bankruptcy. After Labour's victory in the 1945 election, Mr. Ernest Bevin had succeeded Mr. Eden at the Foreign Office, and he took the chair at our meetings. I had been so convinced that there would be a Labour landslide in the election that the relative rarity of this point of view came as a surprise; I wish I had been at home for the event, to win a few bets on the outcome. I had not met one single 'other rank' during the war who was not determined to vote against the party of Baldwin and Chamberlain, and Mr. Churchill seemed predestined to be the victim of this strong dislike of his predecessors. It was on my way back from the Viceroy's visit to Riyadh that I developed a personal antipathy for party politics. We had damaged a wheel in taking off from Buwaib, and our pilot decided to fly to Abadan in Persia for repairs rather than risk a landing in Jedda. We landed safely there and lunched in a U.S. Air Force mess with young men busily involved in the Persian supply-route to Russia, before setting out on the long flight home from Persia to the Red Sea. The King's own aircraft, which he had lent to me, contained an enormous Dunlopillo bed on which I lay, listening to the wireless. The sudden shock of hearing a loved and well-known voice, for years the voice of national unity and of our common cause, raucous with electioneering abuse of the men who had only yesterday been his colleagues, was too much for me.

Mr Bevin, whose sympathies with the Arab sense of grievance over Palestine won him more affection from his envoys in the Middle East than from his own party, was anxious to discover what could be done in each country to assist essential local initiatives with British skills and know-how. He wished to avoid any old-fashioned suggestion of British advisers, but yet to offer to Iraq or Egypt or the Levant States experts, perhaps from a central pool, who might encourage a modern approach to age-old problems of irrigation or agriculture. This is the sort of thing the Israelis have been most usefully and most successfully doing in tropical Africa. It was when my turn came to talk about natural resources, and I had to admit the absence of any tree in Jedda, that Mr. Bevin wanted to know what the hell the dogs did.

Thanksgiving Day, 1946, saw Jane and me married by my old friend Bond at the British Consulate General in Cairo, with Geoffrey Courtney and Pinkney ('Kippy') Tuck, then the American Ambassador, as witnesses. Shepheards Hotel had been bedizened with those vast set-pieces of floral decoration that are Cairo's salute to matrimony, and all of these had to be abandoned to the chambermaids. We took an evening train to Luxor, and our railway-carriage, also, was a small Chelsea of flowers. Mahmoud Ghazali Pasha, a valued counsellor of Oriental secretariat days, was now Governor of Cairo and he had sent a sergeant and a file of police to the station to do us honour. Nothing I could say or do, leaning out of a bower of blossom to take farewell of many friends, would persuade the rigidly saluting constables to break it up and go home, and we left them, still saluting. We were then free to jettison about a hundred pounds worth of expensive flowers along the railway-track to Giza.

Ghazali's bright ideas had reached the Keneh Province. On arrival at Luxor, we were told by an allegedly secret policeman that his orders were not to leave a yard between us during our stay. Him I was able to dismiss, and we reached the hotel unescorted. As expected, our stay in Luxor was a delight.

Jedda welcomed us back with a sandstorm.

T

Our house was comfortable, and our little landscape was attractive enough. On three sides we looked out on high pink and yellow coral houses with their tracery of *mushrabiya* (lattice) casements and huge carved doorways, and on the traffic of Arab and African merchandise. On the west side, beyond the dusty city wall and its sinister domed dungeon, the green water of the reefs stretched to the haze of the open sea, and lateen-sailed *sambuks* wove their way through jagged channels to the water-gate. Every day had a blue and gold morning, musical with street-cries and bright with the great fish brought in to market, still luminous as rainbows from their lost water, flashing green and purple and maroon, and soon to lie unidentifiable and grey. After sunset, when the green ray of the sun's eclipse had signalled the beginning of a new day, darkness fell like a sudden curtain, leaving us only a flicker and bobbing of lanterns in the long canoes of the fishermen off-shore.

The demolition of the walls and prison had started before we left the Hejaz. Jedda is now an open city.

With the opening of all the prison-doors of King Hussein's time, we were no longer immured; liberty was ours for the taking. We could picnic and bathe at an enchanting creek, some miles to the northward; and this became a Sunday habit. In the summer of 1945, the Emir Khaled had given me a beautiful Saluqi bitch, whose name I changed from Nejma to Laila. She was, unfortunately, as stupid as she was beautiful, and after three years of life in the desert she was never at home in a house.

She was a joy and a curse on our picnics. She would float sunlit round our car, as we drove across the desert, with side-excursions to pursue desert foxes. But the process of collecting her to go home again, which for her involved the hated routine of getting into a small closed space, was interminable. Only Jane could persuade her to accept capture. Laila would stand gold-shimmering in the evening light, with the sun aflame in the feather of her ears and tail, daring us to imprison anything so desert-free and lovely.

Other picnics assembled us at a time-battered Turkish fort, some way up the Mecca Road, where the Americans produced un-Arabian refreshment among the green and yellow stones of the ruins. Also, of course, to the Quarantine Islands south of the town. Here sharks still closely patrolled the narrow beaches and we had to step warily among the great clam-shells lest one might snap sudden upon a foot and remove it. Twenty-five years before, I had sailed one evening to the islands for a quiet week-end away from King Hussein and, when we were through the reefs, the full moon had risen, in full eclipse, giving to our boat and sails and ourselves a sudden unreality. This phenomenon I never saw again; but our trips to the Islands and back were full of colour and surprise.

In 1920, our old launch had been manned by two all but naked brothers, the younger of whom, a victim of chronic St. Vitus's Dance, was known as 'Agitato'. Now we had a smart young technician in uniform, who looked after our air-conditioning in his spare time. As we slid through the channels in the reefs, small sting-rays started up into the air by our launch-side and, more alarmingly, bigger ones, six foot and more across, would hurl themselves out of the water and flop splashing back. The coral was cauliflower-innocent to look at and death to our launch to touch, and the orchid jellyfish floating among it were exotically floral. Busy little creatures—black and white bulls-eyes, ears of corn, scarlet mushrooms—darted about beside and beneath us.

Jane and I would walk in the crowded bazaars, dodging the snarling baggage-laden camels in the crowded alleyways. Or, after a drive along the coast, we would send the car ahead of us and walk home. On one walk she exclaimed at a waste of spilled olives on the sand; I pointed to a camel and explained: 'Olive-tree!' Once when we had shared our lunch with a golden oriole in a palmgrove, we filled an Arab child's hands with cubes of ice from our thermos. He was bewitched, and scampered off to show this treasure to his mother; but he did not get far with it.

Sometimes, when the moon rode splendid in the sky, we set out to lose ourselves in a black and silver town. Every street and lane was dust-carpeted and hushed, and we would take every hazard of twist and turn in a world without echo, following white walls to a distant glimmer of lantern or to some black conclusion;

enjoying an extreme remoteness from Anglo-Saxon circumstance. The trick was to get safely home again without asking the way. My First Secretary would have found much to condemn in this exercise. Our half-savage kitchen-cat, christened 'Hitla', would have applauded it.

★   ★   ★

The eldest of Ibn Saud's many sons, of whom there were thirty-seven living when I knew him, was Turki, a young man of great promise, who had already deputised for his father as commander of the Wahhabi forces, when the influenza plague of 1919 struck Riyadh and he died, at the age of eighteen. Saud, later named by his father as Crown Prince, was born in 1902; Faisal in 1905. I was rather incredibly informed that a gap of eight years separates Faisal from the next oldest son, Mohammed; and the series ended with a child born in 1947, when the King himself was sixty-seven years of age. He once named to me twenty-three of them, standing in order of age in an impressive row, on our way to dinner. They were a handsome lot, stamped, every one of them, with their father's royal and personal signet. Two of the number were to become kings, and one was to be a murderer. For on November 16, 1951, the Emir Mishari, a moody stripling of nineteen years old whom the Ousmans had befriended, went berserk on a hot Sunday afternoon and opened fire from the street through their open window. Cyril Ousman was mown down where he stood; Dorothy only escaped other blasts of the Prince's tommy-gun by hiding behind a cupboard. This young man's mother was an Abyssinian slave-girl.

Sudan government passports used to describe the complexions of Sudanese holders as either 'wheat', 'green' or 'blue'. Nobody was black. There were no blues in Ibn Saud's family, but a few whose darker skins traced Abyssinian descent. Most were Arab wheat, sons of Sudairi women (there were at least three Sudairi wives), or of daughters of the houses of Ibn Rashid of the Jebel Shammar, and Shaalan of the Ruwallah. Saud was of the Beni Khaled family of al-Hasa on his mother's side, which is itself of the Äl-Saud. Faisal's mother was of the respected family of

280

Al-Shaikh a descendant of the Abdul Wahhab who imposed the Saudi disciplines of religion two centuries ago. Mohammed, and the next brother, Khaled, were connected through their mother with another powerful branch of the Äl-Saud, for she was sister of Abdel Aziz ibn Musaid ibn Jiluwi ibn Saud, the Amir of Hail. Side by side with these double-barrelled Beduin princes stood a number of other, notably handsome, brothers whose birth had brought them no influence likely to survive their father's lifetime. Mansour's mother was an Armenian concubine; the mother of Tallal, Nawwaf and five others, was a Circassian slave-girl called Munaiyir. Nasser, the darkest of the sons, had a Moroccan concubine as mother. Possibly because he felt a special responsibility for these children of fortune—possibly, in the case of Munaiyir's sons, out of love for their mother—the King seemed to hold this brood in especial affection.

He was a doting father, but discipline was firm. The late Shaikh of Kuwait told me that he had once arrived on a visit to Riyadh and entered the King's presence to find him belabouring one of his sons with his stick. And rightly so, for the young man had been operating a private and illicit still. No one seemed to know, or care, how many daughters the King had fathered.

I was worried lest the dutiful dependence of sons might dissolve after Ibn Saud's death into a strife of brothers, with horrid reflection in civil war, and that is why I tried to chart this first generation in terms of the support which each might expect from his mother's family and friends once the wide protection of a royal father was removed. I had no doubt that Faisal, the more intelligent and experienced of the two, would loyally respect his father's choice of Saud as his successor, but I wondered whether Saud would willingly inherit his father's family as a burden additional to his own, and whether there might not be found one at least who would risk rebellion for a crown. For this Shakespearean role, the most probable candidate was the third son, Mohammed, a bull-necked, violent man, with a reputation for both ambition and lack of scruple, whose own personal connections were influential and turbulent. These speculations did Mohammed an injustice, and Saud also, for my fears on both scores were unrealised. The Crown Prince retained, on accession, the loyalties of all his brothers, and Ibn Saud's wishes were respected by all his sons.

I always paid a visit to the Emir Saud in the course of my visits to Riyadh, where he lived rather dimly in the shadow of an overwhelming father. He was himself something of a shadow of Ibn Saud, such as a flickering lamp might throw on a wall: as tall or taller, as large or larger, with blurred edges of outline and no clear angles; fleshily soft and insecure. He had to wait too long for real responsibility and could not rise to it when it came.

The Emir Faisal was a very different man, fine-drawn and cautious; his hawk-face sardonic with a twist of constant pain. He had travelled widely on his father's business and had found things to admire as well as to despise in the western world. As Viceroy of the Hejaz and Minister for Foreign Affairs, he received me often, in the Jedda palace or in his home at Taif, and I always left him impressed by a refreshing commonsense and tolerance (within limits), and an unfailing courtesy. When he and his brother Khaled first visited the United States, Jane in another incarnation had been responsible for their entertainment. This involved not only dinner-parties and receptions, but busy mornings of shopping. The Emir Faisal wished to replenish the wardrobe of his *harîm*—he is understood to have had only the one, Turkish wife—and the mannequin parade was heady stuff for his bodyguard and suite. The bodyguard, great gold-embroidered negroes with curved scimitars, may well have been heady stuff for the mannequins. Jane's advice was sought, and she advised a formula of tea-gowns. The four dozen that found favour probably did so less on their own than on their wearers' merits. *Cotonnades* for the serving women were also filtered through Jane's approval, but one particularly horrific design, obviously attractive to the Emir, turned her thumb down. Faisal smiled deprecatingly and bought the whole bale. The American detective in charge of the party found all this, and the sight of a glut of gold wrist-watches shovelled across Cartier's counter, very boring indeed.

★   ★   ★

The Personnel Department of the Foreign Office does a most ungrateful task surprisingly well, but I sometimes wished, when in Jedda, that its criteria in staff-selection had erred on the side of normality. Personal eccentricities which in less peculiar surroundings would pass unnoticed became, in our little goldfish-bowl, obtrusive and even objectionable. The hundred-and-one competitive interests which fought for advertisement in my Head of Chancery's teeming mind prevented him from concentration on any one subject—the Chancery work of the moment, for instance—for more than minutes on end. As in that strange place outside Naples, a torch thrust down one hole in the ground set off a hundred others in eager flame. When I heard that another Secretary locked himself for long hours in his lavatory, threatening any servant who claimed his attention there with keyhole-thrusts of his consular uniform sword, I suggested to London that a change would be a good thing.

Thanks to Jane, I made new friends. One of the Ali Reza sons of the *Qaimaqám* of my earlier days had married an American girl, and I was allowed to visit her. The French wife of Ibn Saud's director of mines, a gifted Palestinian called Izzeddin Bey Shawa who had a King's College, Cambridge, degree, was also at home to us. These two 'mixed' marriages were examples of extremes: the rigours of Moslem convention imposed on the little Californian had no place in Izzeddin's household. But such marriage adventures are always hazardous. By and large, French women seem to make a better thing of marriage to a Moslem husband than their British sisters, who are more easily disconcerted by the smaller irritations. The one advice I always gave to parents enquiring about the chances of a daughter's happiness was that her marriage should be performed only according to Koranic rites, with written-in permission for mutual divorce. This protects the girl not only from the loss of British nationality, so enabling British consular assistance, but also from the real risk of finding herself married in British law to a man not legally bound by the same ceremony. Some strains, those set up by religious conscience, for instance, are resistant to all remedy; when these become obtrusive, it is already too late for any relief but a nervous breakdown.

One of our Moslem women friends tempted Jane with the suggestion that she should put on Arab clothes, shapeless and darkly veiled, and visit Mecca under friendly escort, to enjoy the entertainment of legendary bazaars. I have no doubt that she could have done this twenty times without risk of discovery, but I could not allow it.

The sacrosanctity of Mecca was more than once breached, in all innocence, by the British military mission which we had persuaded Ibn Saud to accept, under Brigadier Baird, an Irishman from the Sudan Defence Corps which was stationed at Taif, north-east of Mecca. The main road from Taif to Jedda runs through the Holy City, with only secondary deviation around it. Baird's driver missed a hair-pin turn, and the Brigadier was shaken to find himself passing a petrol-pump which had no place on his route. He roared blindly through the town, and we had a lot of explaining to do. Later, I heard, this happened again.

The American pilots of the Dakotas which then served Saudi Arabia were instructed to give Mecca a very wide berth, by flying north from Jedda towards Rabegh before turning inland to Riyadh. Once when I was flying to visit the King, sitting next to Philby, he gripped my knee and pointed to a landscape I had never dared hope to see. Our pilot must have miscalculated his course, for Philby was showing me the blur of Mecca and the hill of Gebel el-Nur, the Mountain of Light where Mohammed first received his revelation; the little settlement of Muna, and beyond it the Mountain of Mercy, Mount Arafát, whose visitation bestows the title of Pilgrim. I was indescribably impressed. Having acted with obvious pride and pleasure as my aerial *mutawwif*, or cicerone, Philby reported the pilot for disciplinary action on our arrival in Riyadh.

The year 1947 opened auspiciously for me with a K.B.E. on New Year's Day, which meant that my friends had to probe for a Christian name never used outside a shrinking family circle. A hardly less surprising novelty was the sound of a sharp explosion which tore us from sleep at 3 o'clock one morning. A ball of blue flame, the size of a child's football, was floating in the air in our bedroom as if in some small draught of wind. Twice more it bounced on the tiled floor, with a loud explosive pop, and then it drifted back through the open casement to the outer air.

A very welcome visitor to Jedda was Wilfred Thesiger, who came to us from one of those lonely crossings of the dreaded *Rub' el Khali* or Empty Quarter of Arabia which have made him outstanding in British desert exploration. In the teeth of Ibn Saud's disapproval, alone with two or three *bedu* whose fears he refused to share, he had made a journey no Arab would willingly attempt, including one nineteen-day march across shifting dunes between one well and the next. Here was cause enough for admiration. But what delighted his Jedda host and hostess was the Gargantuan appetite he brought with him from his ordeal. 'When I can eat, I do!' he said. To watch him eat was a clinical satisfaction.

I had expected to remain in Saudi Arabia for three or four years, with a vague hope of the Bagdad Embassy to follow, but a Foreign Office telegram in the Spring of 1947 asked whether I would accept another, apparently subordinate appointment. This I regretted, but it is a good rule never to refuse even an unattractive offer, unless a better one has already been made and accepted. I cabled my acceptance immediately. In the event, I never served in the post proposed.

When I asked for an audience to say goodbye to the King in Riyadh, he suggested that my wife should accompany me there. Ibn Saud had always assumed that the real merit in marrying me off was his own, because of those drenchings with essential oils, and his allusions to this responsibility for my happiness were frequent and heavily delicate. Before we left, a large bundle of exotic clothing arrived for Jane's accoutrement.

For town wear she was given no alternative to black—billowing and all-embracing black robes and a double thickness of black veil which reduced her, and Dorothy Ousman who accompanied us, to the starkest anonymity. Within doors, all was to be colour and light. A choice of long silken shifts, emerald or rose, heavily patterned with sequins and scrolls of gold, were to be worn under a tent-like robe of transparent, gold-embroidered black. This had sleeves of a depth to sweep the ground, and the fullness of each sleeve made one half of a coil of head-dress. The embroidered panels below were handholds for comfort when walking.

The little guest-palace outside Riyadh where we lodged had a prospect of palm-groves, and we slept on the roof under the stars to a lullaby of water-wheels. There were three or four of these *sakiehs* around us, their wooden ratchet-wheels endlessly engaged in the wooden gear which brings brimming water-tins from a well to spill over into irrigation. A creaking strain of wood on wood does not suggest sweet music, but there are few lovelier sounds than the blending drone of distant water-wheels, each tortured cry as clear as an African horn. Only an air-raid siren is as instantly evocative as this. The heavily blindfold camel turning the wheel plods on in his long journey to nowhere, thinking perhaps that he is crossing unknown sands but really treading a prison circle of a few yards diameter.

Saudi Arabia had a king and many princes, but no queen and no princesses. It was Ibn Saud's senior wife who received Jane in her apartments, and his chief concubine, in her neighbouring apartments, who assisted her. A French-speaking Syrian girl interpreted, and a flutter of children came and went. The room was oppressively furnished with velvet sofas and fauteuils, but the immense meal was served and eaten on the floor. The wall-paper was a gay design of railway trains, then non-existent in Nejd, and over the curtained entry hung the tinselled bobbles of a Christmas-tree. Conversation had to be condensed to suit local experience. The question where Jane had come from and how she had come to Arabia was not to be answered in purely geo-graphical terms, for no one had heard of Atlantic or Mediter-ranean. She was applauded for the courage that had brought her across the sea: this the ladies thought far more hazardous than the air, which they knew supported the weight of an aeroplane. In water, things generally sank.

The Emir Khaled, the present heir apparent, calling to renew his acquaintance with Jane from New York days, sent both ladies, to whom he was unrelated, to their veils; a young person of six years old also thought fit to scamper with them from the room, her rainbow-coloured *tulle* head-dress tossing behind her like a butterfly-swarm.

The King's great sprawling mud-brick palace of *Qasr-el-Murabba* is now dust and rubble. As my car threaded its way round the twists and sudden corners of its approach, which made its defence no problem, I could not know how soon the golden flood of oil royalties would engulf Ibn Saud and his capital, and with them the stern standards of austerity he had imposed. I knew that, for me, this was the end of Arabian experience, and I could not expect to see him again. The years had brought him failing health, embittered by nagging irritation at the passing of youth's effortless achievement and by a resentment of the new challenge of the times.

To my pleasure, the King spoke warmly of the excellent job done by British contractors in bringing the sweet water of the Hadra oasis to relieve the age-long agonies of Jedda. In an atmosphere of intense American competition, such opportunities for British enterprise were rare, and this task had been impeccably performed.

Ibn Saud's words of farewell seemed to go some way beyond the formal, but such illusions are familiar. On my side, I confess, there was a respect and an affection which I hope he recognised as sincere. I was presented with the ritual gold sword and instructed to live for ever. When I reached London, I found that two outfits of miniature Arab clothes had been sent ahead of me, as a gift from the King to my two schoolboy sons.

Ibn Saud lived for seven years after my farewell (he died on November 9, 1953) confused by great wealth and by the vicissitudes of time. In a sense, like many other great men, he outlived himself. But his life had been on the grand scale, as male dominant and as desert ruler. Also, perhaps, as one manifestation of the will of Allah, for this great Leopard of the Desert wore willingly and without chafing his Master's leash and collar.

Tombstones and all other memorials of mortality are anathema to a true Wahhabi. His Majesty King Abdul Aziz ibn Abdurrahman al-Faisal Ăl Sa'ud lies in the sands, wrapped only in a shroud; and today one must ask of the desert winds and of the cold Arabian stars to find his resting-place.

Index